THE EU'S FOR

G000109124

Commentators have often projected their own hopes and fears onto the EU and its Common Foreign and Security Policy (CFSP). Does the EU, in its foreign policy aspects, represent a 'post-modern' world of persuasion and public-spirited action or is it just a hapless would-be state that has to appeal to the United States, as in Bosnia and Libya, to act effectively? The contributors to The EU's Foreign Policy – from Europe and the three most important Asian countries – reject this simplistic dichotomy, exploring how EU policy actually functions and describing its contributions to modifications in the structure of world politics. How the influence of the EU can be maintained despite financial crisis and long-term recession, and increasing German dominance, remains a major question, not resolved but illuminated by this thoughtful volume.

Robert O. Keohane, Princeton University, USA

The EU's Foreign Policy is a welcome addition to the literature on EU foreign policy, as it critically assesses the changes that have been implemented since the Lisbon Treaty entered into force, and considers the EU's influence in the increasingly multipolar world of the 21st century. The contributors are all highly respected experts, and include academics from well beyond the EU's borders. Highly recommended.

Karen E. Smith, London School of Economics, UK

This volume is original and useful for three main reasons: it provides a conceptual framework for grasping the EU's idiosyncratic international power and diplomatic action; it offers a fresh analysis of the EEAS, its structure and relationship to the EU external action system; and it offers new research on EU diplomacy in action in the near and far abroad. In addition, contributions from scholars from China, Japan and India provide an invaluable perspective from the outside-in. The book will be especially useful for Master's and PhD students in EU studies.

Kalypso Nikolaidis, St Anthony's College, University of Oxford, UK

Globalization, Europe and Multilateralism

Institutionally supported by the Institute for European Studies at the
Université libre de Bruxelles

Mario TELÒ, Series editor (mtelo@ulb.ac.be)

International Editorial Board

Salma BAVA, JNU, New Dehli
Shaun BRESLIN, University of Warwick
Andrew GAMBLE, Cambridge Un.
Peter KATZENSTEIN, Cornell Un.
Robert O. KEOHANE, Princeton Un.
Christian LEQUESNE, CERI, Paris
Leonardo MORLINO, LUISS, Rome
Ben ROSAMOND, Copenhagen Un.
Vivien SCHMIDT Boston Un.
Karen SMITH, LSE
Jan ZIELONKA, Oxford Un.
Michael ZÜRN, WZB, Berlin
ZHU Liqun, Beijin, CFAU, Beijin

Frederik PONJAERT, ULB, Series manager (fponjaer@ulb.ac.be)

The Institut d'Etudes Européennes de l'Université Libre de Bruxelles (IEE-ULB) is a leading research institution, with a large global collaborative university network. As part of successful research consortia, the IEE-ULB was awarded two EU funded programmes. The first is an international multidisciplinary doctoral program in Globalisation, Europe, Multilateralism funded by the DG Culture and Education EU Commission. Over a seven year period, this programme will fund up to 50 PhD students as well as hosting PhD school seminars on every continent. The second programme is GR:EEN (Global Reordering: Evolving European Networks), funded by DG research EU Commission. This is an integrated research project including 16 universities on five continents. The remarkable quality of these senior and junior scholars included in the project allows extensive research both in EU studies and in global governance. Volumes in this series share innovative research objectives around Globalisation, the EU's evolution within it, the changing Multilateral cooperation, and the role of transnational networks; emergent multipolarity and international order; comparative regionalism and interregionalism; EU's foreign policy and external relations.

The series includes collaborative volumes, research based monographs and textbooks with the aim of contributing to the innovation of European Integration and International studies. Every book is reviewed by an international referees process, scientific workshops discussing the first drafts, anonymous referees and advice by the International editorial board members.

The EU's Foreign Policy
What Kind of Power and Diplomatic Action?

Edited by

MARIO TELÒ
Université Libre de Bruxelles, Belgium

FREDERIK PONJAERT
Université Libre de Bruxelles, Belgium

ASHGATE

Published by
Ashgate Publishing Limited
Wey Court East
Union Road
Farnham
Surrey, GU9 7PT
England

Ashgate Publishing Company
110 Cherry Street
Suite 3-1
Burlington, VT 05401-3818
USA

www.ashgate.com

British Library Cataloguing in Publication Data
The EU's foreign policy : what kind of power and diplomatic action?. --
(Globalisation, Europe, multilateralism series; v. 1)
  1. European Union. 2. European Union countries--Foreign relations--21st century.
  3. Constitutional law--European Union countries. 4. Treaty on European Union (1992).
  Protocols, etc., 2007 Dec. 13.
  I. Series II. Telò, Mario. III. Ponjaert, Frederik.

Library of Congress Cataloging-in-Publication Data
The EU's foreign policy : what kind of power and diplomatic action? / [edited] by Mario Telò and Frederik Ponjaert.
    pages cm. -- (Globalisation, Europe, multilateralism series)
  Includes bibliographical references and index.
  ISBN 978-1-4094-6451-8 (hbk) -- ISBN 978-1-4094-6452-5 (pbk.) --
ISBN 978-1-4094-6453-2 (ebook) -- ISBN 978-1-4094-6454-9 (epub) 1. European Union countries--Foreign relations. I. Telò, Mario, editor of compilation. II. Ponjaert, Frederik, editor of compilation.

  JZ1570.A5.E97145 2013
  341.242'2--dc23

2012038187

Reprinted 2013

ISBN 9781409464518 (hbk)
ISBN 9781409464525 (pbk)
ISBN 9781409464532 (ebk – PDF)
ISBN 9781409464549 (ebk – ePUB)

Printed in the United Kingdom by Henry Ling Limited,
at the Dorset Press, Dorchester, DT1 1HD

Contents

PART I: THE EU: A CONTROVERSIAL GLOBAL POLITICAL ACTOR WITHIN AN EMERGENT MULTIPOLAR WORLD

PART II: AFTER THE LISBON TREATY: THE COMMON FOREIGN SECURITY POLICY AND THE EUROPEAN EXTERNAL ACTION SERVICE

PART III: ASSESSING CFSP AND THE EU'S EXTERNAL RELATIONS IN ACTION: NEAR AND FAR ABROAD

List of Figures and Tables

Figures

Tables

List of Contributors

Ummu Salma Bava is Director, Europe Area Studies Programme, Centre for European Studies, Jawaharlal Nehru University, New Delhi, India and a guest faculty at the Foreign Service Institute, Ministry of External Affairs (New Delhi) and Associate Fellow, Asia Society (New York). One of the leading experts in India on contemporary European and Indian foreign and security policy, she was recently conferred with the prestigious Bundesverdienstkreuz (Order of Merit) by the German President.

Caterina Carta, PhD, is an assistant professor at Vesalius College and associated research at Institute d'Etudes Européennes (IEE) at ULB, Brussels. In the framework of the FP GR:EEN, she works on a research project on the EU as a discursive actor. She has published *The European Union's Diplomatic Service: Ideas, Preferences and Identities* (London: Routledge, 2012).

Andrew Gamble is Professor of Politics and Director of Polis, Department of Politics and International Studies, University of Cambridge. He is Fellow of the British Academy and Coeditor of *New Political Economy*. His books include: *Regionalism and Wold Order* (with T. Payne, 1996), *Politics and Fate* (2000), *Between Europe and America: The Future of British Politics* (2003), *The Spectre of the Feast* and *The Politics of Recession* (2009). His current research, supported by the Leverhulme Trust, is on Anglo-America and the problem of world order and the current economic crisis.

Richard Gillespie holds the established Chair of Politics at the University of Liverpool and is the founder-editor of the journal *Mediterranean Politics*. His recent research project on the Union for the Mediterranean resulted in articles in a range of journals, including the *Journal of Common Market Studies* and *Geopolitics*, and a book co-edited with Federica Bicchi.

Giovanni Grevi is the Acting Director of the Fundación para las Relaciones Internacionales y el Diálogo Exterior (FRIDE). Before joining FRIDE, he served as a Senior Research Fellow at the Institute for Security Studies of the EU in Paris (2005–10) and as a Policy Analyst and Associate Director of Studies at the European Policy Centre in Brussels (1999–2005). He holds a PhD in International Relations from the Université Libre de Bruxelles and an MSc from the London School of Economics.

Jolyon Howorth has been Visiting Professor of Political Science at Yale University since 2002. He is also Jean Monnet Professor ad personam of European Politics and Emeritus Professor of European Studies at the University of Bath. Recent books include: *Security and Defence Policy in the European Union* (Palgrave, 2007; 2nd edition 2013); *Defending Europe: The EU, NATO and the Quest for European Autonomy* (Palgrave, 2003, ed. with John Keeler); *European Integration and Defence: The Ultimate Challenge?* (Paris, 2000).

Christian Lequesne is Professor of European Studies and currently director of the Centre d'Etudes et de Recherches Internationales (CERI) at Sciences Po, Paris. He graduated from the College of Europe in Bruges and received his PhD from Sciences Po, Paris. He has been director of the Centre français de recherches en sciences sociales in Prague, Czech Republic, and Sciences-Po LSE Alliance Professor at the London School of Economics. His recent publications include 'Senior Diplomats in the French Ministry of Foreign Affairs: When an Entrance Exam Still Determines the Career' (with Jean Heilbronn), *Hague Journal of Diplomacy*, 7(3), 269–85; 'Old Versus New', in *Oxford Handbook on the European Union* (Oxford: Oxford University Press, 2012); *The Member States of the European Union* (edited with Simon Bulmer) (Oxford: Oxford University Press, forthcoming 2013).

Hartmut Mayer is Official Fellow in Politics (International Relations) at St. Peter's College, University of Oxford. He studied history, politics and drama at the Free University of Berlin and International Relations at Tufts University's Fletcher School of Law and Diplomacy, at Harvard University and at the University of Cambridge (MPhil, Gonville and Caius College). He received his doctorate (DPhil) from St. Antony's College, Oxford. Visiting researcher in Florence (EUI), Berlin (SWP), Helsinki (UPI), Tokyo (Waseda University) and Hamburg (GIGA). He has been visiting professor at Hitotsubashi University (Tokyo) and Hamburg University. He worked as a freelance journalist in Germany for about 10 years and as external analyst on Europe (Region Head) with Oxford Analytica.

Hidetoshi Nakamura is Associate Professor of International Relations, Faculty of Political Science and Economics, and also Deputy Director of the European Union Institute in Japan (EUIJ) at Waseda University. He studied Politics and International Relations at Waseda and the University of Oxford. He was Associate Professor at Siebold University of Nagasaki, Japan. With Hartmut Mayer and Paul Bacon, he is editing a book on EU–Japan cooperation in a changing global order.

Frederik Ponjaert is researcher and lecturer at the IEE-ULB and the KULeuven and associate lecturer of comparative regionalism at Sciences Po, Paris. His research is centred on comparative regionalism with a focus on European and Asian realities; the foreign policies of Germany and Japan; and regional policy processes. He has been a visiting researcher at Princeton University (Fulbright

Fellow), Tokyo University and the University of Warwick. Guest lectures include, amongst others: the Diplomatic Academy of Vietnam, Seoul National University and the University of Giessen. Recent publications include: *Public Research Projects in Europe and East Asia: Cooperation or Competition? A Comparative Analysis of the ITER and Galileo Experiences in East Asia* (London, 2010); 'The EU and its Far-Abroad: Interregional Relations with Other Continents', in *EU and Global Governance* (London: Routledge, 2009) and 'Japan in East Asia: The Dynamics of Regional Cooperation from a European Perspective', in *Studia Diplomatica* (Brussels, 2007).

Mario Telò is J. Monnet Chair ad personam and Vice-President of the IEE-ULB, Member of the Royal Academy of Sciences and also teaches EU institutions at LUISS-Rome. Visiting professor in several European, East Asian and American universities, he has served as advisor to European council presidency, EU Commission and EU Parliament. Among his recent books one might note: *State, Globalization and Multilateralism* (2012), *International Relations: A European Perspective* (2009) – published in English, French and Mandarin; *The EU and Global Governance* (2009); or *The EU and New Regionalism* (2007).

Chen Zhimin is a professor of International Relations and Jean Monnet Chair of European foreign policy at the School of International Relations and Public Affairs, Fudan University, Shanghai. He is a member of the Advisory Board of *The Hague Journal of Diplomacy* and a member of the editorial committee of *The Pacific Review* and *Asia Europe Journal*. His major publications in Chinese include: *China, the United States and Europe: Cooperation and Competition in a New Trilateral Relation* (2011); *Contemporary Diplomacy* (2008); *Foreign Policy Integration in European Union: A Mission Impossible?* (2003, with Gustaaf Geerarts); *Subnational Governments and Foreign Affairs* (2001). He also co-edited (with David Zweig) *China's Reforms and International Political Economy* (Routledge, 2007). Professor Chen was a visiting fellow at Harvard University (1996–7) and has also been a visiting scholar at Queen's University, University of Durham, Lund University, Sciences Po, and Keio University.

Foreword

H.E.M. Pierre Vimont
EEAS Executive Secretary General

The practitioner is always a bit worried – maybe even irritated – when opening an anthology of articles about the organization in which he works. Is he afraid of not being correctly understood? Of secrets being brought out in the open? Whatever the reason, one is worried.

This is not the case with this work. The anthology of articles coordinated and edited by Professor Mario Telò gives us an exhaustive and outstandingly well documented study on one of the most important innovations of the Lisbon Treaty. This treaty was intended to give a new impulse to the foreign policy of the European Union and let it acquire a strength and coherence that it often lacked before. This ambitious objective, I think, comes down to an idea that is rather simple but at the same time fundamental: bring more politics throughout the instruments and procedures used almost daily by the different actors of the external action of the European Union. In other words: set out a clear direction for the European foreign policy and so create coherence and continuity in the European initiatives throughout the world.

To make a success out of this goal, important institutional reforms were necessary: the new function of the High Representative/Vice President of the European Commission for foreign policy was created, and also a new administration, the European External Action Service (EEAS). Definitions of new working methods were also needed to coordinate the work of all those acting in the field of external action. Lastly, a new administrative culture had to be introduced at the heart of the EEAS, jointly carried by experts transferred from the European Commission, the General Secretariat of the Council and by diplomats from member states. Time and patience are needed for this reform to succeed. One does not always realize how big a change of method and state of mind it represents. This will come progressively and will have to invent and innovate on the way forward. Hence many definite judgments – good or bad – that are being made these days look somewhat premature and may deserve later to be reviewed.

But the observer of a reality as complex and extraordinary as the European project must go further than the mere analysis of institutional and operational changes introduced in the European foreign policy by the Lisbon Treaty. Indeed, one must broaden the thinking by studying the substance of this policy and consequently examine the place and the role of the European Union on today's international scene. Today's world wherein national or multinational diplomacies must operate has upset all our certainties and habits. This world is at the same time multipolar, interdependent, unstable, uncertain. It presents new problems that were barely mentioned a few years ago. And it is subject to a phenomenon of general acceleration that puts constant pressure on diplomats and national authorities faced with tensions that succeed each other in the world without interruption. In this context, Europe has to find its new role. But one tends to forget that Europe is not the only player to confront these difficulties: the great traditional powers like the United States or Russia, the emerging nations, or the regional powers, all face the same uncertainties, and they too feel the need to redefine their responsibilities in our globalized world. No nation today can avoid this necessary introspection. The European Union must do the same, and however difficult this is, it is at the same time a sign of hope and progress.

One does indeed see that the contribution by the European Union to the stability of the international community has certainly not been negligible but is still incomplete and, at times, may even appear a bit self-satisfied. Faced with the challenges of the new realities of the international scene, Europe cannot see itself anymore as a normative power, a 'soft power', whose influence remains uncontested. Should this ever have been a temptation, then the current financial and economic crisis affecting Europe has reduced any such ambitions to their just proportions. From these ordeals, and from the innovations in the Lisbon Treaty, a more lucid Europe should slowly emerge; one more open to the others, and more pragmatic as well. The 'comprehensive approach' promoted by the European leaders can, if used with determination and confidence, bring more efficiency to the external action of the European Union. Europe can then hope to become in the future an essential actor in managing and solving regional crises. Today, already, Europe is a valued and sought-after partner for authorities in the Arab world and in Africa. There is an almost natural action field for Europe where the new European diplomacy can prove itself and shape a new role worthy of its ambitions.

Ultimately the merits of the work done by Professor Telò and his colleagues are that they have avoided the twin pitfalls of indulgence and denigration; and thus invite us to engage with a lucid and realistic reflection on the external action of the European Union. Their analysis confirms again that Europe remains an exceptional adventure full of possibilities that could open the way to real progress on condition – and this is by no means negligible – that its members show the political willingness to proceed in that direction.

List of Abbreviations

ACP	Africa-Caribbean-Pacific States
ARF	Asian Regional Forum
ASEAN	Association of South East Asian Nations
ASEM	Asia-Europe Meeting
AU	African Union
BRIC	Brazil, Russia, India and China
BRICS	Brazil, Russia, India, China and South Africa
BTIA	Bilateral Trade and Investment Agreement
CAN	Andean Community
CARICOM	Caribbean Community
CARIFORUM	Caribbean Community + Dominican Republic
CFSP	Common Foreign and Security Policy
CMPD	Crisis Management and Planning Directorate
COREPER	Comité des représentants permanents; Committee of Permanent Representatives
CPCC	Civilian Planning and Conduct Capability
CSDP	Common Security and Defence Policy
(E)CSDP	(European) Common Security and Defence Policy
CSG	Council Secretariat General
DCI	Development Cooperation Instrument
DG	Directorate General
DG AGRI	Directorate General for Agriculture and Rural Development
DG BUDG	Directorate General for Budget
DG COMM	Directorate General for Communication
DG DEVCO	Directorate General Development and Cooperation-EuropeAid
DG ECHO	Directorate General International Cooperation, Humanitarian Aid and Crisis Response
DG ECOFIN	Directorate General DG for Economic and Monetary Affairs
DG ELARG	Directorate General for Enlargement
DG EMP	Directorate General for Employment, Social Affairs and Inclusion
DG IA	Directorate General DG for International Affairs
DG Mare	Directorate General for Maritime Affairs and Fisheries
DG REGIO	Directorate General for Regional Policy
DG RELEX	Directorate General External Relations
DG Trade	Directorate General Trade
DPJ	Democratic Party of Japan
EBRD	European Bank for Reconstruction and Development
EC	European Commission

ECB	European Central Bank
ECFR	European Council on Foreign Relations
ECOWAS	Economic Community of West African States
EDC	European Defence Community
ED ENLARG	Directorate General Enlargement
EDF	European Development Fund
EEAS	European External Action Service
EEC	European Economic Community
EED	European Endowment for Democracy
EFSF	European Financial Stability Facility
EIB	European Investment Bank
EIDHR	European Instrument for Democracy and Human Rights
EMP	Euro-Mediterranean Partnership
ENP	European Neighbourhood Policy
ENPI	European Neighbourhood Policy Instrument
EP	European Parliament
EPA	Economic Partnership Agreement
EPC	European Political Co-operation
ESDP	European Security and Defence Policy
ESM	European Financial Stability Mechanism
EU	European Union
EUMS	EU Military Staff
EurAsEC	Euro-Asian Economic Community
Euromed	Barcelona Process
FAC	Foreign Affairs Council
FAO	Food and Agriculture Organization
FPI	Foreign Policy Instrument Service
FPRs	Foreign Policy Relations
FTA	Free Trade Agreement
GAC	General Affairs Council
GCC	Gulf Cooperation Council
GDP	Gross Domestic Product
GNSS	Global Navigation Satellite System
HoG	Head of Government
HR	High Representative (for Foreign and Security Policy)
HR/VP	High Representative-Vice President of the Commission
ICI	Industrialized Countries (Cooperation) Initiative
IfS	Instrument for Stability
IO	International Organization
IMF	International Monetary Fund
IPA	Instrument for Pre-Accession
IPE	International Political Economy
JAP	Joint Action Plan
JHA	Justice and Home Affairs

LAC	Latin America and Caribbean
LDP	Liberal Democratic Party of Japan
MaMa WG	Council Working Group Maghreb-Mashrek
MERCOSUR	Mercado Común del Sur
MES	Market Economy Status
MFA	Ministry of Foreign Affairs
MoF	Minister of Foreign Affairs
MoFA	Ministry of Foreign Affairs (Japan)
MS	Member State
NATO	North Atlantic Treaty Organization
NGO	Non-governmental organization
PEC	President of the European Council
PRC	People's Republic of China
PSC	Political and Security Committee
QMV	Qualified Majority Voting
RIP	Regional Indicative Programme
RoK	Republic of Korea
SAARC	South Asian Association for Regional Cooperation
SADC	Southern African Development Community
SEA	Single European Act
SG	Secretariat General
SICA	Central American Integration System
SitCen	Joint Situation Centre
SPRING	Support for partnership, reforms and inclusive growth (programme)
TEU	Treaty on the European Union
TFEU	The Treaty on the Functioning of the European Union
TFEU/TEU	Lisbon Treaty
TPC	Trade Policy Committee
UfM	Union for the Mediterranean
UK	United Kingdom
UN	United Nations
UNGA	United Nations General Assembly
(UN)MDG	(United Nations) Millennium Development Goals
UNSC	United Nations Security Council
US	United States
WEAMU	West African Economic and Monetary Union
WG	Working Group
WMD	Weapons of Mass Destruction
WTO	World Trade Organization

Introduction

Mario Telò

A New Approach to the EU's Foreign Policy System and a Fresh Working Method

This edited volume is a direct product of the GR:EEN multidisciplinary research initiative on multilateral global governance. It is also the first publication of the new GR:EEN-GEM book series.[1] Accordingly, this research must acknowledge the support of both the FP7 large-scale integrated research project GR:EEN – Global Re-ordering: Evolution through European Networks (European Commission Project Number: 266809)[2] and the GEM Erasmus Mundus Joint Doctorate on 'Globalisation, the EU, and Multilateralism' (EACEA Project Number 2010-0010).[3] Both of these endeavours pays a great deal of attention to the EU's evolving foreign policy and external relations. As such it addresses a two-pronged question: at the policy level, how to assess the EU's capacities and performances on the one hand; on the other, at the polity level, how to capture the evolving nature of the EU as a distinctive type of global player.

The GR:EEN-GEM book series which welcomes this volume as its initial publication exemplifies three main innovations:

A Commitment to a Truly Global Research and Publication Strategy

The global dimension of the network of authors and discussants is a defining feature of the series. This is, in our understanding, not a secondary option, but

---

1   The GR:EEN-GEM book series as a whole is directed by M. Telò and F. Ponjaert. The latter deserves a special mention and thanks for his collaboration in the editing process of this book, and notably for the edited volume's Introduction.

2   It includes 16 universities and research institutions from five continents – i.e. Beijing University; Nanyang Technological University – Singapore; Waseda University Tokyo; NUPI-Oslo; Copenhagen Business School; Universiteit van Amsterdam; CEU – Budapest; ISPI-Milan; FRIDE-Madrid; FLACSO-Buenos Aires; Cape Town University; Boston University; Université Libre de Bruxelles (book series editor); University of Western Australia and University of Warwick (project coordinator).

3   The global GEM PhD school includes nine world-class universities – i.e. Fudan University-Shanghai; Waseda University-Tokyo; Boston University; ITAM-Mexico; Université de Genève; University of Warwick; LUISS-Rome; United Nations University-CRIS and the ULB as central coordinator – and will over the course of seven years (2010–17) provide funding for up to 50 doctoral projects.

rather a determining pledge with regards to how, in researching and publishing on European affairs, non-European scholars are to play a seminal role alongside and in conjunction with their European counterparts. As such, they are expected to assume all possible roles in this concerted research and publication effort, ranging from designated discussant of European authors' contributions – thus providing them with a fresh point of view; up to book editor – thus contributing towards the definition of joint research initiatives, by way of the author of a given chapter offering an outsider's analysis of the EU. Sustained and structured transnational communication with critical external partners will allow for their perceptions of the EU's foreign policy to permeate the series as one of its fundamental tenets. Ultimately, this commitment ensures that the series eschews any excessively Eurocentric or inward-looking approaches to the EU's international role. This volume, the first one in the series, sees both transatlantic and Asian views included amongst the chapters; whereas Russian, South American and African perspectives were proactively included in the workshops and policy forums which moulded the publication's content.[4]

A Commitment to Both a Collective Enterprise and Original Research

Rather than collecting a patchwork of disparate essays without any shared focus, the series is dedicated to the publication of original, coherent and qualitative ensembles. This commitment to quality and originality is reflected in the series' innovative production process. Fostering and channelling an intensive interplay within the standing global group of researchers is a concrete and highly effective way of implementing our innovative approach. The first and second drafts of the 12 original chapters published in this volume were submitted to a non-diplomatic exercise combining both group and individual peer-review reinforced by an internal discussion nurtured through the Internet interaction and a dedicated scientific workshop. The workshop was organized in Brussels according to an original method – where 90 per cent of the available time is dedicated to direct communication and mutual criticism based on the papers circulated beforehand.[5]

---

4   Besides the authors included in the volume, we would like to acknowledge the useful and constructive contributions from colleagues, hailing from Brazil (A.Valladao and M. Patriota); South Africa (Spies); China (Zhu Liqun, from CFAU), and Mark Entin (MIGMO) and thank them for their precious insights.

5   We would like to take this opportunity to make a special mention of M. Johan Robberecht – the GEM PhD School's central manager and out-reach officer; and offer him the editors' sincere thanks as neither the workshop nor the subsequent publication would have seen the day of light without his support.

A Commitment to a Meaningful Dialogue with the Policy-Making Community

The series editors foster significant and repeated interactions with the policy-making community. Authors of research papers are provided with several opportunities to take the challenging inputs from outstanding high-level EU servants into account. Participating voices might hail from any institution relevant to the EU's external actions: the Commission (BEPA, DG Trade, DG Research, DG Education) and the EEAS; but also other international organizations.[6]

All three of these commitments helped define a collective research and cooperation methodology, and ensure that the EU's foreign policy is not reduced to that of a sovereign (proto-)state. The GR:EEN project and the GEM PhD School both favour pluralistic approaches to global governance which shun teleological understandings of the EU as a state in the making, and European integration as a process whose end goal is a perfectly coherent and consistent political unit.

The series strives for excellence by coalescing authors who provide a critical and empirically informed know-how distinct from the expertise provided by commentators, councillors or lobbyists. Steer clear of conjuring up future scenarios conditioned by the obstacles thrown up by the 'egoism and narrow minded interests of national governments'. Forty years after the ever controversial UK membership; 20 years after the founding in Maastricht of a critically unbalanced monetary union; almost 10 years after the start of the challenging Eastern enlargement of 2004–7; even the most convinced Europeanist cannot content themselves merely with the optimism of functionalist theories. Equally, uncertainties about the future of the European construction are too serious to leave the analysis of their features and causes to the prejudices of Eurosceptical streams. Accordingly, far from either the Cassandras and their doom scenarios or Panglossian reassurance, the GR:EEN-GEM series strives to offer the Commons informed and dispassionate insights aimed at empowering the wider debate on the EU whilst furthering the rich dialectic between International Relations Theory and EU Studies.

Furthermore, as an international Brussels-based network of scholars, we are fully aware after a decade of EU-funded research on comparative regional cooperation[7] that the EU is the most integrated regional grouping, and has a

---

6 Notably this project allowed for a first meeting in the Berlaymont building, headquarters of the EU Commission, co-hosted with the BEPA and DG Research, which all clearly added value. A first policy forum already took place in Brussels on 19 March 2012 with the participation of M.J. Rodrigues, J. Zeitlin (Amsterdam University), Ding Chun (Fudan), Basso (of Van Rumpuy's cabinet), Patriota (Brazilian presidential office), representatives of the ILO, the Belgian government and other organizations such as Zhu Hong (CASS Beijin). We thank all the participants from the institutional EU side in no particular order, and without being exhaustive: A. Olljum, A. Conte, P. Dun, A. Mogni, J. Marques Almeida, A. Liberatore, S. Stunz, the directors from BEPA DG Research and of DG Culture and Education.

7 For outcomes see Telò (2009 and 2012).

uniquely sophisticated role in coordinating neighbouring member states and societies whilst simultaneously stabilizing peace, domestic democracy and relative prosperity at a quasi-continental level. Of course, after the combined impact of the EPC, the subsequent foundation of the CFSP, and the difficult process of Treaty reform which brought about the current Lisbon Treaty, the EU's foreign policy is a complex and advanced institutional system which nevertheless clearly expresses its will to contribute towards regional and global governance through enhanced institutional efficiency and legitimacy. This leaves the research community with two fundamental challenges: on the one hand, to provide a realistic analysis of the changing capability–expectation gap; and on the other, to tackle the thought-provoking theoretical issues at stake. The shortcomings and far-reaching consequences of the long economic crisis have only made said issues even more pressing. When studying such an unprecedented political actor, several conventional paradigms have proven useless and fresh research rooted in the interplay between theoretical innovation and realistic performance assessments is sorely needed.

Why do we need a new wave of EU external relations and foreign policies studies? First, because the early stages of EC/EU studies almost wholly ignored the policies' external dimensions, as it focused exclusively on the inward-looking integration process amongst the six, nine and 12 member states. Since the 1980s and particularly the 1990s, the interest in EC/EU external relations and foreign policy has grown exponentially. However, the mainstream interpretations formulated during this second stage were biased in favour of the EU's self-definition as a 'post-modern' entity in opposition to a non-European world mainly perceived as a potential recipient of Europe's principled message. Foreign policy was conceived of as the projection of a civilizing, gentle and soft European power emanating from a post-Westphalian island of peace and democracy surrounded by global context, which was often erroneously reduced to a monolithic Westphalian sovereignty-enhancing system. This was possibly defensible during the unipolar momentum which opposed the EU's multilateralism to the United States' unilateralism, but said position became particularly arrogant as of the incipient years of the emergent multipolar order. The EU as a normative power, and a benevolent federal state in the making, was expected to overcome its internal complexity and incrementally play its civilizing mission focused on worldwide peace, democracy and human rights. It would thus emerge as a coherent, consistent and fully unified actor, speaking with a single voice.

This collective book aims to contribute to an emerging body of knowledge which aggregates the study of the EU's reality as an unprecedented power (and notably its foreign policy/external relations), not in opposition to, but as a component of, the currently changing, uncertain and heterogeneous internal and international context, while focusing on the actual and possible interactions between its internal complexity and the external world. A decentralized EU and a multipolar context imply both risks and opportunities. The book's shared assumption is that the EU has to be analysed on its own merit rather than as it ought to be according to abstract patterns from the past or ill-defined fears of the future. Consequently, the EU's complex and *sui generis* foreign policy system would be neither fundamentally opposed to an ideally state-styled EU echoing the unification path of the United States; nor impervious to exogenous pressures from the external world. A (re-)conceptualization of the EU's foreign policy and a novel assessment of its performance in both the near and the far abroad, are to be developed through the confrontation of inter-disciplinary dialogues and cross-theoretical dialectics. Also, the necessary empirical research is also rooted in specialist knowledge of the EU's real-world functioning.

Three Key Angles: the Global Context; the Institutional Setting; as well as Near and Far Abroad Partnerships

EU Power in the Global Context

First, this publication is a coordinated research focusing on the international context, notably the possible shifts in global power as conjectured in a set of alternative scenarios for the twenty-first century and their implications for the EU's position. In Chapter 1, A. Gamble offers a detailed assessment of both the kind(s) of global multipolarity which might emerge as well as what the added impact of the worst financial and economic crisis since the 1930s could be. Howorth in turn (Chapter 3) provides a forecast of the evolving transatlantic security regimes which remains a central feature of the international space known as the West. Finally, Telò addresses the actual and potential interplay between external and internal variables of the EU's foreign policy (Chapter 2).

All three authors offer dispassionate and realistic analysis of the global and regional political changes as well as an evaluation of the direct fallout from the worst economic crisis since 1929. They all focus their gaze on likely scenarios regarding the international development of the EU. Gamble provides the book with an overall picture of the external variables of the post-Cold War era, which largely condition the EU's evolving role. Overall, if the United States still has significant resources, it can no longer single-handedly frame the current international transition; whereas emerging powers, in spite of their extraordinary economic dynamism and relatively sheltered position within the global crisis, are still hobbled by underdevelopment, lack of environmental policies and important domestic uncertainties. In this context, an EU weakened by the asymmetries between the monetary union and a want for economic and political union, looks fragile in an increasingly interdependent world wherein institutionalized cooperation faces more and more challenges. However, the EU's resilience is often underestimated. According to Gamble, a neo-multilateral scenario – the most suitable scenario for the EU's development (even if an adaptation of European regionalism to a neo-mercantilist scenario is not excluded) – remains on the table even if this virtuous scenario is forced to face domestic political deadlock; declining unipolarism;

controversial bipolar (US–China) tendencies; and the partial return to balance-of-power logics. However, neo-multilateralist tendencies will be more likely than in the past, given the pluralism of poles and the urgent common challenges calling for better global governance.

J. Howorth's chapter focuses on the effectiveness and impact of security and defence policies in light of the evolving link between the CSDP and NATO. According to Howorth, the 'archetypical scenario' of the EU's performance before and during the Libyan war and the dramatic spending cuts due to the Eurozone crisis are in open conflict with one of the Lisbon Treaty's main objectives: the making of the EU into a credible international security actor through the new Treaty provisions and notably the stronger leadership, the legal personality, the 'structured cooperation' fostering military capabilities. As the Libyan intervention would not have been possible without NATO, the illusions of 'une *Europe puissance*' as an independent security actor seem to have been definitely routed. However, this provocative chapter does not advance a new version of the unipolar scenario alternative identified by Gamble; quite to the contrary, what the author is suggesting is a rethink of NATO and the Common Security and Defence Policy beyond both a hegemonic context and a mutual perception as rivals and contenders. He concludes by outlining 'a CSDP autonomous through and within NATO' and a 'more proactive role for the EU in regional crisis management'.

How to combine this largely shared realistic assessment of the CFSP 20 years after the Maastricht Treaty and almost three years after the Lisbon Treaty with a credible perspective for the EU as a distinctive international power and diplomatic actor? Telò's chapter, while honing in on internal variables, shares Gamble's vision of the ambiguous and uncertain interplay between the evolving EU and the shifting global powers. A balanced assessment must be twofold. On the one hand, the EC/EU was able to gradually reform the relevant Treaty provisions in the hopes of a better coordination and effectiveness of its external relations and foreign policy (the double-hatted HR and the EEAS among others). On the other hand, 2011 and 2012 revealed that the 'king (still) has no clothes', in other words that the capability–expectations gap is still unresolved. Disappointments include: the performances of the CFSP and CSDP in Libya, and in general as the Arab Spring unfolded; the inward-looking impact of the Eurozone crisis; the irresistible demilitarization of the nearly ruined European states; and the negative consequences of the growing institutional complexity. What about the way out of the current crisis? The second part of the contribution recalls the strengths of the EU as an economic, trade, knowledge and civilian power and their external impact. Against conventional wisdom and beyond old myths of a global state-styled power of classical magnitude, coherence and ambition, this chapter illustrates why and how the EU, even with an inevitably enhanced German leadership, could contribute to better global multilateral governance. This will only be possible by combining the structural foreign policy in the long run with a more coordinated and proactive diplomatic action. Beyond two opposite alternatives – a marginalized, irrelevant and inward-looking EU or the missionary zeal of the some of the past decades –

this third way centred on gradually transforming the Westphalian order remains a possible way out of the current deadlock.

The three authors agree both on their disaffection with the past dual conceptualization – the EU as an idealistic 'normative power' and a 'global security actor in the making' vs. the EU as an irrelevant entity – as well as on the need to address in innovative ways the existing deficit of theoretical conceptualization of the EU's institutional set and policies.

Strength and Weaknesses of the EU's Institutional Reform

The increasing complexity of the foreign policy system is the common hypothesis of the chapters provided by Carta, Mayer and Lequesne. In Chapter 4, C. Lequesne frames his analysis of the EEAS within the historical EC/EU objective of setting an institutional body (initially, the secretariat of the Council) charged with coordinating foreign policy. The EEAS has three main functions: strengthening horizontal and vertical coordination, improving circulation of information and providing the EU with new ideas. The chapter's conclusions are twofold: on the one hand, against conventional realist wisdom, he underlines the achievements of the EU and EEAS in managing the bureaucratic side of the EU's external relations; on the other hand, as high politics and urgent international challenges are concerned (Libya, Syria, Palestine, UNSC) the Treaty implementation confirms that we are witnessing a diplomatization of the EU, rather than a Europeanization of the national foreign policies. The lack of visibility and the weakness of the public discourse coming from the Brussels institutions are disappointing, with inevitable consequences, notably the decline in legitimacy.

In Chapter 5, C. Carta's provides a sophisticated analysis of the EEAS building process within the whole context of the CFSP's executive bodies after the Lisbon Treaty. A robust theoretical conceptualization frames a detailed research on the four stages of the CFSP: a) policy initiative; b) policy formulation; c) discourse making; and d) implementation. The research outcome focuses, along the four mentioned stages, on: the crowded leadership table, the unresolved legacy of the pillarized structure, the multiplication of actors, the overlapping competences and tasks, the weaknesses of the coordinating mechanisms, the further compartmentalization, and the confused financial responsibilities.

In Chapter 6 H. Mayer's directly addresses a crucial theoretical issue: why the repeatedly affirmed objective of foreign policy consistency and coherence has never been reached by the EU, despite a multitude of Treaty reforms. He consequently provides an analysis of the five spheres of coherence: a) horizontal and interpillar; b) vertical consistency; c) strategic consistency; d) rhetoric or narrative consistency; e) external consistency related with interaction and communication with other actors. Its real advances notwithstanding, the Lisbon Treaty proved unable to overcome the early dualism between Council and Commission. Also external variables, notably the rules of IOs, make improving vertical consistency an impossible task. In a context where both legal means and the narrative of 'a single European voice' towards consistency and coherence appear exhausted, Mayer concludes by suggesting a more modest and pragmatic, but more credible, external action, stripped of any unrealistic or teleological rhetorical symbols.

The three chapters converge with Part I in so far as defining: the objective of the EU as a unified political and military power as a typically early twentieth-century one, rooted in normative and idealistic symbols of the past which fit neither the current historical evolution nor recent international relations theories. International relations theory, notably when combined with comparative politics, can only strengthen the relevance of neo-institutionalist approaches. Accordingly, rational choice analysis of the reduction of the transaction costs allowed by the creation of the EEAS and Keohane and Goldstein's research on the innovative role of ideas are picked up by Lequesne; public policy analysis resting on the 'policy cycle' theories described in the seminal work of H. Lasswell and others permeate Carta's contribution; and finally, historical institutionalism and 'path dependency' ground the argumentation developed by Mayer.

All three contributors recognize that comparing the EU's foreign policy machinery with national diplomacies is an assignment fraught with danger. Indeed, comparing the EEAS to a Ministry of Foreign Affairs may be just as misleading as a simple comparison between the HR and a Minister of Foreign Affairs. Additionally, even US literature (see Allison and Zelikow) has convincingly argued the end of the realist myth of the unity of state which favoured a single interpretation of 'the' national interest. H. Milner is even clearer when dealing with the United States' WTO negotiations which are seriously influenced by conflicting domestic lobbies. Lequesne is particularly clear when distinguishing between high politics (still in the hands of the larger EU member states) and routinized foreign relations where gradual and partial Europeanization is possible. His conclusion recalls the distinction proposed by T. Lowy regarding the three levels of US external relations: fragmented routine relations; centralized high politics; and polyarchic middle range issues. That which is distinctive to the EU's central institutions is its relative abnegation of high politics issues. However, all the book's authors share the idea that the current world is not characterized by the trivial opposition between a decentralized and post-modern EU and monolithic and centralized emergent powers, be they the BRICS, the United States or any other major actor. Conversely, decentralization not only concerns federal states like the United States, India, Brazil, Russia, Canada, Australia and South Africa; but has also to a different extent even affected China, where political and military centralization can hardly be considered as the internationally most commended consensual feature of the Chinese state structure.

Foreign Policy and External Relations Assessment: Near and Far Abroad

The book's third part presents both the general context of the EU's policies towards its near and far abroad, as well as an assessment of its respective performances. It covers three kinds of external relationship: the ENP which is broached through the lens of the challenging Mediterranean partnership (Gillespie, Chapter 7); the assorted basket of interregional relations the EU has developed over time and throughout the globe (Ponjaert, Chapter 8); finally, the 10 'strategic partnerships' it has set up are to be analysed both as a whole (Grevi, Chapter 9) and through a critical exploration of its three largest Asian components (i.e. China, India and Japan), which are to be respectively assessed by Chen, Bava and Nakamura (Chapters 10, 11 and 12).

R. Gillespie's chapter offers a balanced and rigorous evaluation of the gap between the EU's slow abandonment of past support of authoritarian regimes and the very rapid pace of events in the region since the outbreak of the so-called Arab Spring on the one hand; and the progress the EU had made towards a more differentiated and democracy supportive ENP, on the other. Among the four criteria used to dispassionately assess the ENP's performance since the introduction of the Lisbon Treaty: leadership and strategic vision show the poorest record; whereas the EU's foreign policy discourse has gained in coherence and its overall legitimacy appears to have been upheld. As in Howorth and Telò's chapters, the Libyan crisis is considered a moment of truth for the EU's ongoing partnership with its Southern-rim, and again the relationship seems even more byzantine than before. The reasons behind the relationship's difficulties are multiple, serious and difficult to cope with. Not only the shortage of material aid (from the EEF and a revised EIDHR) hampers the relationship's deployment, but the legacy of different national interest, the narrow scope and vision of the UfM, the complexity of the new Treaty provisions, and competition of external factors all conspired to weaken the EU's action. In conclusion, two questions are raised: first, whether bilateral conditionality within the ENP and ranking the partner states may paradoxically generate a demand from the Southern-rim for a new sort of multilateral architecture; second, whether the EU's reputation in democracy promotion may be affected by the internal yet visible divergences regarding the appropriate methods, civil society linked networks, and types of negative conditionality.

F. Ponjaert's chapter shows that, from the 1970s to the 1990s, the EU's relations with its far abroad were mainly dealt with through its interregional foreign policy toolbox. Interregional arrangements were thus set up with East Asia (ASEAN started as early as 1972 and ASEM was launched in Bangkok in 1996); with Latin America (after the first set of initiatives in the 1980s the 'Rio de Janeiro process' started in 1999) or other smaller groupings such as the Caribbean nations gathered within CARICOM or the Gulf Cooperation Council. Furthermore, group-to-group partnerships, such as the Mediterranean partnerships (Barcelona process and Union for the Mediterranean) or the revived ACP process (Cotonou, ACP Conference, 2000), can also be added to the list of interregional endeavours. Ponjaert provides, through a comparative exercise, a conceptualization of this distinctive kind of post-hegemonic, non-hierarchical, multidimensional, yet also structural contribution to global governance. The same comparison also allows for an evaluation of its strengths and limits in light of its ability to gradually foster new international, diverse, cooperative initiatives, possibly buttressed by bilateral strategic partnerships.

Bilateral strategic partnerships (SPs) between the European Union and single states representing major global and regional actors are increasingly an emerging feature of the EU's foreign policy. G. Grevi's chapter shows that, despite the considerable scepticism surrounding their development and their patent flaws, the 10 existing strategic partnerships (as of 2012) are not only an important and multi-purpose tool in the EU foreign policy arsenal, but they also potentially fulfil reflexive, relational, preventive and structural goals at the same time. Grevi develops his argument further by introducing new insights into the practical functioning of the SPs' machinery.

The EU's strategic partnerships differ fundamentally from bilateral relationships set up by traditional powers as SPs are not set up in line with *Realpolitik* dictated practices. The EU's strategic partnerships are not principally concerned with security objectives, but rather aim at sublimating bilateral transactions into a factor paving the way to multilateral cooperation. The list of the current SPs includes traditional allies, medium size powers and all the BRICS countries. Grevi remains quite pessimistic when considering the chances of seeing a spontaneous trend towards enhanced multilateralism emerge in today's heterogeneous multipolar world. However, the EU's efforts at strategic partnership building may be 'conducive to stronger multilateral cooperation. As such, they form part of a structural approach to foreign policy, shaping international relations beyond bilateral transactions'. The Durban UN conference on climate change is a good example. In this sense strategic partnerships might connect the distinctive long-term structural foreign policy practiced by the EU (see Chapter 2) to concrete issue-linkage opportunities and diplomatic efforts geared towards fostering rule-based global or regional governance. However, the challenges and uncertainties ahead remain very significant. First, whether more focused, issue-driven, functionally structured SPs can improve their performance compared with past iterations is still to be proven. Second, whether the EU's partners will accept multi-purpose and sovereignty-sharing forms of multilateral cooperation instead of instrumental and sovereignty-enhancing ones is equally uncertain.

The Eastward shift in economic growth and global power makes a common research agenda with our East- and South-Asian partners particularly meaningful. The EU has successfully engaged the three major economic powers of Asia: Japan since 1991; China since 2003; and India since 2004. The final three chapters focus on the commonalities and differences between these key strategic partnerships, all of which are framed by the EU's 'New Asia Strategy' which was published in 1994, and revised in 2001.

The 1991 joint declaration launched EU–Japanese cooperation as the earliest Euro-Asian partnerships, reflecting the EU's initial preference for like-minded partners. However Europe's search for strategic and political convergence with two fellow civilian powers – i.e. Canada and Japan – was a first innovation in the EU's foreign policy outlook as it sought to timidly move beyond its main traditional military ally: the United States. However, as highlighted by H. Nakamura, 'trilateralism' (including the United States) provided the overriding security framework for these initial strategic partnerships, for example NATO has framed the partnership with Canada, while the 'Trilateral Commission' and the G7 has done so with Japan.

Asserting that economic ties were the driving force for expanding bilateral partnership with emerging economies is only partially true. According to Z. Chen, the subsequent relationship between the EU and China experienced its highest point just after the launching of the formal bilateral strategic partnership on 31 October 2003, and this in parallel with the booming bilateral economic ties. Chen argues that, after serious disappointments, the history of this particular SP has recently entered a third stage which is more fluid and thus rich in both risk and opportunities. The first years after 2003 were characterized not only by booming trade but also by a political convergence against US unilateralism. Furthermore, according to S. Bava, a common aspiration for a more autonomous international role also explains the upgrading of the India–EU partnership in 2004, and its associated 2005 Action Plan. All in all, this first stage marked by the initial multiplication of partnerships was rooted in very optimistic forecasts about the emergence of an international role for the EU and its supposed convergence with like-minded new emerging global powers.

All three authors conclude by most accounts that the initial results of the SP were not in line with their initial expectations. For Nakamura the weak leadership on either side of the EU–Japan relationship was to be blamed for failing to seize upon the opportunities created by the potentially high impact of the convergence between two civilian powers. When assessing the poor record of implementation of the ambitious Action Plan of 2005, the critical perception put forward by Bava underlines what she defines as the EU's twofold arrogance: as a normative entrepreneur and a discriminating defender of its own economic interest. Furthermore she mentions the double standard compared with the more intensive pro-China commitment and the resistance of Europeans to the change of the international status quo demanded by emergent India. The value-based diplomacy plays a relevant role in the criticism presented in Chen's chapter as well. Moreover, he adds two explaining factors: an enhanced political divergence due to the return to the primacy of the transatlantic relation (under the impetus of Merkel and Sarkozy) and the negative consequences of the Eurozone crisis: inward-looking trend, the image of declining power, re-nationalization of external policies complicating the EU's two-level foreign policy system. However a third stage is maybe open, starting with the Lisbon Treaty paving the way to alternative scenarios, according to the three chapters: the prioritization of bilateral national partnerships with EU member states, or a more pragmatic, functional, search for win-win compromises between the two sides on their respective key concerns.

Strategic partnerships are alternatively considered either as nothing more than rhetoric for a strange power like the EU (missing military might, a classical strategic culture, and bold relationships with traditional and new powers), or as possible only with a state-styled evolution of the European political union. In both cases, the EU's foreign policy would be definitely unable to cope with the emergent mutipolar world. This book's authors support a third, more understated but vibrant hypothesis which is also a research agenda unto itself. After a hard learning process characterized by Eurocentric approaches and normative diplomacy, and provided an integrative exit out of the Eurozone crisis, the EU's bilateral strategic partnerships may represent a post-hegemonic and innovative form of global governance. Even if it is uncertain whether with the EU's interregional relations; outwardly SPs could also potentially translate the EU's long-term structural foreign policy into compromise ready diplomatic action, thus paving the way to wider and less contingent multilateral cooperation.

PART I
The EU: A Controversial Global Political Actor Within an Emergent Multipolar World

Chapter 1

The EU and the Evolving Shift of Power in Global Governance

Andrew Gamble

Abstract

The world order was transformed by the end of the Cold War, which allowed the US-dominated liberal world order to incorporate most of the rest of the world. This unipolar system was short-lived partly because of the ambitions of the EU to make itself a global actor, but mainly because of the emergence of rising powers, particularly Brazil, China and India, which raised the prospect of a fundamental shift of power in the way the world order was governed. The financial crash of 2008 and the Eurozone crisis since 2010 underline the growing relative weakness of Western states, and accelerated trends towards shifts in power between established and rising powers. What form these shifts will take is uncertain, and will depend in part on whether and how the political deadlocks both at domestic and international level such as those in the United States and the European Union are resolved, and what kind of new world order then emerges. A number of scenarios as to how the international economy and the international state system might develop are set out, together with their implications for the European Union.

Introduction

The contemporary world order was transformed in 1991 by the collapse of the Soviet Union, which created for a time a unipolar world in security terms, the apparent triumph of the West, and the consolidation and extension of the multilateral liberal market order which had been fashioned under US leadership. It freed the European Union from dependence on the security guarantees of the United States, and led to attempts from the Maastricht Treaty to the Lisbon Treaty to turn the European Union into a global political actor (see Chapter 2 in this volume) developing a common foreign and defence policy while extending the already existing common economic policy to embrace monetary union. This new assertiveness and distinctiveness of Europe was accompanied by the rise of new powers, in particular Brazil, India and China, which many observers interpreted as signalling the emergence of a new multipolar world, opening up possibilities for both multilateral and bilateral cooperation as well as conflict between the main players, along with new forms of regional economic and security cooperation.

The emergence of the new rising powers has led to speculation about a fundamental shift in power in the world order, as they become leading players and seek to alter the system in their favour. Their challenge is to the Western-dominated liberal world order of the last 200 years which in the nineteenth century was shaped and sustained first by Britain and subsequently by the United States. The future of this system in the twenty-first century was already looking uncertain with the prospective return to a multipolar world, and this uncertainty has been magnified by the crash of 2008 and its aftermath, and the significant economic weakness in North America and Europe it has revealed. The robustness of the political and economic foundations of the growth of the rising powers has also however been questioned. There seems no easy transition to the next stage in the evolution of the international economy and the fragmented state system which is an integral part of it, and it is difficult to imagine concretely what that next stage might be. There are optimistic and pessimistic readings of the political and economic outlook, and the future of Europe. The European Union has been through many difficulties, but the crisis over sovereign debt in the Eurozone since 2010 is threatening to become a fundamental existential crisis over the future of the European Union itself – whether the predictions of a steady decline of Europe's influence and importance in the world will be proved right, and even whether the kind of association between states which the European Union has pioneered can survive (see Cramme 2009; Lucarelli et al. 2011; Marquand 2011; Telò 2009; Tsoukalis 2009).

The crisis in the Eurozone has also raised questions over the feasibility of the EU becoming a global political actor, a major aim of the Lisbon Treaty (see Chapters 2 and 3 in this volume), and rising powers such as India and China have been reassessing the importance for them of having the EU as a strategic partner in the future (see Chapters 10, 11 and 12 in this volume). As the balance of power in global governance continues to evolve, the weaknesses exposed in part by the Eurozone crisis may make it difficult for the EU to play a full part in shaping the outcome.

The End of Bipolarity

The opening of the Berlin Wall in 1989 and the collapse of the Soviet Union in 1991 brought to an end four decades of Cold War between the Soviet Union and the United States, and the bipolar structure which had come to define both the international state system and the international economy after 1945. The sudden collapse of the Soviet Union was not anticipated by many analysts, but in retrospect it was not considered a surprise (Halliday 2000). The competition had been unequal from the start, and the bipolarity existed because the USSR possessed nuclear weapons rather than because it was a genuine competitor which might have supplanted the United States across all dimensions of power.

The security threat posed by the Soviet Union helped the United States to weld together its allies into a relatively cohesive and successive international economy and security alliance. The European Union had grown up within that context, and with American support.

The end of bipolarity with the disintegration of the Soviet Union left the United States without any serious challenger. In military terms it was now overwhelmingly dominant. Most of the other major military powers, including those within the EU, were its allies and likely to remain so, although the EU now felt able to plan its own defence and security policy. The international economy was reunified under the control of the institutions which the United States had set up after 1945. For the first time since before 1914 the international economy was once again one economy, with many economies that had formerly stood outside it, including China and India, now engaging with it. Free market capitalism and liberal democracy appeared unchallengeable as the ideological principles for this new unified world, and the spread of both to all parts of the international system of states was confidently predicted (Fukuyama 1992).

During the 1990s the liberalisation of the international economy begun in the 1980s combined with the expansion of the world market to promote a new boom in the international economy. The era of stagflation which had afflicted the United States in the 1970s was definitively banished, and many countries now experienced steady rates of growth and low inflation. Some of the most successful economies of the Cold War period, Germany and Japan, did not participate in this success, Germany because it was struggling with the costs of reunification, and Japan because it was coping with a severe deflation after its financial implosion at the end of the 1980s. But the relatively subdued performance of these two former engine rooms of the international economy was more than compensated by the high rates of growth achieved first by China and then by other rising powers, including India and Brazil. The flood of cheap imports from these countries pushed inflation down to historically low levels in the more developed countries, while providing surpluses which were recycled through an increasingly inventive financial system and created ever higher levels of demand. The twin supports for this boom were thus increasing personal, corporate and public debt made possible by an expanding financial services industry, and low cost manufactures, made possible by the industrialisation and urbanisation of major countries in Asia (Glyn 2006).

This boom was taken as another signal that the United States and the political and economic order over which it had presided since 1945 now incorporated the majority of states in the international economy, with only a few remaining outside or resistant to it. The discourse on globalisation became dominant in the 1990s, with the talk of a borderless world, and dreams once again of creating a perpetual peace (Hay and Marsh 1999; Held and McGrew 2007). The European Community, which had been so important in binding together the countries of Western Europe during the Cold War, now emerged as the promoter of a new post-Cold War model of multilateral integration, with proposals for a full Union embracing monetary cooperation and defence cooperation. The idea of Europe as a model for the liberal world order, promoting a relatively open form of regionalism, took hold (Telò 2005).

The era of liberal peace, however, soon became one of liberal war as a number of small-scale wars against failed states and against states labelled terrorist states erupted. While US military dominance remained unquestioned, it proved very difficult for the United States to translate its military superiority into control over particular states. This was illustrated by the 9/11 terrorist attacks on New York which led to the United States declaring a war on terror and embarking on interventions first in Afghanistan and then in Iraq. These wars and their messy outcomes underlined how far much of the world was from embracing a single set of values and institutions, or accepting without question US leadership. It also displayed the vulnerabilities of the United States and led to reassessments of the different kinds of hard and soft power which the United States had at its disposal (Nye 2003). While the United States remained world's only superpower, or hyper-power as some preferred, its reach was shown to have limits. The strong movement of opinion in the United States in favour of US primacy and in the forceful assertion of US power which had been such a strong feature of the neo-conservative critique of US foreign policy in the 1990s, and helped shape the US response to 9/11, has been checked by the difficulties encountered in Iraq and Afghanistan, and induced a new mood of disengagement in the United States (Fukuyama 2006).

One of the results of the more proactive US foreign policy after 2001 was to divide Europe into those governments which supported the United States in its war on terror, and those which disassociated themselves from it. EU governments were split, although EU public opinion much less so, and it led to some angry exchanges between European and US politicians and commentators, with Europe being perceived as too weak and divided to provide for its own defence, yet unwilling any longer to support the United States (Kagan 2003). Although much diplomatic effort was spent repairing the rift, the division was an increasingly real one, with most European countries choosing to spend much less on defence than the United States (see Chapter 3 in this volume) and being unwilling to sanction overseas intervention without explicit UN authorisation. The United States found its political and ideological authority waning, and its position as the undisputed leader of the West weakened.

The other looming challenge was the rise of new great powers – China above all, but also India, Brazil and a reorganised Russia. Unlike the EU these states had not been incorporated into the American-led West, and they now appeared as potential challengers to the US liberal world order, China being particularly singled out by many US commentators as the next potential threat to the liberal world order and US hegemony within it (Friedberg 2011; Halper 2010; Swaine 2011). The liberal world order of the last 200 years has maintained a relatively open international economy based on liberal principles encouraging free movement of goods, capital and labour and instituting common rules for the conduct of trade and international affairs. While proclaiming universal principles it also served the immediate interests of its leading powers, first Britain and then the United States. The challenges to it had come initially from Germany and the United States before 1914, but the United States ultimately sided with Britain and France against Germany. That war however fractured the liberal world order and attempts to rebuild it failed. A new wave of challenges now came from Germany, Japan and the Soviet Union. After the defeat of Germany and Japan made possible by the alliance between the United States and the USSR, there followed a long stand-off between the two former allies. The liberal world order so badly damaged after 1914 had taken 80 years to be fully restored (Van der Pijl 2006).

It was however a very different liberal world order. Europe was no longer central to it, and the colonial empires had disappeared. Through the European Union Europe had overcome its internal fragmentation and divisions which have caused two world wars, and now emerged as a zone of peace and prosperity, comfortably within the American security umbrella, with its own distinctive model of welfare, human rights and democratic governance. The EU was not a great power in the traditional sense, its decision-making structures were opaque, and formation of a unified political will and common policies was slow and difficult. After the disintegration of the USSR the EU began to enlarge further, gradually admitting new members from Eastern Europe. By 2008 it had 27 members, with several more states seeking to join. The EU was now the largest economy in the international market with a population higher than the United States. But in most contexts the EU was not treated as a single entity but continued to be broken down into its constituent parts. There were numerous examples of this in international organisations. Britain and France retained their separate seats in the United Nations; Britain, France, Germany and Italy were separate members of the G8; and the G20 when it began to assume a greater role after the financial crash included the same four G8 EU members, an additional seat for the EU as a whole. Other EU states, including Spain and the Netherlands, were given observer status at some meetings. The EU was recognised as an important and essential part of the functioning of international institutions and the international community, but its capacity to exercise leadership was limited, and while European attitudes often inspired US irritation at times, the EU was not seen as challenging the position of the United States. It subscribed broadly to the same set of principles and understood the operation of the liberal world order in the same way as the United States (Anderson 2009; Cafruny and Ryner 2007; Garton Ash 2005).

If there was an underlying shift in world power in this period the threat to the position of the United States came less from the EU than from the rising powers, which precisely because they were rising introduced uncertainty as to their long-term intentions and interests. The scale of the transformation that began to take place in the two decades after the opening of the Berlin Wall and the collapse of communism in Europe marks this period out as potentially one of the great watersheds in modern world history. The Eurocentric character of the governance of the world order in the last 200 years has been much analysed. Even in 2000 the richest and most powerful states were the same as in 1900, with the solitary exception of Japan. States had risen and declined, but the basic hierarchy remained intact (Arrighi 1994). But by 2000 it was already clear that changes were in train which would transform that hierarchy in the twenty-first century. The richest and most powerful states by 2100 are certain to include several of the new rising powers. Even before the 2008 financial crash a key question had become how these rising powers could be fully integrated into the international economy and into its governance arrangements. The size of these states and their economic potential meant that their legitimate interests would have to be accommodated. Such alterations in the balance of power had however rarely been accomplished without friction and conflict. Finding a way to prevent the economic challenge of China becoming a security challenge was acknowledged as a key task for the international community.

The 2008 Financial Crash

The financial crash of 2008 not only brought the boom in the Western economy to an end; it signalled the opening of a new era in the international economy, inaugurating a period of economic and political reconstruction (Gamble 2009). The crash did not affect all states equally; its effects were felt most sharply in Europe and North America. The rising powers suffered some effects from the contraction of demand in some of their most important markets, but this at most moderated the pace of their advance. It did not stop it. The dependence of the rising powers on Western markets was real but not absolute, and the onset of the crisis forced all states to rethink their economic strategies, and what would preserve their economic security and prosperity in the future.

The dimensions of the current crisis are still uncertain, but three years after the initial crisis over the financial system in 2008 it is already clear that the recession in the Western states which has followed is much more than just a normal cyclical correction. There has not been a sharp V-shaped recovery. Instead there was a steep plunge in output of around 6–9 per cent in many Western economies, followed by a weak recovery in 2010, followed by a further downturn in 2011. In 2012 there were again signs of an economic recovery, notably in the United States, but the indicators remained weak, and there were concerns that this recovery too might be reversed. The level of output before the crash has still not been regained in many countries, a sign of strong deflationary pressures created by the overhang of public, private and corporate debt. The difficulties of paying down debt and creating the right conditions for growth is proving very testing for policy-makers across the Western world, and this has led to fears that the Western economy may be entering a prolonged period of stagnation and deflation similar to that endured by Japan in the 1990s (Kaletsky 2010; Koo 2009; Krugman 2009).

The pessimistic assessment of the Western economy is that a period of very slow growth has become inevitable while the debt burden is reduced. Many Western countries, particularly in the EU, have few obvious sources of renewed growth. To the extent that the last boom was kept going by ever increasing levels of corporate, public and personal debt, this is no longer a viable option while levels of debt remain so high, and so many Western banks remain fragile. Major new innovations which revolutionise production by reducing the cost base across industry are proving difficult to identify, population levels in many countries are declining or static, and immigration faces increasing domestic hostility. The explosive growth in some of the populous countries of the world is increasing demand for raw materials and resources, and while this is giving prosperity to resource-rich countries such as Australia, the overall effect is upward pressure on commodity prices. The international economy has so far avoided a return to high inflation, despite the financial measures such as quantitative easing and interest rates close to zero taken by central banks to keep economies afloat after the financial crash. But inflationary pressures are increasing, particularly in China, and governments everywhere may lack the political will to resist them since inflation is the easiest short-term way to reduce the debt burden in the absence of growth.

Political Deadlocks

The model of growth that served so well for almost two decades looks extremely hard to resuscitate, but finding a new model is not easy. One result of the greater economic integration that resulted from the boom is that the world is on some measures more integrated and interconnected than it has ever been, but politically it is still fragmented, and the difficulty of organising cooperation to deal with the many common problems remains perhaps the greatest threat to human societies. The balance of power in global governance may have begun to shift from West to East, but it is doing so in an uncontrolled and unpredictable manner, and no one is sure what kind of world order will come next. Much will depend on how various political deadlocks are resolved, such as the deadlock in the United States over its growing debt. The debt first became an important factor in US politics during the Reagan years. Today it has reached $15 trillion and is still rising. All sides agree that the debt cannot be allowed to go on increasing indefinitely, but there is no agreement on how it should be cut, and a stalemate has developed between President and Congress. Underlying this domestic battle is a much deeper conflict over how the United States is to balance the spending abroad it needs to preserve its hegemony with the fiscal regime at home it needs to maintain domestic support. After 1945 the United States secured for itself a privileged position in the international monetary system because the dollar became the international currency and main international store of value, which has meant that the United States has never been subject to the same constraints as other nations (Eichengreen 1996; Schwartz 2000). Since the early 1960s the United States has been a debtor rather than a creditor nation, spending huge sums abroad and at home which other nations have been prepared to finance. In the latest cycle it is China which has become one of the main holders of US Treasury bonds, recycling the export surpluses which it earns from selling to the United States (Thompson 2010).

These arrangements are in the end not economic but political. Germany, Japan, Saudi Arabia and the UK have all had their reasons in the past for bankrolling the United States. The Chinese have powerful reasons for doing so now. The problem for the United States is whether this is a sustainable long-term basis on which to project power. The dangers of imperial overstretch preoccupied theorists of US decline in the 1980s (Kennedy 1988) and the problem has not gone away. The United States possesses significant reserves of strength; it still has a dynamic and diverse economy, many of the world's leading research universities, a relatively young population because of immigration, large natural resources, and cultural power. But like many leading powers before it, the United States is no longer generating sufficient wealth to do all the things it is attempting to do.

Many are now predicting that one consequence will eventually be a shift of power in global governance from the United States and Europe to China and other rising powers. The gap between established and rising powers is still large. China is the world's second largest economy on GDP measures, but measured by income per capita it is still a long way below the level of the United States and Europe. The same is true when looking at the impact on the environment. China has recently become the largest single emitter of greenhouse gases (17 per cent of the world's total, as opposed to 16 per cent for the United States). But in terms of emissions per head, China is only 25 per cent of the US level, and half the European level. India is still further behind. Such statistics are used by China and India to argue that they are still developing countries and cannot be expected to shoulder the burdens of leadership borne by rich countries. While China on present trends will become the largest world economy fairly soon, it will need to maintain its present rate of growth for several more decades until it matches the United States in terms of its productivity. There is no certainty that China can sustain its present rate of growth, or that the United States will remain locked into low growth (Breslin 2007). When the United States was a rising power at the end of the nineteenth century its productivity was already ahead of its rivals. None of today's rising powers are in a comparable position to that of the United States in the 1920s, still less to its position in 1945.

What the rising powers possess is enormous potential, because of the size of their populations and distinctive cultural traditions, and also because of the opportunity they have to adopt the techniques and technologies already pioneered in more developed economies. The major problem confronting the rising powers, and China in particular, is finding a way to continue their rapid modernisation, industrialisation and urbanisation in ways that both avoid frictions with established powers and maintain internal domestic legitimacy. This is a tightrope demanding extraordinary political skill, and the main question mark over the rising powers is whether they have the kind of culture, institutions and independent civil society which can generate the political leadership to secure them (Hutton 2006).

The drama playing out in the Eurozone also reflects the policy dilemma at the global level. Political fragmentation in the Eurozone prevents the adoption of solutions to the financial crisis, just as political fragmentation in the G20 prevents adoption of workable solutions to global problems, whether of international financial architecture, nuclear proliferation or global warming. The single currency assumes a single economy with a single political authority standing behind it. Without that there will continue to be major divergences in productivity between different parts of the Eurozone, and therefore an underlying balance of payments problem which the markets recognise but the institutions of the Eurozone do not. Trying to deal with divergences in productivity and balance of payments problems through fiscal compacts and austerity packages will not work, because they will always be insufficient, and will not command the confidence of the bond markets. Only full fiscal union is likely to satisfy the bond markets that the monetary union can be sustained, but full fiscal union means in effect a federal state, for which there is little popular support. There is a European demos but it is weak compared to those of the nation-states, and during this recession nationalist and populist forces on both left and right have been gaining ground in many member states.

The EU in a Changing World Order

The shift of power from West to East in the international economy and the international state system is still potential rather than actual. The financial crash in 2008 has highlighted the relative economic strength of the rising powers and their ability to keep growing, while the Western economy is predicted to endure many years of slow growth, debt deleveraging and austerity. If this forecast turns out to be accurate it will strengthen the case for reform of global governance institutions, particularly voting rules in the IMF and World Bank, and even the UN Security Council, and the consolidation of the G20 rather than the G8 as the main forum for the discussion of common issues. This would represent a move to a much more multilateral system of global governance, one modelled on the institutional forms which have emerged in the EU. But it would need the other leading powers, particularly the United States and China, to agree.

In the period since 1945 the governance of the international economy was organised under US leadership, with the Soviet Union and its allies excluding themselves. It combined both multilateral and unilateral relationships, hegemonic and imperial logics, and various forms of regionalism (Ikenberry 2004: 609–30; Telò 2007). But the United States was always the prime mover in organising these different relationships in both security and economy. In the present period the position of the United States is no longer guaranteed. It still has the capacity and the will to reassert its leadership. No other country can begin to match its strengths and advantages (Nye 2011) but this is against a background in which its underlying structural power is declining relatively and can be expected to go on declining as the rising powers realise their potential. There is no new hegemon waiting in the wings in the way that the United States was when Britain began its decline, and therefore any new pattern of global governance which emerges will either have to be multilateral or bilateral and regional. As the EU has learned, however, such relationships evolve slowly and take enormous patience and skill to manage. There are not many incentives for a declining hegemon to participate, and this increases the risk of political fragmentation.

Four possible scenarios for the development of the international state system and the international economy are sketched in Table 1.1.

Table 1.1 Scenarios for the development of the international economy and the international state system

	Geopolitics	Political economy
Scenario A	**Unipolar** US leadership maintained Challenge of rising powers postponed Reinforcement of existing international rules and institutions	**U-shaped recovery** Further globalisation Return to finance-led growth
Scenario B	**Bipolar** United States shares leadership with China (G2) New cold war or mutual dependence Bilateral bargains	**W-shaped recovery** Short weak rallies Competition for energy, water, resources, regional influence
Scenario C	**Multipolar – multilateral** **United States shares leadership with G20** Multilateral bargains on environment, trade, nuclear proliferation Rewriting of rules Rebalancing of power	**V-shaped or U-shaped recovery** Conditions created for new boom Green New Deal Eco-modernisation
Scenario D	**Multipolar – regionalism and US decline** Disengagement from leadership Division into blocs Spheres of influence	**L-shaped recovery** More protectionism Less trade, less interdependence, less growth Energy, population, resource pressures

In each scenario a different assumption is made about the role of the United States in global governance and the kind of recovery which takes place in the international economy, and particularly in the Western part of the international economy. The most positive of these scenarios is scenario C, which assumes there can be a grand multilateral bargain at the international level brokered by the United States, made possible by the overcoming of the internal deadlocks, and the creation of conditions for renewed growth in the whole international economy. The most negative is scenario D which assumes US disengagement and return to a more isolationist posture, and a consequent development of relatively closed forms of regionalism and political fragmentation. Scenarios A and B are in between. Scenario A is the closest to business as usual, in which the United States reasserts itself, and another phase of the development of the international economy proceeds under US leadership, with minimal change either to the dominant growth model or to global governance arrangements. Scenario B assumes the emergence of a new bipolar world with the relationship between China and the United States critical for global governance. This could be accompanied by increasing friction and competition between them.

These scenarios suggest different futures for the EU and the Eurozone. The EU has much greater resilience than many of its critics allege, and although its shortcomings have become rather visible in the last few years, its strengths tend to be overlooked. It faces a testing time in holding together through the sovereign debt crisis, and in particular finding a growth model which will work for the whole Eurozone. Domestic political constraints on all the members of the Eurozone are severe, and this complicates the task of finding durable solutions at the EU level. Several member states are also sitting on the sidelines refusing to get involved. The EU will thrive best in scenarios C and D. In scenario C a multilateral grand bargain would be the echo of the grand bargain which Europe itself has been seeking. The EU would be genuinely a microcosm of the wider system of global governance. The EU would be most comfortable in a world of multilateral governance, rather than a world of great powers. The EU is not a great power and is most unlikely to become one (see Chapter 2 in this volume). In the eventuality of scenario D the EU would suffer from the effects of the breakup of the liberal world order, but would be well-placed to organise its own defensive regional bloc. Scenarios A and B pose more problems. In scenario A the EU would not gain greater influence as it would in scenario C, and would more likely suffer a decline of influence, because Europe would have less strategic and economic importance for the United States. In scenario B European influence would also be likely to decline because of the stand-off between China and the United States, in which Europe would be of less importance as a strategic partner for the United States than it was during the Cold War. Other countries, particularly Brazil, India and Japan, would be more significant. In both of these scenarios the EU would have difficulty discovering a new growth model and developing its own strategic partnerships with the rising powers, and would tend to continue its relative decline to other parts of the international economy.

The size and wealth of the European economy, the prestige of its social model and its system of multilateral governance means that the EU will remain a significant player under all these scenarios, but failure to resolve its internal problems may mean that it becomes less central in shaping how the world is governed, and becomes a less important strategic partner for the other major players, including the rising powers. This may be unavoidable. As in previous shifts of power it is impossible for all states to retain their former positions. The rebalancing of the international state system and international economy is rooted in material factors, the reality of which has eventually to be accepted. States can manage to adjust to relative decline; it is absolute decline which poses much sharper problems. To avoid an absolute decline the EU has to resolve its conundrum of too much debt and too little growth. It has to overcome its internal deadlocks and find new leadership and direction, and establish a new coherence in its foreign policy and in its strategy as a global actor. If it fails then it may become steadily more marginal in international affairs, as power and influence move elsewhere.

Chapter 2

The EU: A Civilian Power's Diplomatic Action after the Lisbon Treaty. Bridging Internal Complexity and International Convergence

Mario Telò

What is rational is real and what is real is rational.
– G.W.F. Hegel, *Preface to 'The Philosophy of Right'* (1821)

Abstract

Is the post-Lisbon Treaty EU's foreign policy system fit to cope with the emergent multipolar world? This chapter will critically analyse the legal/institutional achievements (throughout the long revision process until the Lisbon Reform Treaty), arguing that each progress towards enhanced coherence was paradoxically increasing internal complexity, to some extent explaining the serious shortcomings of the EU's international performance of 2011 and 2012. However, quantitative/ qualitative indicators illustrate the EU's actual international influence, multiple contributions to regional and global governance and unprecedented civilian power. By the same token the hypothesis of an emerging more 'German EU' is thought of as a confirmation of previous trends rather than an inflexion. The second part of the chapter provides an analysis of the concrete ways ahead, as well as some implications for the EU's structural foreign policy and diplomatic action within a changing, heterogeneous and porous multipolar context.

Introduction

This chapter is part of a research effort aiming to answer a twofold question born from the extraordinary progress the EU accomplished with the Lisbon Treaty with regards to its aims of enhanced efficiency and democratic legitimacy. First, the internal pace of reforms is both too slow compared with the rapid global and regional changes, and is far from giving birth to a state-styled political power. Beyond past illusions, the EU is however a relevant economic, trade and civilian power, capable of producing structural foreign policy. The difficulty is what is exactly meant by this distinctive external action, and how to combine it – after the Lisbon Treaty – with a flexible bilateral and multilateral diplomatic action?

Second, to what extent and how, is the EU, even if weakened by the economic crisis, a proactive part of the emergent global governance? Multilevel and multifaceted communication looks not only possible but is an everyday experience through bilateral as well as multilateral networking, be it with the near or faraway partners. The multipolar world is not a homogeneous, compact and threatening context for a post-modern EU. On the one hand, the EU is internally complex because of the influence and weight of the intergovernmental logic; and on the other hand, even the BRICS are a varied, internally differentiated group with varying degrees of openness to more binding global governance. Is a third, more modest and realist but also more communicative and flexible way possible for EU diplomacy beyond the Eurocentric illusions of the past? An alternative between irrelevance and conflict with the rest of the world, either of which would mean an irresistible decline?

Improving the EU's Institutional Capabilities from Maastricht to Lisbon: Strengths and Limits of a Complex Foreign Policy System

Power depends on both the changing context and internal resources. Provided a correct evaluation of the weight of the international context as a crucial variable of the EU's political integration, it is possible to understand the role of the internal demands of developing a foreign policy in a more consistent, coherent and unified way. Only after 1989/91 could the EC/EU upgrade its previous international profile as a modest US junior partner, more likely to be a possible victim of history rather than proactive player. The end of the Soviet Union's nuclear threat made it possible to address the challenge of increasing its political autonomy from the United States and look beyond the region and update its institutional set accordingly. Previous foreign policy declarations (the 'Venice Declaration' on Arab-Israeli conflict, 1980, support for the 'Contadora Group' in Central America, 1985, among others), when relevant, were rhapsodic, ephemeral and without practical consequences. The large gap between the economic/trade giant EC and the political dwarf could eventually be addressed – at least in a fledgling way – thanks to both internal pressures linked to the integration process (the modest EPC was included in the SEA since 1986) and external, systemic, changes related to the end of the bipolar world. Relevant steps forward were achieved during the subsequent two decades.

However, confronting the absolute progress with the acceleration of world history towards a new unipolar/multipolar world wherein the EU risks marginalization and irrelevance is definitely necessary. It is uncontroversial that the biggest success of the EU's foreign policy over the last 20 years was the implementation of an objective which is not traditionally classified as a foreign policy one: the Eastern enlargement and the peaceful organization of Europe at a quasi-continental scale. What about the foreign policy, as a policy independent from enlargement policy?

On the one hand, the 1992 Treaty of Political Union signed in Maastricht set up the new dual institutional architecture of the EU's external relations by creating a second pillar (CFSP) characterized by special intergovernmental procedures in opposition to the 'community procedures' of the first pillar's external relations (trade policy, development, humanitarian aid policy, etc.). On the other hand, article C of the new Treaty of the European Union established a 'single institutional framework'.[1] As the vertical consistency between member states and the EU is concerned, articles 19 and 20 of the TEU aimed at enhancing the low degree of loyalty and coordination, notably of the largest member states, and so put into practice the idea of shared sovereignty and collective power.

This institutional progress looks relevant compared with the EC of the 1970s and 1980s. Functionalists, neo-functionalists and federalists argued that since the foundation of the first European communities the European construction made progress towards integration through internal crises (failure of the EDC in 1954, the 'empty chair crisis' in the 1960s). Systemic schools emphasized the role of international changes like 1945–7 and 1989–91 (origins and end of the bipolar world). Both matter, yet was this step fit for the post-Cold War world?

The Maastricht Treaty is historic in nature; as a product of single market pressures in favour of a common currency on the one hand, and of Franco-German interpretation of the end of Cold War as political opportunity for the EU to grow up as a political actor, on the other. However, it was not a true common foreign and security policy that was institutionalized by the Treaty, but rather a soft form of intergovernmental coordination, not that far removed from the previous EPC. Over the last 20 years the CFSP offered more added-value to smaller states than to bigger ones which loathe coordination, notably when high politics are concerned. Its objectives were missed on several occasions, for example during the former-Yugoslavian conflicts or the Iraq War (2002–8). The Europeanization of national foreign policies is advancing slower than expected, whereas diplomatization of EU intergovernmental institutions is far from disappearing.[2]

---

1 Article C: 'The Union shall be served by a single institutional framework which shall ensure the consistency and the continuity of the activities carried out in order to attain its objectives while respecting and building upon the "acquis communautaire". The Union shall in particular ensure the consistency of its external activities as a whole in the context of its external relations, security, economic and development policies. The Council and the Commission shall be responsible for ensuring such consistency. They shall ensure the implementation of these policies, each in accordance with its respective powers.'

2 Three forms of Europeanization are taking place: a) top-down policy convergence; b) bottom-up national projection; and c) socialization/internalization of Europe in national identities (see Wong 2005). The concept is interesting in the extent to which it brings together institutions and identities. Since the independent variable is the regional integration process, Europeanization is stagnating in a period of economic crisis despite the role of non-state actors and of various neo-functionalist pressures from within. Wong's

The very poor performances outlined above clearly demonstrate a degree of inefficiency and lack of effectiveness of the new 'second pillar'. Consequently, the CFSP was revised by the Amsterdam Treaty (1997), notably with regards to its visibility (High Representative – even if supported by a very limited staff) and efficiency (QMV procedure is possible in the Council regarding individual actions, provided that a strategy has been previously and unanimously approved). However what may have been enough during the 'Liberal peace' of the 1990s was not appropriate during the 'Liberal war' (Gamble 2012): the Iraq crisis and the calls for resistance to the unipolar momentum. The 'Laeken Declaration', approved in December 2001, called for a new stronger EU global role. The European Convention of 2002–3 subsequently showed commitment to reconciling the serious internal political divergences with new provisions strengthening external coherence and consistency.

The Lisbon Treaty entered into force on 1 December 2009. It was the outcome of a 20-year-long, complex, sometimes dramatic constitutional debate, wherein the enhanced role of the EU in the world was one of the main guidelines. This debate stagnated between 2002 and 2003 as some of the main member states actively supported the Iraq War. This can account for the limitations of the institutional compromises reached in 2003/4 regarding the 'European Security Strategy' and the Constitutional Treaty. The latter, even if rejected in 2005 as a result of the French and Dutch referenda, eventually revived in 2007 as the Lisbon Treaty. According to the literature, the realm of external relations counts amongst the treaty's most relevant innovations. Why?

A New Institutional Environment

First, the previously independent posts of High Representative for CFSP and Commissioner for External Relations (Commission Vice-President) were merged. Contrary to the advice given by the first High Representative J. Solana, the challenge of increasing the CFSP's horizontal coherence and vertical consistency was addressed by this relevant but extremely complex institutional change: a double-hatted authority, chair of the new Council of Foreign Affairs, and provided with the support of an integrated ('two hats') European external action service. Second, the permanent President of the European Council underlines continuity and unity of the EU's external representation. And finally, the EU's single legal personality is also expected to replace the three pillars structure and support the integration of the full external action within the EU's institutional system. Furthermore, hopes of enhanced consistency are also underpinned by a new, more comprehensive, concept of external action.[3] However, the second pillar procedures remain mainly

---

article ignores the pressures coming from beyond the EU, external threats and/or threat perceptions.

3   Article 22 of the TEU brings evidence of both innovation and complexity: '1. On the basis of the principles and objectives set out in art. 21 the European Council shall identify

intergovernmental and the multiple legacies of the Maastricht Treaty's baroque architecture are far from disappearing (Dony 2010).[4]

A New Bureaucratic Agent

In order to partly diminish one of the institutional causes of the famous 'expectations–capabilities gap' (Hill 1996) the new European External Action Service was created. It merged the two branches of the EU external relations administrations and 140 external delegations (www.eeas.europa.eu). This also brought the crisis management institutions (CMPD, EUMS and CPSCC) within the EEAS, requiring them to report to the HR.

Renewed Coordination

The Treaty also aims at strengthening the vertical coherence between the EU's external action and the member states' foreign policies. While the 'EU's foreign policy system' (Hill 1996) remains fundamentally decentralized and multi-layered, the Treaty fosters a higher degree of centralization and coordination. Even if it is not at all a full-fledged federalizing institutional step, it seeks to address both the original split of competencies between states and EU, and the bicephal structure of the EU's external relations. Intensive transgovernmental networks (Slaughter 2004) are fostered. The open question is whether member states, Council and Commission are merely transferring their differences into

---

the strategic interest and objectives of the Union. Decisions of the European Council on the strategic interests and objectives of the Union shall relate to the common foreign and security policy and to other areas of the external action of the Union. Such decisions may concern the relations of the Union with a specific country or region or may be thematic in approach. They shall define their durations and the means made available by the Union and the Member states. The European council shall act unanimously on a recommendation from the council adopted by the latter under the arrangements laid down for each area. Decisions of the European Council shall be implemented in accordance with the provisions provided for in the Treaties. 2. The High Representative of the Union for foreign affairs and security policy, for the area of common foreign and security policy and the Commission for other areas of external action may submit joint proposal to the Council.'

4   Look for example at the very relevant art. 40 which mentions the Treaty for the functioning of the EU (art. 3 and 6) regarding the clear share of competences in three groups (exclusive, mixed and only allowing EU supporting measures) and the different procedures to be adopted: Article 40(ex Article 47 TEU): 'The implementation of the common foreign and security policy shall not affect the application of the procedures and the extent of the powers of the institutions laid down by the Treaties for the exercise of the Union competences referred to in Articles 3 to 6 of the Treaty on the Functioning of the European Union. Similarly, the implementation of the policies listed in those Articles shall not affect the application of the procedures and the extent of the powers of the institutions laid down by the Treaties for the exercise of the Union competences under this Chapter.'

a new institutional context rather than overcoming them. Research should address the question of the impact of the new degree of socialization between the transgovernmental networks and cross-fertilization within the Brussels epistemic community and among national diplomatic cultures. However, the challenging events of the post-Lisbon Treaty years show that, even if it exists, improved internal efficiency does not necessarily mean enhanced external effectiveness in coping with the international challenges.

2011, *Annus Terribilis*: Three Shortcomings Affecting the Post-Lisbon EU's International Role

2011 was a terrible year for the EU's post-Lisbon foreign policy system. Critical analysis needs to move beyond superficial explanations such as: personal leadership, the EEAS's short training period and lack of resources. In 2011, the combined effects of the economic clash and the Libyan crisis revealed three unexpected European weaknesses.

Lack of Political EU's Leadership

Worldwide, Europe is singled out for its responsibility in the oscillating international management of the Mediterranean region. The internal divisions regarding Palestine[5] and the Arab Spring were further deepened by the Libyan crisis. The EU as such was expected to act, but it was unable to because of the vertical division between two leading states: France and Germany (who abstained like China/Brazil and Russia at the UNSC and did not take part in the intervention). Immediate fallout from the Libyan crisis included: a revitalized NATO and re-nationalized defence policies. In political terms, the lack of Franco-German unity was confirmed as a paralyzing factor for the Common Foreign and Security Policy as Germany confirmed its low international profile. We will address the question of why, contrary to some superficial comments, Germany simply confirmed how low-profile its regional hegemonic role is and this despite its increasing economic leadership.

Notwithstanding the initially strong international legitimacy of NATO's intervention in the Libyan crisis – UNSC resolution 1973 – the EU-CFSP was silent and unable to implement either its distinctive civilian approach, or its understanding of the 'responsibility to protect' or 'responsibility to rebuild'. This allowed for the European military intervention – mainly provided by France and UK air forces (with the support of Italy and other member states) – to evolve into a regime-changing mission after having stopped the threat to the Benghazi

---

5 EU states did show their divisions already in October 2011 in the case of the UN vote about the application of Palestine to UNESCO permanent membership (welcomed by France, but rejected by Germany, with the abstention of Italy and the UK).

population. Regime-change is neither included in the list of 'Petersberg tasks', nor in the 'Solana paper',[6] whereas it is included in the 2002 US Security Strategy. This continued up until Qaddafi was dead and a new and controversial regime installed. Moreover, the crisis raised explicit questions regarding the Lisbon Treaty provisions' capacity to bolster both member state loyalty and the EU's international profile.

A Weakening of Europe's Traditional Military Powers

The same crisis revealed not only the low profile of the first European power, but also the weaknesses of the two traditional European military powers, the UK and France. This is a fundamental point because the most persuasive critics of the civilian power EU thesis are based on the existence of two great conventional and nuclear powers among the member states. During the Libyan campaign, the clearly deficient military capacities of France and the UK, further weakened by the recent budgetary cuts, risked exposing to the world their incapacity to maintain a sustainable military commitment, even of this limited kind. Such a blazing piece of news radically questions the traditional appreciation of the nature of the EU as a 'complex subsystem of international relations' (Hill and Smith 2005) including at least two 'would-be' great powers. As such, the national military might of France and the UK would underpin a European 'puissance'. After the Libyan campaign, their decline is no longer a matter of debate. In 2011, both states signed a bilateral defence cooperation reflecting a growing awareness of their apparently deficient capacities. Rather than exaggerating the Libyan 'victory' (*Foreign Affairs*, March–April 2012) a serious observer should highlight these shortcomings and remember the related withdrawal from Afghanistan, and the inconceivable option of military pressures on Iran and Syria.

　　Can these political and military deficits – not only of the EU but of its three leading states – be reversed in the years to come? Comparative analysis shows that the electorates are against enhanced defence budgets. Even if we don't share *Le Monde*'s thesis that 'Europe risks global irrelevance' (1 April 2012) there is increasing evidence that the very nature of the EU's power is changing.

A Debilitating Economic Crisis

The greatest economic crisis since 1929 is about to bury the mainly French idea of 'Europe puissance' as a fully-fledged political and military power (Gnesotto 2011). Germany, the single European state capable of avoiding the recession and coping with international competition, has taken the lead in cutting its military budget. Italy has followed suit. Despite the rhetoric of the 2011 Franco-British entente on defence policy, even France, the UK (and other member states, including Greece)

6　European Council, 'European Security Strategy: A Secure Europe in a Better World', Brussels, December 2003.

are cutting their military budgets on an unprecedented scale for a very simple reason: the combined pressure of international markets, social demands of the national electorates and the new 'fiscal pact' proposed by Germany for balancing the budget. All three of these have conspired to apply budget-cutting solutions to the economic troubles of almost ruined states. The crisis is fostering deeper European integration (even if without Britain), and every step out of the crisis is a step towards enhanced integration. However, the integration in economic governance not only excludes military integration, but is also preventing it. Akin to a zero-sum game at a national level without the balancing effect of a coordination of defence budgets at the European Union level.

The crisis of the Eurozone is seriously affecting not only the EU's power in general but also the its foreign policies. Since internal socioeconomic unity and the euro are at the core of the EU's international influence, the 2010–12 inward-looking years occurred within the context of an external profile in decline, affecting both the EU's foreign policies and image. From a model of regional stability, as it was depicted by the *Financial Times* during the first two years of the global financial crisis, the Eurozone became in 2010–12 the very focus of the economic crisis. The external implications weakened the EU in the near and far abroad.

Even if in a different way, according to their respective objectives (Grevi 2011a) the ENP and all the 'strategic partnerships' are affected to some extent (as their priorities and focus) by the external implications of such an economic recession and the increasingly individualized search for partnerships of many member states (for more details to what extent and in which manner see Chapters 7, 10, 11 and 12, this volume). The EU Council made some improvements by ensuring the follow-up of strategic summits as a matter of fact (compared with the times of the rotating presidencies). However, this progress is not enough to diminish the negative perceptions and image abroad; and recovery will take time and energy.

The Limits of the Lisbon Treaty and its Implementation: Analysis and Theoretical Implications

There are both structural and transitional reasons for these shortcomings. There is evidence that the High Representative does not have the time and the profile to act properly in her role as Commission Vice-President. This means that no satisfactory coordination is taking place with the Commission's extremely relevant external competences. Looking at the Treaty provisions may help when addressing the deep causes. The legal/institutional side has evolved since the Maastricht Treaty for the European Union (1992) in a twofold way, which was not fundamentally changed by the Lisbon Treaty. On the one hand, towards an enhanced role of the political cooperation and several coordinating provisions among the various actions and policies affecting external relations; and on the other hand, towards more complexity, derogations, opting out, exceptions, to some extent making the system as a whole more hermetic, obscure and non-transparent.

The HR and the EEAS are certainly two potentially powerful tools aimed at strengthening cross-pillar coordination. Moreover, as a development of the abovementioned article 3 of the TEU, the new articles 3 and 21 of the Lisbon revised TEU are very relevant as well, as they strengthen the concept of a common institutional framework, where common objectives and principles affect the whole spectrum of external relations.

Second, the Lisbon Revised Treaty expands and clarifies EU discourse in terms of values, principles and common declared objectives: see the TEU, article 3 (principles) and article 21 (CFSP objectives, Title V). What seems strengthened compared with previous treaties?

Article 3 of the TEU presents the EU (point 1) as an organization for peace. Point 5 of the article addresses the EU's external relations: the EU defends its values and interests and protects its citizens. The EU contributes to peace, security, sustainable development (for the first time so explicitly), solidarity and mutual respect between peoples, free and fair trade, elimination of poverty, protection of human rights, particularly of children, and respect and development of international law, notably, respect of the UN Charter principles.

Article 21 of the TEU (an entirely new and long article) mentions the principles and objectives of the EU's external action and presents a general concept of external relations. The link between the external action and the funding principles of the EU itself is particularly relevant: democracy, rule of law, indivisibility and universality of human rights, fundamental freedoms and human dignity, equality and solidarity, and respect of the UN Charter principles and international law. Partnerships with third countries, regional and international organizations are based on the abovementioned principles. The UN is the framework for multilateral solutions to common problems. Second, the EU as a policy-maker is mentioned.[7] Finally article 21 mentions 'the external dimension of its other policies' and concludes by calling for policy coordination as the external action and calls for the responsibility of Commission, Council and HR for ensuring coherence of its external actions.

---

7   According to the article 21 of the TEU: the EU aims for a high degree of cooperation in every field of IR. In particular: defending its interests, values, security, independence and integrity; consolidating human rights, democracy and international law; peace keeping, conflict preventing, international security enforcing consistently with the UN Charter and Helsinki final act and Paris Charter, including external borders; economically and socially supporting sustainable development of developing country with the objective of eradicating poverty; it is supporting inclusion of every countries in the global economy and, gradually, in the liberalization of the global trade; defending and improving through cooperative action environment protection and improvement towards a sustainable development; helping populations by natural and human provoked disasters; promoting the strengthening of the global multilateral system and good global governance.

As for its content, EU international discourse looks like a synthesis of the objectives and values of international organizations, cooperation and regimes. The image the EU wants to project is one of the strongest defenders of the UN Millennium Goals (2000), the 'Monterrey Consensus' (2003), the Rio de Janeiro UN Conference for Environment (1992 and 2012). This evolving discourse matters to some extent even if we have already argued that this distinctive normative basis is not the key variable in defining EU power, and explaining the CFSP in action.

However, ideas are embedded within the institutional foreign policy system. At the institutional level, the abovementioned international objectives should be relevant to all EU institutions and should be of a binding nature; not only for the large array of external relations depending on either pillar, but also for the multiple agencies including external action, for example Eurojust, Frontex, Asylum Office, etc. They all have to comply with the same principles and objectives. For example, respect of the founding values (democracy, rule of law and respect of human rights) of the EU should shape every policy including migration policy, development policy and anti-terrorist policy. The EU commitment to multilateral cooperation is also based on the same internal values (for example The Hague Convention). This strong link between internal and external policies is an essential part of the EU call for coherence.

Conversely, horizontal coherence and vertical consistency are challenged by a number of exceptions and internal differences affecting external relations. This complexity is incrementally expanding and notably so when soft law is adopted and intergovernmental procedures are not revised. Both the second and third pillars are affected. For example, internal decentralization and variable geometries (resulting from the UK, Ireland and Denmark opt-out as the European space for liberty, security and justice) have external consequences:

1. Relevant uncertainties brought about in negotiations on deepening strategic partnerships (and respective action plans) with, amongst others, Russia, China, South Korea and India as strategic partners are often at pains to understand how many and to what extent EU member states are affected by the EU's commitments.
2. Complexity affecting the ENP where the pressure for deepening bilateral partnership is particularly strong (for instance by including energy and immigration).
3. Paradoxical situations are emerging where the EU has to negotiate an international agreement regarding immigration policy with an EU member state as if it were a third party (such as for example Denmark).

Some of these examples come from member states belonging to the 1973 wave of EC enlargement which over 40 years have still not found dynamic solutions regarding the overall integration process. Accordingly, it is hard to stick to functionalist hopes of spillover tendencies towards more integration, or neo-functionalist forecasts for an 'institutional fusion' (Wessels 1997, 2005).

Complexity is increasingly becoming – with the expanding external actions and relations – a very long lasting characteristic of the nature of the EU's institutional set of foreign policies. All in all, this twofold evolution looks similar to the concept suggested by F.W. Scharpf (1996)[8] regarding the EU's polity in the making: every step towards federalist-styled paths is associated with new steps towards increasing institutional complexity through: opting out, derogations, exceptions, etc. Even if distinguished from 'neo-medievalist' governance theories, this concept of complexity goes far beyond the multi-actor-game concept of foreign policy-making applied by Allison and Zelikow to the complex negotiation within the US leadership at the time of the Cuban Missile Crisis (Allison and Zelikow 1999). Not only the weight of domestic factors in foreign policy-making is increased within the highly decentralized EU foreign policy system, but the approaches focusing on polyarchy, fragmented politics (multitude of private and public interests) and bureaucratic politics (see Chapter 5, this volume) confirm their enhanced appropriateness and hermeneutic relevance.

All in all, we should talk about the gradual evolution of a complex foreign policy system rather than of the mature consolidation of a definitive stage. Complexity, fragmentation, derogations rather increase in parallel with the steps towards an enhanced coherence.

1. The inter-institutional relations are increasingly complex and a stable balance has not yet been reached between the new power poles: HR and EEAS, Commission, and the EU Council presidency, despite the declining external competences of the rotating presidency. Furthermore, internal 'variable geometry' affects even intergovernmental coherence and re-nationalization of policy limits the trends towards centralization and loyalty.
2. The EEAS is an unprecedented institutional creation which provides the huge advantages of an information-gathering opportunity (with numerous embassies and delegations abroad), but still remains at the early stages of a learning and identity building process. The very notion of an EU diplomacy is far from being clearly identified in terms of its strategic culture, institutional identity and its policy-making rules, procedures and

---

8   The concept of 'Politikverflechtung' is presented, among others, in his contribution to P. Schmitter et al. (eds) Governance in the EU (Sage, 1995). Other German scholars worked out this more sophisticated version of the merely descriptive concept of multilevel governance, like Rurup and M. Skuballa, and applied it both to the EU and FRG. We can argue that Politikverflechtung means not only means multilevel governance without centre and internal centripetal hierarchies. This concept of political science also means that relevant policy objectives set by public authorities cannot be addressed and implemented independently from an intensive interplay with multiple actors and administrative authorities of different kind, level and nature. Moreover, beyond the formalized administrative and institutional powers, also informal authorities and actors want to play a role at the level of the horizontal and vertical decision-making process, which results in an extremely slow and weak implementation of government decisions.

scope. It is rooted in three different origins (Commission DG External Action, Council and member states). The quality of skills and training is still questioned, its internal structure is not yet consolidated and the balance between geographic and thematic organizational criteria is still evolving. The delegations/embassies feel understaffed because of the extra duties required of them. The financial side and the resources are affected by the current and legal limits of the EU budget (1 per cent of the total GDP of the 27 member states)[9] and by the consequences of the economic crisis.

3. These uncertainties affect the EEAS's consolidation process: first, the degree of acceptance of the new hierarchies and competences – notably, smaller states feeling under-represented and bigger states feeling threatened by a new competitor. Second, the 'esprit de corps' (self-identification) of this relatively large 'epistemic community in the making' looks like a challenging construction. Moreover, the EEAS is also troubled by coping with implementation challenges: the chain of command is not defined clearly enough and some doubts remain on relevant issues, for example, who negotiates on behalf of the EU in areas of the multiple shared competencies.

4. Other bodies matter within the revised complex foreign policy system: first, the rotating Council presidencies, which, despite their relative decline (see the last controversial old-style performance by Spain in 2010), has not disappeared: they remain relevant as far as several crucial external policies are concerned (trade, development, humanitarian aid, etc.) by setting the Council agenda and promoting priorities. Second, the European Parliament, notwithstanding its limited competence in foreign policy, has shown its relevance on many occasions where external relations are concerned, even during the hard starting up debate (2010) about the EEAS budget and status. Its more assertive role is a factor of increasing complexity.

Paradoxically, both the trends towards clarity and simplification, and institutional complexity, are increasing with the new Treaty and its implementation. The financial mechanism (Foreign Policy Instrument) confirms this tendency. Enhanced coherence, combined with increasing complexity and fragmentation, look to many as the paradoxical but quasi-final features of a mature EU polity.

The EU: An Incipient Civilian Power

This chapter's aim is to contribute to the literature on the EU's international power, by going beyond two opposed oversimplified pictures. According to a

---

9   In the current debate about CFSP resources also the shift of the EUISS (a research institute and think tank about foreign policy dependent on the HR) from Paris to Brussels is discussed.

realist critique, the EU cannot be considered as a power at all: it is condemned to internal fragmentation and external irrelevance (a view furthered by evidence that: it is not a fully-fledged military and political power and thus submitted to NATO;[10] it was irrelevant in the face of the Arab revolts, Israeli-Palestinian conflict, Iranian challenge, or the Korean crisis; and it looks unable to cope with its internal complexity). The second, more idealist picture, presents the EU an alternative kind of power, a post-Westphalian values-based community and strategic actor in the making. The European Union has been described in mainstream interpretations as a 'normative power' (Manners 2002), essentially characterized by a distinctive normative basis consistent with the UN Charter, asserted through 'a series of declarations, treaties, policies, criteria and conditions'.

Against either picture, we argue that the EU already is an incipient civilian power; even if it is of an unprecedented kind. The normative features, obvious for every power, are not the very soul of the EU's influence and international role. By updating the concept of 'civilian power', notably by stressing the fact that it is by default when not by design, we want to underline both the impossibility of the EU becoming a 'normal' military and political power, as well as the long lasting alternative basis for the EU's external power, which includes relevant material and immaterial resources – even if traditional military might not be one of them.

The EU is the largest advanced industrialized market in the world (30 per cent of the global GDP, by 2010 – €12,5 trillion,[11] and a 'trading state' (Rosencrance 1987)). It strongly influences international trade as a trading bloc (20 per cent of global trade flows, by 2010), is a leading destination for FDI, a major regulator in global competition policy (Dewatripont and Legros 2009) and standardization (Sapir 2007). With a population of 500 million people who are relatively well trained and educated, the EU is still the most significant Western demographic entity. The Eurozone crisis does not seriously affect the euro's role as the first competitor to the US dollar (as a reserve currency from 18 per cent in 2000 to 25.7 per cent in 2010, with a peak at 27.6 per cent in 2008). The EU is also the first actor working in cooperation with developing countries (as the world's largest development budget, from 2008 to 2013 the European Development Fund accounts for €22.682 million). The European Neighbourhood Policy affects 17 countries belonging to the European region in the broadest sense, from former CSSR members, including the Eastern European neighbours and the Caucasus region, to the Southern rim of the Mediterranean. Enlargement and pre-enlargement policy include Croatia,

---

10   Art. 42.7 of TEU not only states about the mutual assistance clause 'in accordance with Article 51 of the UN Charter', but also about that 'this shall not prejudice the specific character of the security and defense policy of certain Member States. Commitments and cooperation in this area shall be consistent with commitments under the NATO, which, for those States which are members of it, remains the foundation of their collective defense and the forum for its implementation'.

11   http://ec.europa.eu/would/what/international:economic:issues/index.enhtm, mentioned by Damro (2011).

Turkey, Iceland, Serbia and other Western Balkan states. The EU is at the centre of the world's largest network of international arrangements and agreements of several kinds (bilateral, multilateral, interregional and 'strategic partnerships'). Finally, the EU has begun more than 20 missions of a variety of sorts (military operations under the 'Petersberg tasks': civilian missions and mixed). Thirteen missions are currently ongoing – under the umbrella of the CFSP-EDSP, the EU's 'Cinderella'.[12]

The EU is a power because it can use its material might to change and influence other actors' decisions, even against their will. For instance, positive and negative measures can be taken which seriously affect trade partners. Among the positives, there are the conclusion of trade agreements, cooperation agreements, association agreements, tariff reductions, quota increases, grant inclusion in the GSP, and the provision of aid and extending loans. Among the negative measures are embargoes (bans on exports), boycotts (bans on imports), delaying conclusions of agreements; suspending or denouncing agreements; tariff increases; quota decreases; withdrawing GSP; reducing or suspending aid; and delaying granting of successive loan tranches. States, private multinational companies, NGOs and international organizations have been interplaying with these relevant EU powers for decades.

All in all, the EU, in more than 20 years after the end of the bipolar world, was able to transform itself from a regional grouping of neighbouring states, a strictly economic entity, into a global multidimensional actor. However, the EU is unable to consistently use this huge potential for a central state-styled kind of integration of both its institutional capacities on the one hand, and, the large array of external policies, on the other. Even a true coordination of CFSP and trade policy still seems to be out of the EU's current scope.

Beyond Teleological Approaches

According to a traditional school of thought the EU is expected to increasingly comply with its asserted principles and norms and teleological affirmations of progress towards coherence and fusion of its external policies. Several critics are focusing on the gradual transformation of the CFSP into a single voice and action of the EU in international affairs.

However, it is an oversimplification to decry a disappointing reality on the basis of a pre-existing normative model. These critical approaches keep explaining the shortcomings of the EU's integration in foreign policy by comparing it with the stages of development of the United States as a federal state. Contrary to the United States, the EU was not created out of a war for independence where

---

12   Even if the EU confirms as not looking at them as a priority and, in an era of resource constraining, no new missions are foreseen for 2012, despite US pressures for burden sharing.

unifying army and foreign policy were the first imperatives. The pressures from external factors matter, notably threat and challenge perceptions; but not enough to foster a federal union. In any case, Europe faces these on a completely different scale than in the United States' early history.

Contrary to neo-realist analyses (Gilpin, Mearsheimer and others), the Cold War did not play a fundamental role in accelerating European integration, as shown by the failure of the European Defence Community in 1955, the primacy of NATO and the marginality of defence and security cooperation for 40 years. In short, the fear of Stalin was not (or insufficiently) the EU's external federator. However, H. Bull (1977) was right in considering the EC civilian power before the end of the threat of a nuclear war as a '*contradictio in adjecto*' (contradiction in terms). At the time, the EC's internal and external policies had a rather indirect and marginal effect on international relations.

Even the second historical stage, with the transformation of the EC into the EU, provoked similar disappointments and critics from the perspective of the 'United States of Europe'. The systemic change of 1989/91 was actually strong enough to foster an extraordinary expansion of the EU's external relations and the TEU; but not enough to either persuade the member states to delegate to the EU a significant part of their external sovereignty, thus underpinning the creation of a single European voice and action in international affairs; or agree on a single European international strategy, which is considered by many as its precondition. The traditional comparative approach focusing on the US model, argues that what the EU needs first of all is strategic unity similar to the United States. A political strategy in IR demands a shared vision and institutional capacities for implementation. When talking about a strategic vision, what do we mean? When looking at US literature (with the exception of the Allison book and its followers), an internationally coherent strategy has to be systematic, differentiated, deliberate and purposeful, and it should account for at least three elements:

1. A shared vision and narrative, including a shared threat perception.
2. Clear strategic guidelines including common priorities regarding both partners and issues.
3. A stable institutional set and an effective coordination between the Council, the EEAS and the Commission (and the ESDP).[13] This should include rational planning of human and financial resources (of the EU and member states) and avoiding redundancies.[14]

---

13   With the launch of the ESDP, civilian and military structures became two different worlds even if some interplay exists: look for example at the respective funding mechanisms of the civilian (by EU budget) and military missions (by member states).

14   Research is needed: let's take the example of aid to developing countries. On the one hand, the EEAS is now part of the planning regarding priorities and modes of allocating the relative budget. On the other hand, the top-down process of putting the decisions into

In reality, the EU is missing both a sufficiently stabilized institutional set, and clear guidelines/priorities reflected in a shared narrative. After 20 years of intense treaty reform (from the Single European Act to Lisbon), it becomes apparent that the EU is not a federal state in the making and cannot develop a state-styled strategy for international relations. Both the mentioned limits of the EU central budget and the unanimous voting rule in the foreign affairs council are symbolic of this non-state nature. What we have instead of singular strategic action is multiple and multilevel external actions with neither a hierarchy of priorities nor a clear distinctive profile. Lady Ashton's (HR for Foreign Policy since early 2010) first annual report (2011) tellingly emphasizes the number rather than the quality of the EU's foreign policy (more than 400 statements in one year).[15] Even if the EU's discourse, from the 'Solana paper' to the September 2010 European Council conclusions, are about 'more strategic' action;[16] and improved vertical and horizontal coordination is a Treaty obligation, the basic elements of a consistent state styled strategy are still missing.

Regarding capacities, the radically different size of the central budget is often neglected as an obstacle to comparing the EU to the United States. Even 20 years after 1989, the central EU budget remains below the Treaty provision of 1.27 per cent of GDP, which is incomparable with the United States' 20 per cent of GDP (the share of the defence budget is $0.739 billion, which accounts for 20 per cent of the total federal budget for 2012: $3.456 billion). CFSP and ESDP missions are funded at the expense of member states' declining defence budgets, whereas the central administration budget – thought to have more than doubled in 10 years – amounts to approximately €250 million per year.[17]

Second, as far as the institutional capacities are concerned, by explaining the current shortcomings, along the lines of Kissinger's famous joke, realist comments focus on weak central leadership. Others address the objective difficulty of a job (HR) which includes too much, according to the Treaty provisions, and fosters too high expectations. In practice, the HR can look at the EEAS development and follow the everyday international politics, but without a long-term vision, it

---

practice remains the responsibility of the Commission (without a real coordination under the HR umbrella).

15   High Representative for Foreign Affairs Report 2011.

16   EU Council Conclusions, September 2010: 'the EU and its Member States will act more strategically so as to bring Europe's true weight to bear internationally'. The EEAS is called upon to support all EU institutions 'concerning the strategic overview and coordination necessary to ensure the coherence of the European Union's external action as a whole'.

17   Total amount for the period 2007–13: €1.74 billion. Compared with €46 million in 2003, €62 million in 2004 and 2005 and €102 million in 2006, the relative progress is relevant. The budgets allocated in the CFSP budget are nevertheless small compared with the €49 billion available to the Commission for external relations over the period 2007–13 (humanitarian aid – ECHO, development aid, regional cooperation, trade policy, etc.) and ridiculous if compared with the US defence budget.

misses out on the coordination with the Commission which was expected from the Commission Vice-President.

Furthermore, coordination (including between CFSP and trade policy) and strategic action look to some observers as more difficult than before the Lisbon Treaty. For example we are witnessing some backtracking compared even with the Solana paper of 2003 (updated in 2008) which at least looked like an answer to the Bush administration's 'New Security Strategy' (2002) prompted by the will of the Europeans to oppose effective multilateralism to unilateralism; and prevent war or at least avoid the EU's implication in the Iraq War whilst sublimating internal divisions in a dynamic way.

It is true that even the real strategic nature of the 'EU's Security Strategy' – the 'Solana paper' – has been questioned for it looks more like a reactive exercise to the US unilateral strategy than it does an original and distinctive EU strategy, entailing systematic long-term and midterm vision, consistent priorities, policy guidelines and political coordination. However, the effective multilateralism ideology of the 2003 'Solana paper' had the merit to work as a kind of flag against the 'unipolar momentum' and was recognized as such by many of the BRICS as well as by many streams of public opinion. Nothing similar has been proposed in the last two years, whereas public expectations of the EU's international role as a driving force of European integration are confirmed by recent Eurobarometers.

Why does the EU appear to be moving backwards, and why is its international profile declining? The challenging economic crisis explains to some extent the inward-looking tendency of 2010–12 affecting the three main EU institutions' priorities. Furthermore, many member states are multiplying bilateral relations with strategic partners, notably the BRICS, with the aim of attracting investments and improving bilateral trade.

Does this change explain the low profile of the CFSP? This question was broached in December 2011 by 12 foreign ministers. The corollary of this fact is that 15 foreign ministers, including very significant member states, in rejecting vertical coordination, notably regarding high politics, are perfectly happy with the current lacking strategy and weak CFSP. They would oppose a step in the direction wished by the other 12. Public opinion does provide unambiguous signals and demands, even if some NGOs do mainly fear an instrumental subordination of development aid and humanitarian aid to strategic priorities. Overall, Eurobarometers consistently call for stronger and more consistent international action by the EU, as a possible new 'raison d'être' of the European project. However, even if the current HR cannot meet expectations of an enhanced EU global role, the current deficit cannot be identified with a single personality.

In conclusion, seriously analysing the deep causes of the EU's external action shortcomings cannot revive again and again the traditional pleas in favour of a classical state-styled foreign policy which is out of reach for the EU. Although some improvement in the degree of efficiency and coordination are possible, after a change of leadership and further treaty reform (difficult to achieve and ratify by a 28 member-state union), the EU cannot replicate past state-making models. What remains to be explored is rather the existing room for improvements of the current system by reforming practical – formal and informal – governance mechanism on the one hand; and modes of coordination among the member states and between the member states and the central institutions, on the other.

The Controversial Revival of Neo-Realist and Rational Choice Approaches and the Eventual Consequences of German Hegemony

By emphasizing the limitations of traditional federal/functionalist approaches, a 'critical approach' is emerging from the realist mainstream and developing into rational choice institutionalism. It argues that regional polities can only work where a regional hegemony emerges, shaping its own agenda, policies and institutional set, and measured against its own interests and objectives.

Never in the past has democratic Germany seemed a reliable candidate for the EU's driving seat until the periods of the Schröder/Fischer government and the two Merkel coalitions.[18] These distinctive periods largely explain the journalistic and scientific literature about the coming 'German Europe'. There is no evidence that the Franco-British military cooperation, even if strengthened in 2011, is about to build up an alternative hegemony within the EU, whose core remains the Eurozone. Germany is at the Eurozone's centre, the very soul of the EU regional and global power. Could the emergent German leadership grow up from an economic to a political platform? Could it work as the main independent variable for a change of the still decentralized and complex EU foreign policy system? And in that case, which would be the foreign policy of an increasingly 'German' Europe?

During the Schröder/Fischer government (1997–2005), Germany did actually support, both within the EU and internationally, an unprecedented (after 1945) diplomatic assertiveness:

1. Germany secured for the first time the relinquishment of the principle of parity among the four largest states in the Council and Parliament and thus the recognition of population size as criterion for the QMV (starting with the Nice Treaty and confirmed in the Lisbon Treaty).
2. Applied as member of the UNSC through a very large international lobbying and in alliance with Japan, India and Brazil (G4), despite controversies and conflicts with other EU member states.
3. Decided to take part in the NATO military intervention in Kosovo in 1999 (benefiting, from its humanitarian purposes, extensive public opinion support, including leading intellectuals like J. Habermas).
4. In alliance with France, other member states, and the EU Commission, it was able to oppose, between 2002 and 2008, the G.W. Bush administration's

---

18   First, the Grosse Koalition between the CDU/CSU and the SPD (2005–9) and, second, the coalition of the CDU/CSU with the FDP (2009–13).

preventive war in Iraq, even at the cost of the most serious transatlantic rift since 1945.

As a consequence of previous reforms, during the two different government coalitions led by A. Merkel, Germany radically changed its international image as the 'sick member of the European economy' – then mainly opposed to the winning British model – into that of Europe's leader. Not only as the world's first exporting economy, and as the first country to emerge from the worst financial crisis since 1929, but also as the leading force within the European Council as far as the anti-crisis measures are concerned. All of the key decisions between 2008 and 2012 were taken with the main input coming from Germany (with France in the role of supporting junior partner): building three financial market monitoring agencies, strengthening the regional funds – notably the EFSF and then the ESM up to €800 billio, allowing the ECB to distribute €1,000 billion to the European banks, creating a national budget control system (called 'European semester'), firmly asserting, in spite of the self-exclusion of the UK, the new intergovernmental treaty, the 'Fiscal Pact' for stability, which – for the first time – can enter into force with the ratification of only 12 member states. All in all, restoring the EU's economic stability, the very background of the EU's international reliability, within the G20 and the globalized and multipolar world, will be proportional to the shared acceptance of the 'German model'. This provoked a large international debate about the coming 'German hegemony' and even about the transformation of the EU into a 'German Empire' (Beck, U. 2011) with inevitable implications regarding the EU's internal legitimacy, its external image, its foreign policy and international perception.

Is the German pressure in favour of a major role of the European Council in boosting a top-down European convergence and centralization of economic governance paving the way for a German regional hegemony? Only provided the following conditions will Germany become the recognized 'benevolent hegemon' (according to the criteria set by the scientific literature):[19]

1. Disseminating within the EU shared ideas on an innovative and comprehensive modernization culture. Not only the anti-inflationary German culture but also the other sides of its successful model are to be shared: industrial consensus (*Mitbestimmung*), greening the economy, prioritizing the knowledge economy, social inclusiveness (welfare state and expanding high wages to 18 million Eastern Germans) and administrative efficiency. Germany already influenced the so-called 'EU2020' agenda in this direction, but the instrumental interpretation of the 'German model'

---

19   According to the liberal school, hegemonic stability implies providing 'common goods' (Keohane 2004); according to the Canadian school, hegemonic powers are strongly influencing the realm of ideas, perceptions and creating consensus of a large social alliance of interests (R. Cox 1986).

as mere budget austerity is still prevailing which negatively affects its external appeal.

2. Providing the EU with enough support by building new 'European common goods', which means supporting a sufficient regional fund, a banking union and, eventually, also Eurobonds as key elements for a strong economic governance, enhancing both growth and cohesion.

3. Supporting a kind of 'Marshall Plan' for Greece, Portugal, Spain and the southern EU economies as complementary to authority policies (for instance, through investments in solar energy, as suggested by the EP president M. Schulz in 2012).

Even if Germany still has a long way to go to be recognized as a benevolent hegemon, we can take into consideration a possible 'German Europe' scenario and its implications for the CFSP. The alternative hypothesis of a Franco-British hegemony, along the recurrent 'St Malo model' (UK-France Declaration, 1998), looks fragile, considering its receding economic and institutional foundations and the declining nuclear power. No foreign policy leadership is possible in the EU without the background of such an economic/monetary and institutional soul based on the euro as its core. Germany's experts are aware of the multiple historical, domestic and constitutional obstacles for this leading role to be fully implemented (Bava 2001; Bulmer 2010; Telò and Seidelmann 1995). However, according to many this possibility for change – which could be explained through a combination of instrumental institutionalism and discursive institutionalism (Schmidt 2012) – cannot be excluded. A caveat: mere instrumental institutionalist approaches to EU Treaty reform can only make the internal democratic deficit more serious. In any case, what about the eventual impact in terms of foreign policy of a more German Europe? Will this German leadership build the driving force and be the simplifying factor allowing the internal EU's complexity to be transformed in an efficient way towards a full, effective and more independent global security actor?

The comparative analysis with other states brings evidence, in the aforementioned scenario, that old labels such as the Bismarck-centred expression 'German Empire' or 'German power' will be unfit to define the unprecedented international profile a post-1945 and post-1990 German leadership would increasingly provide the EU. At the institutional level the EU would remain a multilateral entity (combining supranational and intergovernmental procedures) and the institutional framework would evolve towards an enhanced role of the 'community methods'; at the level of policies and identity, the model of a 'civilian power' would be rather confirmed than denied, both as a default policy and as a design. This deep correspondence of the EU with the new Germany has also been underlined by a pluralist stream of scholars like Habermas (2006), Maull (2006), Czempiel (1999) and others,[20] on the basis of several strong arguments: weight of

---

20   On the similarities with Japan see Chapter 11 in this volume.

history, constitutional limits, inevitably low international profile of defeated states, etc. Some of the recent evidence confirms this forecast:

1. Germany is, in the EU, the leading country regarding the European trend towards substantially cutting the national defence budget, which is currently downgraded below 1 per cent of GDP.
2. Germans have been internationally qualified as 'timid Teutons' because of public opposition and government prudence in military interventions (1991 Gulf War, Southern Lebanon Mission of 2007, etc.) and the early 1990s expectations of an emergent 'Fourth Reich' have quickly been shown to be preposterous.
3. The Libyan crisis of 2011 and the German abstention at the UNSC on resolution 1973 allowing an intervention to stop the imminent Benghazi massacre and the subsequent regime change, have shown that Germany is ready to pay the double price of deepening the CFSP crisis and dismantling its own previous 'G4 strategy' (application as permanent member of UNSC) in order to keep its international profile low and oppose the Europe puissance scenario.[21]

All in all, analysing the neo-realist and rational choice interpretations, and arguing in favour of a 'German EU', brings us to the conclusion that: first, Germany is still far from becoming a recognized regional hegemonic power; and second, as the eventual implications on the CFSP and CSDP are concerned, it would rather confirm the 'Civilian power' thesis, including its demilitarizing dimensions.

The critical argument made by J. Howorth in Chapter 3 (a weak CSDP calls for a merging between CSDP and NATO within a rebalanced NATO) can be answered in two ways: on the one hand Germany and a more 'German Europe' would be in favour, not of simply remodelling but rather of radically transforming the alliance from the traditional Cold War-styled Atlantic alliance towards a 'Europeanized NATO' (Sommer 2012). This transatlantic link, under a changing NATO umbrella, depends inevitably on one of two swing scenarios: it seems credible in the event of a multilateralism-focused US administration conscious of the difficult management of a 'No one's world' (Kupchan 2012); but it is unrealistic in times of a unilaterally acting US administration (as shown in the years between 2002 and 2008) which provoked a 'divided West' and a more marginal EU (Habermas 2012; Kagan 2002 as well as scenario A in Chapter 1 of this volume).

Commitment to the European Union and its supranational institutions, Europeanization of the transatlantic alliance, a balanced partnership with Russia, a special relationship with China and the BRICS, low political and military profile: an emerging 'German Europe' would be in continuity with the traditional pillars of the European approach to foreign policy.

---

21   For a critical French perception, confirming these trends see: Allemagne: le défis de la puissance, Questions internationales, n.54, 2012.

The Foreign Policy of a Regional Entity

After decades of international debate about the nature of the emergent EU power, discussing some of the theoretical implications of what has been written above should imply both a *pars destruens* (critical) and a *pars construens* (normative). The EU is an institutionally sophisticated regional entity, but not a federal state in the making. Transforming an internally differentiated regional grouping of neighbouring states into a coherent international actor is a difficult challenge. The EU is hardly able to transform either its internal diversity and decentralized polity or its increasing institutional complexity into a single voice or a single action. Neither federal/functionalist approaches nor hegemonic stability theory offer persuasive arguments of a coming 'big bang' concerning the EU's internationally relevant features. What we need is an evaluation of the EU's international role as it is, not as it should be.

A Very Partial Military Actor

Not only has the EU confirmed its limits as a military power, but in the context of the current crisis and despite the current international rearmament it has further deepened them. The EU has not and will not have in the foreseeable future the centralized institutional set of a sovereign political power, which can expend the '*jus ad bellum*' as a core feature. The still decentralized polity prevents it from any military intervention which is not based on the UN Charter, UNSC legitimating decisions and limited in scope and objectives by the 'Petersberg tasks'.[22] EU diplomacy does not – and will not have in the foreseeable future – have the capacity to play 'the full array of options' card (not only at EU level, but also less and less at the level of the member states) as the United States, Russia, China and other states still do on a regular basis. Regarding military capabilities, the various forms of 'variable geometry', like the current EU Battlegroups system,

---

22   See art. 42 of the TEU (former art. 17) '1. The Common security and defence policy shall be an integral part of the common foreign and security policy. It shall provide the Union with an operational capacity drawing on civilian and military assets. The Union may use them on missions outside the Union for peace-keeping, conflict prevention and strengthening international security in accordance with the principles of the United Nations Charter. The performance of these tasks shall be undertaken using capabilities provided by the Member States'. And art. 43: 'The tasks referred to in Article 42(1), in the course of which the Union may use civilian and military means, shall include joint disarmament operations, humanitarian and rescue tasks, military advice and assistance tasks, conflict prevention and peace-keeping tasks, tasks of combat forces in crisis management, including peace-making and post-conflict stabilisation. All these tasks may contribute to the fight against terrorism, including by supporting third countries in combating terrorism in their territories'. The Council votes by a unanimous voting procedure.

and the hypothetical 'permanent structured cooperation'[23] are unlikely to develop into a standing army as was planned in 1952 in the failed EDC. The EU-CFSP will continue to act with a distinctive kind of balance between diplomacy and coercion, leaving to NATO the 'dirty jobs' such as in the Libyan crisis. The Treaty paragraph on collective defence does not change this feature: it fundamentally means nothing more than loyalty to the UN Charter and recognition of the complementary role of pre-existing military alliances such as NATO.[24] The current 21 missions are by and large civilian or mixed and those (five) of military kind are focused on making the EU's civilian presence (in the framework of the 'Petersberg tasks') more credible and reliable.[25]

A Fragmented Actor

The EU is not and will not easily become in the foreseeable time a fully-fledged political actor consistent with any classical path towards sovereign power. The functionalist, neo-functionalist and 'fusion theories', expecting a gradual merging of the EU's institutions competent in external relations, are radically questioned by the complexity of institutional developments. It will not become a major political player in the sense described by Carl Schmitt when talking of actors able to face an 'emergency situation'. In other words, it fails, and will continue to fail, to cope with hot and urgent high politics challenges. Libya is not an exception; it is the rule – at least for a foreseeable time.

The EU's foreign policy will remain a two-level system of a regional entity coordinating member states thus slightly enhancing internal convergence. The true question is to what extent institutional dynamics of coordination can improve, diminishing their dependence upon the member states. According to a rational choice institutionalist approach the EU is not very much more than an instrument of the largest states (Hill 1996; Moravscic 1998). And if one of them is seemingly emerging as a leader, we already analysed the reaffirming consequences of an ever-increasing impact of the German approach to foreign policy. However, the

---

23 'Those Member States which wish to participate in the permanent structured cooperation referred to in Article 42(6), which fulfil the criteria and have made the commitments on military capabilities set out in the Protocol on permanent structured cooperation, shall notify their intention to the Council and to the High Representative of the Union for Foreign Affairs and Security Policy'. This treaty provision has not yet been implemented.

24 The new art. 42, paragraph 7, states: 'If a Member State is the victim of armed aggression on its territory, the other Member States shall have towards it an obligation of aid and assistance by all the means in their power, in accordance with Article 51 of the United Nations Charter. This shall not prejudice the specific character of the security and defence policy of certain Member States'.

25 In 2012, the 21 ESDP missions are taking place in Africa (eight), in Asia (six) and in Eastern Europe (seven).

instrumentalist paradigm is unlikely to really grasp the CFSP dynamics and the EEAS emergent action. We must take other variables into account.

A Historically Determined Actor

The balance between continuity and change largely depends on internal and external variables. Historical institutionalism better explains both the EC origins and its transformation into the EU. Changes matter in EU history, but they converge in underpinning an international low profile: between 1945 and 1960 all the major European countries lost a war, either the Second World War or a colonial war. Civilian power is first of all the typical profile of defeated powers. Comparative analysis of Italian and German constitutions shows how relevant the weight of the history is, which is difficult to capture through mere rational choice approaches. Why the contagion to others? The winning states of the Second World War were losers of colonial wars during the next two decades, which also explains the declining international capabilities and profile of the Netherlands, Belgium and even of the UK and France (and the consequences on the EU). The contribution of new members, the neutrals, Iberians and the CEECs, did not change the EU's low profile, and neither did the neutral latecomers. Whereas the two world wars and decolonization look as crucial change, the external threats of the twenty-first century appear insufficient to provoke a fundamental change according to the path of a classical international power.

A Regional Actor

There exists a clear discrepancy between the regional nature of the EU's polity and the rhapsodic ambition of some EU institutions or leaders to act as a traditional kind of state power. For example, such emulation can be found in the option to focus strategic partnerships on high politics. Such choices have not yet been sufficiently analysed. The incident at the UN General Assembly of September 2010 (Lady Ashton unsuccessfully applied to take the floor) is an interesting case study: it is symptomatic of 'a frog wanting to be a bull' (see the famous La Fontaine fable). This led to serious misunderstandings with other regional entities (e.g. CARICOM, ASEAN, etc.) and necessitated intensive diplomatic work, resulting in the compromise of 3 May 2011. The incident also revealed a diminishing interest on the EU's part in regional cooperation abroad; that is in comparison with the Commission's interregional external policy during the decade 1990–2000. This may provoke further incidents and is strategically misleading because unrealistic. For example, how can the EU hope to multilateralize the emergent powers and frame their sometimes assertive sovereignty-enhancing policies, without the institutionalization of regional cooperation in East Asia, South Asia and in Latin America?

Discussing the EU's evolving global shaping power implies also a *pars construens*: the EU has been defined as an 'oil tanker' actor (rather than a battleship), by literature focusing on its long-term policies and a distinctive approach to IR. The most efficient EU foreign policies are the external projection of internal policies (the euro, market policy and so on) and some civilian external policies.[26] We have already drawn attention to the EU's market power (competition policy, trade policy, agricultural policy) (Damro 2011) but not yet on its 'linkage power': both horizontally and vertically, between internal policies and external policies (see Commission Communication of June 2006 and the European Council Declaration of December 2007), beyond the traditional distinction between high politics and low politics. Horizontally, trade policy negotiation for instance is often linked to concessions in environmental policy; cooperation in research and education (technological transfers, patents, 'Galileo', first of all, but also, for example, the Erasmus Mundus and the 7th framework programme, etc.) is offered as part of packages including economic cooperation and political dialogue; also international support to the euro could be situated within strategic dialogues aiming at a reform of multilateral organizations and maybe towards a new global monetary system. A wiser exercise of its 'linkage power' is a key element of a greater EU success in international relations.

Furthermore, we have emphasized that, contrary to Eurocentric post-modern dreams, a certain degree of coercion is an essential part of the cooperative and diplomatic game. An example is provided by sanctions. There is a distinctive EU approach to emphasizing diplomacy, regional solutions, legitimacy through the UNSC as the only basis for economic and trade sanctions.

In any case, according to the EU's approach, strengthening global regulation from above or from outside needs to be combined with increasing legitimacy by way of both the international community, the epistemic community and NGOs; as well as, internally, the national democratic bodies. The EU's external action is inevitably under additional pressure as it seeks a less contingent legitimacy not only as a normative ideal, but as a practical necessity because progress towards multilateral regulation inevitably demands more democratic accountability and legitimacy such as within the EU laboratory itself. These features bring arguments for both the perspective of the EU's 'structural foreign policy' and an unprecedented diplomatic action, able to adjust to the multipolar heterogeneous and multilevel world.

A Structural Foreign Policy

A decade ago, a part of the research community started qualifying the distinctive features of the EU foreign policy as a 'structural foreign policy' (Keukeleire 2004; Keukeleire et al. 2012; Telò 2005). The word 'structural' is however highly polysemic and needs a deeper conceptual definition. 'Structural foreign policy'

---

26 The negative side is also remarkable: agricultural policy for example, where relations with the developing world are hindered by internal policy.

has nothing to do with the Marxian opposition of structure (modes of production) to superstructure (politics and ideology), nor with the French structuralist school originated by De Saussure and influencing anthropology (notably C. Levy-Strauss) and social sciences. On the contrary, this conceptualization cannot overlook the already established focus within international relations theory on the global political structure (anarchy) and the neo-realist legacy about the notion of power. *Hic Rhodus hic salta.*

In international relations two concepts are still particularly relevant: the first one was elaborated by K. Waltz, and the second by S. Strange. K. Waltz proposes that the anarchy of the international relations system is structural in the sense that it is eternal and fundamentally conditions the units (states). A structural foreign policy in Waltz's understanding is impossible because the structure is impossible to change. However, not even realists are satisfied with the rigidities and static features of Waltz's concept of structural anarchy as it is accused of not explaining the issue of systemic change (Keohane 1986).

Structural change, according to one of Waltz's most brilliant pupils, R. Gilpin, can however only come through hegemonic power cycles and wars (Gilpin 1981). He does not accept the possibility that a declining hegemony of a superpower may allow a systemic change without any alternative superpower or increasing international anarchy. On the contrary, R.O. Keohane has argued as early as 1984 that institutionalized cooperation may continue even in absence of a global hegemonic power (see also Keohane 2004). J. Nye (1971) and E. Haas (1964) and a large multidisciplinary literature added that not only did global regimes continue to expand, but so did regional groupings of states. However, according to a realist understanding of IPE, regional entities – provided that they actually exist – are merely the result of emerging regional hegemonic powers, rather than the product of individual bottom-up choices by states as this latter interpretation would leave the system-units in the driver's seat. First conclusion: a structural foreign policy agenda is changing the structural international anarchy without necessarily the stabilizing factor of a hegemonic power.

Furthermore, R. Gilpin still welcomes the classical international power hierarchy, which allows hardly any relevance to the European regional power – i.e. first, military power, then political power, then economic and lastly cultural. By contrast, S. Strange overcomes this traditional hierarchy when opposing 'structural power' to 'relational power' (classical definition of power relations). Furthermore, power is a changing concept also in international relations theory: financial power, economic power and 'knowledge power' may matter more than military power and affect political power.

This critical analysis of the concept of international structure as established by K. Waltz, on the one hand, and of 'structural power' as proposed by Strange, on the other, may underpin a less empirical definition of the EU's 'structural foreign policy'.

Our next step is defining a structural foreign policy according to the following criteria which can be conceptualized as 'civilian power', and which are not limited to the EU but are also applicable to other national and regional entities.

1. A structural foreign policy is mainly based on continuity and coherence between internal policies and external governance. IPE provided a theoretical framework. In practice, the Commission's and the Council's statements between 2006 and 2010 emphasized this need of enhanced coherence between inside and outside. External policies should be more consistent with internal policies. Why? Because the very soul of the EU's international power is rooted in domestic policies like competition policy, market policy, internal trade policy, social policy and modernization policy, space of freedom, security and justice, all of which entail crucial external dimensions and implications for the EU's external influence.

2. A structural foreign policy addresses long-term challenges, rather than short-term conflicts: climate change, peace, balance between North and South, eradication of poverty, conflict prevention, etc. Consequently, sustainability is the main objective of such a foreign policy.

3. Contrary to any idealistic definition of the EU as a normative power, a structural foreign policy not only focuses on universal norms but also on second degree norm setting (standardization for example), procedures, diplomacy as mutual learning and dialogue. The efficiency and legitimacy of the EU's leading role as laboratory for global governance, is that internal compromises result from negotiations between 27 member states which may provide the global negotiation with sophisticated insights.

4. As Keukeleire and Justaert argue (2010), a structural foreign policy is characterized by comprehensiveness and coordination of all relevant actors: on the one hand, a holistic approach including different levels – i.e. national, regional and local; on the other, enhancing coordination of all relevant actors – i.e. headquarters in Brussels, delegations outreaching and also member states. Communication with domestic actors and existing institutions within partner states is crucial, and a key to sustainability.

How to Measure the Successes and Failures of Structural Foreign Policy?

The first successful structural foreign policy of the EC/EU is what J. Habermas calls the 'internal foreign policy': the end of the internal historical European anarchy, the internal conflict prevention, the transformation of the continent in a continent of peace where security dilemmas no longer matter. The second is enlarging, with various degrees of success, this 'security' to an increasing number of new member states – i.e. from six to 28. This regional model, limiting anarchy and changing the traditional notion of power, is not an isolated European case as supporting its spread in every continent is also matter of structural foreign policy. Third, setting a series of agreements with neighbouring countries, and interregional relations with regions abroad, based on limiting conflicts, building cooperation-regime, and supporting democracy and human rights. The EU influences the surrounding world and its far abroad as such, for the very simple reason that it exists as a voluntary, democratic, prosperous and peaceful grouping among neighbouring states. According to many observers, the EU's regional cooperation and integration is a model: the EU's soft power does not imply explicit policy-making, but rather diffusion by example and the benefits of economic cooperation among neighbouring countries and societies.

However, within the emergent multipolar world, the long-term structural policy is only one of the main tools of the EU's international influence and actorship. A more political actor in the making needs a second one: a consistent and distinctive diplomatic action. Structural foreign policy should be reflected in the way of understanding and implementing concrete ENP, interregional and strategic partnerships as shown in Chapters 7, 8 and 9.

A Distinctive Diplomacy in the Making

At least on paper, the EEAS will, within a few years, be one of the world's largest and most relevant diplomatic services. The literature has already addressed several relevant questions during the preceding 'unipolar momentum' and even more at the early stages of the emergent multipolar order.

1. Is a civilian power's diplomacy possible when the major global actors play according to a different playbook? Or is it no more than a type of declaratory foreign policy? Assessing the evolution of the international context is the crucial variable: the literature is still divided with regards to the nature of the current multipolarity, or the room for regional and civilian actors to emerge. Uncertainties remain as to the multilateral and multilevel network ability to frame the exercise of national sovereignty.
2. Second, to what extent and how can the EU foreign policy effectiveness, institutional efficiency and material capabilities be improved? Can it adjust to a non-European world? Can it comprehend the nature of the external challenges, in order to cope with a rapidly changing international context?

We will attempt to answer by focusing on five distinctive features of the EU's diplomacy in action.

Innovating the Policy towards the Near-Abroad

Providing the 'near abroad' with a solid cooperation architecture which is a viable alternative to both enlargement policy and foreign policy has been an EC/EU priority since the 1970s (early *Ostpolitik* and Mediterranean partnership). Contrary to the successful enlargement policy, the multiple European Neighbourhood

Policies are often mentioned as a case of the EU's quasi-failure, despite the two democratization waves (1989 and 2011) and the spread of several EU values.[27] Competition with Russia in the East and Islamic movements in the Arab world looks increasingly problematic. The key elements of the current difficulties are considered to be, on the one hand, 'realist' compromises with authoritarian regimes; and a want for comprehensive and effective policies regarding two of the most crucial challenges of the macro-region (regulating immigration and energy), on the other hand. These have provoked a series of unintended consequences. However, despite a series of shortcomings, no debilitating security dilemmas have emerged within the relationships entertained with the largest non-EU partners in the region, and the EU inescapably remains their main partner.

The ENP has a sound foundation in the Treaty (art. 8, TEU) and in the EU's interest in shaping the continental and Euro-Mediterranean macro-region in light of a common polity, a shared institutional architecture framing common policies. The EU is facing a fork in the road: either the temptation of old bilateralism and policy re-nationalization, or engaging a new multilateral approach with regards to the surrounding macro-region. The latter should, according to the Commission papers of 2011–12, be shaped by experimental forms of external governance, civil society democratic networks and a new macro-regional common architecture.

A regional power such as the EU has the responsibility of organizing through common principles and rules a larger territory beyond the strict borders of the actual member states: the enlargement policy (based on the Copenhagen criteria of 1993) and the European Neighbourhood Policy (since 2003) are the two tools for these pan-European and Mediterranean policies. In both policy fields the EU could better implement a typical civilian power's approach at macro-regional level. Many of these policies are bridging between external governance and internal governance, even if at different degrees of conditionality. As such, soft law and mutual learning work as a kind of 'open method of coordination' (Tulmets 2010). The combination of conditionality and open method of coordination could inspire neighbourhood policies. The internal complexity may be complementary to external flexibility and the degree of coercion/conditionality would evolve towards new forms more acceptable to neo-sovereign states. These features will become more relevant if they are supported by further Europeanization, notably if national diplomatic and organizational cultures of the member states would be enticed towards an increased coordination within the new EEAS, even if full integration is not viable. What would matter is the elaboration, between the Commission and the Council, of an emerging third mode of governance of external relations transcending their respective working methods, modes of governance and professional cultures (with two different modes of governance and procedures: community method and intergovernmental).

---

27   See Chapter 7.

A Deeper, Broader and More Legitimate Multilateralism

The second challenge the EU external action is facing is gradually building a 'new kind of multilateralism' (scenario C described in Chapter 1). This means combining its internal experience of a deeper and very binding kind of multilateral cooperation with an open and outreaching policy. It must look for convergence with as many players as possible, including the ones which are implementing merely contingent, instrumental, ad hoc approaches to multilateral cooperation.

To some extent, the EU is already exporting its modes of multilateral governance and aiming to strengthen a rule-based multilateral cooperation. It developed a procedural international identity focusing on deepening multilateral cooperation. Look at two examples of multilateral negotiation, climate change and trade. The climate change issue is a very good case study showing opportunities of inclusive regime building (from Kyoto to Bali) but also obstacles and failures (Copenhagen 2009). However, the Copenhagen UN Conference illustrates the risk of a unilateral and Eurocentric understanding of 'binding measures' which lack communication with other global players. The challenge is by contrast combining binding multilateral regimes with self-constraining and national targets allowing the largest inclusiveness (China and the United States), and looking for a third way between the EU-styled and the merely instrumental multilateral cooperation. Communication seems possible with major players abroad, provided the EU is ready to compromise between its supranational multilateralism and the partners' contingent, ad hoc, functional or even short-term and rent-seeking types of multilateralism. The recent UN Durban Conference on climate change is considered by many a success: for the first time the EU's approach in favour of a self-constraining treaty was welcomed by China and other BRICS. This was achieved thanks to a convergence between the most threatened countries belonging to the G77, some of the BRICS and the EU.

The example of trade diplomacy also highlights some of the EU's distinctive features and their complex implications for negotiations. The Commission acts as the EU's sole representative (exclusive competence) often without consulting the EEAS or the HR. The EU asserts a controversial combination between trade bilateralism, regionalism and multilateralism. Whereas its ideology favours global multilateralism and liberalization, its competition with the United States and other major trade actors fosters bilateralism. While its model is diffuse reciprocity, the EU is increasingly demanding specific reciprocity, notably in its relationships with weaker southern neighbours on the one hand; and with the strategic BRICS, on the other. This is done regardless of the EU's supposed greater ability to engage in win-win scenarios and in multiple issue linkages within a multilateral relationship: for example trade concessions in exchange for a partner's stronger commitment to common objectives related to global issues.

More generally, EU diplomacy has little choice but to look for multiple bridges and communication channels between its internal multilateral complexity and the rapidly changing external world. However, that does not mean mere adjustment to the other's views as the partner's preferences are far from being static and fixed. In other words, it could take stock of internal diversities and improve communication channels with the heterogeneous and changing non-European world.

Is this enhanced communication possible or is the EU an isolated entity within the multipolar world and '*hic sunt leones*'? Contrary to Manichean visions opposing the EU and the rest, a large literature is providing evidence that, in spite of fundamental differences, even state-diplomacy abroad is evolving beyond the classical Westphalian script (Pigman 2011).[28] Several observers argue that in the current post-Cold War era, nothing has proven any real effectiveness of the military option in conflict resolution and peace building (look at the Iraqi and Afghan examples) (beyond those in the purview of the realm of the 'Petersberg tasks'). Second, regional cooperation is spreading up on every continent, often as a better way to ensure conflict prevention and conflict settlements. Often regional cooperation, such as the Union of South American Nations, is considered both a security provider and sovereignty enhancing mechanism. However, four of the BRICS – Brazil, India, South Africa and Russia) – are federal states, familiar with the issue of sovereignty sharing and multi-level governance. The first three are vibrant democracies with a recognized track record regarding the respect of the rule of law and fundamental rights. The two remaining are part of multiple multilateral regimes both at global and regional level, which are fostering respect of rules, procedures and principles. All these factors, among others, are gradually questioning the still asserted nineteenth–twentieth century principle of 'non-interference'.

When talking about the defence of the 'common European interests' the treaties are fostering a move beyond the classical nineteenth-century Westphalian concept of 'national interest'. The latter is far from being uncontroversial even outside of the EU. Its interpretation varies in time according to the specific context and the shared global challenges affecting every state and which foster cooperation rather than competition. For example, even China's foreign policy has for years included concepts such as 'multilateralism' and 'responsibility' towards global challenges (Chen 2012). In the current world, windows of opportunity and possible bridges

---

28   This book provides analyses of the multiple post-Westphalian tendencies in the world diplomacy abroad: changing actors, venues, processes and functions of diplomacy multilateral organizations, supranational polities, global firms, civil society organizations and diplomats functions of representation and communication (including economic, military and security, and cultural diplomacy). An interesting historical example (mentioned as a part of the comparative literature) is provided by the early experience of the United States, before T. Roosevelt's imperial presidency: the early United States was no more than a democratic trading state even if confronted classical Westphalian challenges (UK, Spain, France) and was able to combine for several decades its internal 'republican dilemmas' between representation and external power with an effective soft external policy. The EU is not a federal state in the making and comparing it with the US evolution could be misleading.

exist for the EU to foster moves towards an open, multi-level, rule-based, post-hegemonic understanding of multilateral cooperation.

However, for several decades to come, convergence and divergence will coexist in the multipolar globalized world and this in spite of common reference to multilateral cooperation. No doubt that, even in the case of increased international regime building and the further institutionalization of international life, an important dialectic will emerge between the EU's understating of diffuse reciprocity (opposed to specific reciprocity to the extent that the expected exchange can be both postponed and based on issue linkage) and the partner's often contingent approaches (Green and Gill 2009; Calder and Fukuyama 2008; Telò 2012; Timmermann and Tsuchiyama 2008). Paradoxically, both near and far partners may improve their own coordination, and in turn demand a revised multilateral framework that the EU would need to respond to. The EEAS's ability to look for allies, convergences and issue linkages will be crucial.

The Opportunity Offered by the European Diplomatic Service

The EU's diplomatic service will inevitably be characterized by several distinctive features and specific challenges within the evolving multipolar context:

1. It will tend to measure the efficiency and effectiveness of its diplomatic action in the context of a long-term structural foreign policy.
2. It will have to prove its internal legitimacy and added value on a daily basis, and this in light of both sceptical member states – ever present through the internal interplay between 28 national foreign ministers, and particularly those hailing from the largest member states; as well as the need for improved horizontal coordination.
3. Beyond the mere role of EEAS as a coordinating service, it will aim to develop a third kind of shared identity, between Council and Commission, and compile a single external message rather than a single voice, one that is distinct from both the national ones or the UN style one.
4. For all that to work, it has also to address remaining legal uncertainties: for example, whether the EU ambassadors have to be listed as full ambassador of list 1, or as IO representatives? Which status for EU delegations? (e.g. which right of protection of the staff in case of emergency?)

Prioritizing a Non-Contingent Democratic Legitimacy

What about the external projection of the EU democratic values? In the EU's understanding, democracy is an essential component of external relations and foreign policy. This is not only a consequence of the EU treaties' asserted values (see paragraph above) and of an internal identity evolution since the Iberian and Greek enlargements. Solana's 2003 concept of 'efficient multilateralism' does not underline enough the profound link between efficiency and democratic legitimacy in the EU foreign policy. Linking democracy and foreign policy is excluded by 'realist' arguments as well: however, many local crises (Arab countries, Myanmar) confirm that democracy means sustainability. Also, non-contingent legitimacy is a welcome complement to both multilateral regime making as well as more effective global and regional and global governance – see the famous 'governance dilemma' (Keohane 2004). Underlining the democratization side of the EU's external action is not only a matter of idealism but also of policy sustainability, as long-term effectiveness opposed to short-term effectiveness.

New Enforcement Mechanisms

Value-driven conditionality may entail coercion. Inducement increases the cost of provocations and lack of respect for international arrangements. If new multilateralism demands enhanced legitimacy, it will inevitably include Kofi Annan's concept of 'responsibility to protect' (R2P) which has to be clearly dissociated – after the Libyan conflict – from regime change. The EEAS and the EU are expected to elaborate a more sophisticated combination of diplomacy and coercion, amongst others as a development of the previous notion of R2P. Regarding this very relevant tool of the diplomatic game, in contrast to the United States the EU drastically excludes the notion that the 'goal of the coercer is usually not total destruction but the use of enough force to make the use of future force credible to the adversary' (Byman and Waxman 2002: 5), a logic which can include air strikes or even, if need be, the threat of nuclear attack.[29]

Furthermore, international literature recognizes the growing relevance in the twenty-first century of other instruments of coercion which for many years have been available and deployed by the EU as complementary to diplomatic action: political sanctions (South Africa); diplomatic isolation (Austria); economic sanctions (Iraq); indirect and direct support of internal opposition to authoritarian regimes (Myanmar); support of provisional governments (Libya); and always provided further legitimacy to humanitarian interventions by the international community (UN). In a context of declining support from domestic public opinions and growing credibility gaps, the issue is however becoming more controversial.

Are trade sanctions effective as a foreign policy tool? Research emphasizes that the legal framework matters as the varying degrees of efficacy are concerned:

---

29   A comparison with France and the US national coercion policy clarifies the structural differences with the EU: according to the former Defence Minister P. Joxe, France can develop a strong diplomatic action because it has the 'force de frappe' available since De Gaulle which has not only to be seen as a dissuasion tool but also a way to make foreign policy and diplomacy with more effectiveness and efficiency. The same with the United States: Truman was a new man in Potsdam 1945 because he had, contrary to the Russians, the N bomb in his arsenal. However, these arguments can be considered as legacies of the nineteenth and twentieth centuries and even rational choice realists have to recognize that the N bomb has never been used.

sanctions under the ACP art. 96 umbrella prove more successful than the measures under CFSP (Title V, TEU) (Portela 2010: 163). The Council is prevented from legally committing to CFSP sanctions because of the division among member states when faced with challenging and controversial cases. Conversely, in the case of the ACP and art. 96, material and immaterial consequences of the suspension of the treaty (including development aid) and the clarity of the 'contract' make pro-democratic sanctions more effective. The procedure of QMV in the Council, the commitment of the Commission, the proactive role of neighbouring countries, explain both the enhanced efficiency and the effectiveness of this course of action.

At a later stage, the 'Petersberg tasks' underline the distinction between peace-keeping and peace-enforcing missions. The first (before the conflict) imply compliance, whereas the second (after the armed conflict exploded) need combat forces and deterrence, be it immediate or general. The EU may be pressed into playing this last card in the Caucasian, African or Mediterranean regions. This is not in contradiction with the civilian power approach: it would only make the civilian role more credible. However, the balance between the civilian and military side is crucial to the success of any mission started under the CFSP and EDFP.

What Can Realistically be Improved?

What could be improved at the level of the EU's concrete political actorship within the multilateral system and its bilateral partnerships?

Increasing the EU's 'Multilaterability' and its International 'Procedural Identity'

First, this is a matter of international 'procedural identity' and will depend on both internal (further Treaty reform) and external factors. At the moment, the EU's direct representation is very limited (FAO) and the EU has a mere observer status within IOs, which affects its international effectiveness. The EU's treaty revisions may implement the objective of enhanced external coherence and member state loyalty, provided that the political will of member states to increasingly unify their external representation exists, at least for example within the IMF. Currently, internal obstacles and opposition from some member states to unified external representation still prevails. However, if the Europeans want to be more credible on the international stage, they should diminish the contradiction between their own multilateral internal practice and asserted multilateral identity, on the one hand; and the European states' overrepresentation within the IMF, G20 and other multilateral bodies, on the other. Such self-restraint of the European states with regards to IO reform (already begun with the 2011 IMF shares reform) could be balanced out by a united representation of the EU such as within global multilateral governance institutions.

Increasing the EU's 'Multilaterability' and the Position of Associated States and Regions

Second, the resistance of the UN system and other international organizations to welcoming regional entities as full members is a possible further obstacle. In spite of the EU's strong commitment to UN values and practical cooperation with the UN, the international organization's charter constitutes a real obstacle because it depends on the other's willingness – i.e. that of third-party states and regional entities. The UN General Assembly is an intergovernmental body, its members are states: the EU still sits among observers (despite the 3 May 2011 UN resolution) and this even though Europe provides 55 per cent of the funding and aid. In September 2011 seven member state leaders took the floor before President Van Rompuy. An enhanced role for the EU within the UN system can only be achieved provided: an alliance with other regional groupings, on the one hand; and treaty reform strengthening internal cohesion, vertical consistency and loyalty on the other.

Strategic partnerships could also be improved beyond the Council conclusions of September 2010. Focusing on big powers is an obvious corollary to the EU's rising international political status. However, the actual strategic partnerships should be better differentiated from each other, be they also at same time deeper and more inclusive (to allow issue linkages and deal making) and more prioritized.[30] Second, thanks to the European Council presidency, the follow-up activities in the time between summits should be more detailed and enhanced involvement of a plurality of actors should be encouraged (several commissioners, several epistemic communities, civil society networks, etc.). Finally, not only the EU's diplomatic action, but also its structural foreign policy risks to be affected in case of open competition between the bilateral strategic partnership with regional leaders, and the interregional partnerships set by the EU during the 1990s according to its nature of regional entity: Mediterranean partnership (1996), ASEM (1996), 'Rio Process' (1999), new ACP convention (Cotonou conference, 2000).[31] Improving coordination between bilateral, interregional and multilateral relations is a crucial challenge and a matter of improved practical governance.

Increasing the EU's 'Multilaterability' by a Closer Cooperating Hard Core

The current institutional set allows for more flexibility and differentiation within the integration process. A new treaty is not necessarily needed to strengthen a driving group of states (as in the case of economic governance): 'closer cooperation' among member states, strengthening integration, which is in line with EU objectives and open to latecomers is possible provided that at least nine member states take part in it (TEU Title IV, art. 20 and TFEU, articles 326/334).

---

30   See Chapters 9, 10, 11 and 12.
31   See Chapter 8.

The Libyan crisis illustrates why such a hard core has not yet seen the light of day and that it will never coalesce around hard policy objectives such as imposing 'regime change'.

Conclusion

The EU's foreign policy and diplomatic service will be that of a sophisticated regional grouping and will never be a copy of previous or existing state powers, not even federal ones. Both the multiple forecasts sensing an eminent EU superpower (Leonard 2005), as well as the recent opposite theories of a declining and marginalized EU have been rubbished. The EU is geared towards continuing to elaborate new ideas and experimental governance (Zeitlin 2009), including in its external relations. Institutionalization matters as a kind of set, civilized power. As such, the EU can combine either in a confused or in a smart way a large array of soft means, for example in its approach to external conditionality. Its main realms of action are and will be the regional and global multilateral processes where a rigid power hierarchy does not yet exist: environment, climate change, health, human rights protection, financial stability and other transnational challenges.

The EU is not an isolated case study as it reflects a more general trend: the diffused call for new forms of institutionalization of international life that bind state behaviour without substituting itself to the state. This is a great idea for international relations in the twenty-first century, provided that it is not identified with merely disseminating copies of the EU's kind of institutionalization.

The EU is not an isolated case study also because a structural foreign policy is a current and diffused feature of global governance: 'New Regionalism' is spreading on every continent and ushering in a 'world of regions' (Katzenstein 2005); even more so as a multi-regional world takes shape wherein pluralism and regional multilateralism is becoming a structural form of global governance. However, regionalism is making global governance more complex and multi-level, and its democratization is increasing complexity even more. Within the emergent multi-layered, many factors are increasing global governance's complexity: the expanding regional cooperation, interregional relations, multi-actor negotiations, transnational networks, and pressures for a more diffuse reciprocity, the increasing weight of domestic demands for decentralization and also for democratization. The EU's internal complexity is not an exception; it is part of a general decline of the old path of sovereign national state power. The hypothesis that the EU is less and less an isolated case study is even more realistic than the opposite one. European networks are modestly but seriously strengthening a kind of new regional and global post-hegemonic '*koiné*', where social actors are sharing common global concerns and looking for common solutions.

The EU, with or without German hegemony, will remain an unprecedented power: an incipient civilian power. However, power is also changing elsewhere within the current interdependent multipolar/apolar world. Multiple and different forms of power are emerging in different issue areas. A gradual revision of the Westphalian order is occurring even if along a variety of paths. This urgently calls for a re-conceptualization of power and multilateral cooperation (including more 'diffuse reciprocity' for example) rather than a post-modern dream or a U-turn back to old conceptions and practices based on mere power politics.

The European Union is not an isolated case study as far as its new diplomatic service is concerned. The EEAS is an extraordinarily relevant experiment of socialization and identity building, in both its intergovernmental and supranational nature. If adjusted to current challenges, the European structural foreign policy and diplomatic action may to some extent suggest and foster solutions for the twenty-first century's regional and global governance as it anticipates modern tendencies which are *in nuce* emerging elsewhere in the world. We are witnessing the spreading on every continent of several forms of new diplomacy: the interplay between internal complexity and new combinations of diplomacy, societal networking and external conditionality are also emerging in other global actors.

Against idyllic visions a mix between imperial tendencies and a completely new context is emerging in all parts of the world wherein fragmentation, interdependence and multilateralism, including deeper forms of multilateralism, matter as well. Europe is a strange part of the same planet where a more traditional kind of power is surviving. When talking about a possible 'new multilateralism' we are not opposing an idealized EU-styled approach to the others, but drawing the attention to existing similarities and exploring the possible convergence scenario. Ultimately, allowing the EU to become better at combining complexity and external efficiency whereas the emergent powers are to become more responsible, complex and less 'sovereign' in the classical sense. Needed are dialectic interactions between innovative and more legitimate forms of multilateralism, on the one hand; and traditional, pragmatic and contingent forms of intergovernmental relations, on the other. A dynamic relationship will then be possible between oft diverging interests, practices and visions. Such a mix of cooperation and competition can improve the common evolving multilateral context, as a kind of revival of the post-Alexandrian hellenistic '*koine*', a shared rule-based framework (scenario C described in Chapter 1) fostering transnational people-to-people meetings and networking.

The external context is actually a largely independent variable as we argued at the beginning. The relevance of the EU and its performance will depend upon what in 1513 Machiavelli called the combination of '*fortuna*' (objective circumstances and material conditions: in our case, the rise of the rest of the world) and '*virtus*', the subjective variables (institutional and human capacities). The only viable scenario for the EU is the global 'convergence scenario' and this in the inevitable context of multiple paths towards modernization and conflicting values. However, thanks to the weight of various favourable internal and external trends and societal pressures, a dynamic cooperative mix might still prevail.

Chapter 3

The Lisbon Treaty, CSDP and the EU as a Security Actor

Jolyon Howorth

Abstract

The immense promise of the Lisbon Treaty for a new impetus to CFSP/CSDP has been disappointed. Part of the explanation has been the global (and European) economic crisis, which has resulted in 20 member states reducing their defence budgets from 2009–10, while most other consequential actors have increased theirs. Three further events over the past year have exacerbated this crisis: the EU's 'defection' during the Libyan operation; Robert Gates's stark warning in June 2010; the January 2012 US Strategic Review.

The Libyan crisis was in many ways the archetypal scenario for which the EU, through CSDP, had been planning since the Balkans fiasco 20 years earlier. Yet, when the moment arrived to organise military intervention, the EU was absent, the victim of its own internal divisions and lack of leadership. *Operation Unified Protector* was *formally* a NATO mission, led by France and the UK, with the United States taking a back-seat role; yet without US inputs, the mission could not have succeeded. Since the Libyan operation, CSDP has been somewhat regenerated through the initiatives of the EDA, the Weimar process, the Polish presidency and the Ghent Framework. But it still suffers from incoherence, inadequate projects for pooling, sharing, specialisation and rationalisation – and from an all-pervading sense of gloom about the direction of the EU. The initial project of CSDP 'autonomy' from NATO and from the United States has run out of steam. The future for CSDP therefore lies in ever greater integration with NATO. As for the Alliance, its 'American' future (the global alliance or League of Democracies), which Europeans never accepted, has been fatally compromised in Afghanistan. The contradictions in the *New Strategic Concept* are stronger than ever. NATO should therefore return fully to Europe and its hinterland, probably change its name and progressively merge with CSDP.

Introduction

Prior to its ratification in 2009, it was widely believed that the Lisbon Treaty had the potential to make a more significant difference to the functioning and impact of the EU as a global actor than any single document since the founding Treaty of Rome. In particular, the mechanisms and dynamics of the Common Foreign and Security Policy (CFSP) and the Common Security and Defence Policy (CSDP) were widely expected to acquire considerable new impetus. This has not happened. What nobody foresaw on the eve of ratification was the depth and scale of the financial crisis which was to hit Europe the following year. This has had a seriously negative effect on defence budgets and military spending and has contributed to calling into question the EU's capacity as an international security actor – a role for which it had been preparing for 20 years. This chapter will address the CFSP/CSDP innovations of Lisbon; the balance sheet for CSDP since Lisbon; the impact of the Libyan crisis in 2011 on the EU's potential as a security actor; and the future relationship between CSDP and NATO.

Lisbon came into being because it was seen by the member states as necessary in order to increase the efficiency, effectiveness and impact of the EU itself, both internally and externally (see Chapter 1 in this volume). Nowhere is this more evident than in the field of CFSP/CSDP. Of the 62 amendments to the previous treaties introduced by Lisbon no fewer than 25 concern CFSP/CSDP. Moreover, with the exception of the confusion in Ireland over that country's traditional neutrality, the national debates over these foreign and security aspects of the Treaty gave rise in no member state to any particular issues of concern. Opinion polls across Europe consistently suggest that there is considerable popular support for the view that foreign and security policy ought logically to be conducted at European level rather than exclusively at national level.

The Main CFSP/CSDP Treaty Changes

The CFSP/CSDP changes introduced by Lisbon can be grouped under the headings of general provisions, institutional innovation and new procedures.

General Provisions

A new article 46A appears in the Lisbon Treaty and states, succinctly and seemingly innocuously, that 'The Union shall have legal personality'. What this implies in international law is that the EU acquires the *capacity* to act in the international arena, but not necessarily the *competence* – which continues to depend on the agreement of the member states. Nevertheless, the acquisition by the EU of 'legal personality' henceforth gives it a status in international law which ought only to enhance its capacity to speak with a single voice. These developments do not, of course, undermine the sovereignty of the EU's member states, but they do mean that, increasingly, the EU should be in a position, *in parallel with its member states*, to be seen and heard on the international stage (de Schoutheete and Andoura 2007).

Chapter 1 of the Treaty, on 'General Provisions of the Union's External Action', goes into great detail concerning the underlying principles and values of CFSP and CSDP. The Lisbon Treaty's article 10a states that:

> The Union's action on the international scene shall be guided by the principles which have inspired its own creation, development and enlargement, and which it seeks to advance in the wider world: democracy, the rule of law, the universality and indivisibility of human rights and fundamental freedoms, respect for human dignity, the principles of equality and solidarity, and respect for the principles of the United Nations Charter and international law. The Union shall seek to develop relations and build partnerships with third countries, and international, regional or global organisations which share the principles referred to in the first subparagraph. It shall promote multilateral solutions to common problems, in particular in the framework of the United Nations.

The lengthy articulation of these rather grandiose principles and aims makes it very clear what the EU formally considers to be the underlying normative framework for its interaction with the rest of the world. The problem, however, lies in the implementation of these principles. The General Provisions of the Lisbon Treaty in effect lay down the guidelines for moving from wishful thinking to increasingly coordinated action. This begins with institutional reform.

Institutions

The Treaty created two key new positions: President of the Council and High Representative for Foreign Affairs and Security Policy-Vice President of the Commission (HR-VP). These positions were filled, respectively, by Belgium's former prime minister, Herman Van Rompuy, and by the UK's Catherine Ashton. I have examined elsewhere, at length, the performance of these two actors on the world stage since their appointments in late 2009 (Howorth 2011). The former position (Council President) was always widely assumed to be a *Chairmanship* rather than an executive function. The fact that the hypothetical candidacy of Tony Blair was overwhelmingly rejected speaks to the lack of desire on the part of the Heads of State and Government to find themselves in a position of being browbeaten or coerced by one of their own. Whatever ambitions Van Rompuy might have entertained to turn the job into one of real executive authority, those ambitions were rapidly squashed. The main policy challenge facing the Union since 2010 – the financial and sovereign debt crisis – ensured that the only power-brokers capable of reaching a solution (Germany and, to a lesser degree, France) would take the reins. Under these circumstances, Van Rompuy had little alternative but to act as a 'Secretary General' of the EU. In that capacity, and given the constraints imposed by the Treaty upon his position, he is widely judged to have been relatively effective.

The same cannot be said about the HR-VP position. In early 2012, Ashton's 'half-term reports' were generally quite negative. One problem was that it was never clear quite what the job entailed or what exactly was expected of the incumbent. By selecting an individual with no experience of foreign and security policy, who was almost bound, at least initially, to find herself vulnerable and hesitant, the member states could stand accused of having set the position off on a path of minimal effectiveness. Ashton was far from being the strongest candidate for the job. Her appointment was felt by the large foreign and security policy community across the EU as a major disappointment. She made many initial mistakes which exacerbated the situation. It has not been all bad and there have been both mitigating circumstances and some positive outcomes (Korski 2011; Ruger 2011). But on balance the record is almost universally perceived as poor. In February 2011, 300 European officials and decision-shapers, questioned by the public-relations firm Burson Marsteller about the second Barroso Commission, ranked Ashton as (by far) the least effective Commissioner, with 37.7 per cent judging her performance to be 'disappointing', 29.1 per cent to be 'below average' and another 17.8 per cent to be merely 'average'. Only 9.9 per cent gave her a score of 'good' (Badr 2011). Many say that the job is impossible for one person. If that is the case, then it should be re-thought. If it is not the case, then it needs to be carried out more effectively. Either way, Europe as a post-Lisbon global institutional actor seems to have got off to a very bad start.

New Procedures

There is little in the Lisbon Treaty dealing specifically with the development, on the part of the Union, of effective *military capacity*. This is an ongoing process. In the Council's Declaration on Strengthening Capabilities of 11 December 2008 (Council 2008), it was agreed that the EU should develop the capability to mount a number of overseas missions simultaneously: two major stabilisation and reconstruction operations, two rapid response operations of limited duration, an emergency operation for the evacuation of European nationals, a maritime or air surveillance/interdiction mission, a civilian-military humanitarian assistance operation lasting up to 90 days, about a dozen CSDP civilian missions of varying formats. A significant measure of agreement has now been reached by all member states (including the UK) on the necessity of *pooling, sharing and specialization* of military capacity (EDA 2012).

One aspect of this is *permanent structured cooperation* (PESCO), a new procedure introduced by Lisbon to encourage member states to coordinate their military capacity in a variety of ways. Article 28A/6 calls for:

> Those Member States whose military capabilities fulfil higher criteria and which have made more binding commitments to one another in this area with a view to the most demanding missions shall establish permanent structured cooperation within the Union framework.

The procedures whereby member states may enter into permanent structured cooperation are laid out in detail both in the main body of the Treaty and in a separate Protocol. The most important feature is that the dynamics of this procedure must be as *inclusive* as possible (Biscop 2008). The objective is to mobilise the maximum capacity of which the EU is capable, drawing on whatever instruments are available from whatever source. CSDP cannot and will not work if it relies massively on a few contributors, with the others as bystanders or paymasters. If PESCO can be made to work as intended, it could have a significant effect on the generation of EU military capacity. This will increasingly be required, not only to carry out the missions referred to under the Declaration on Strengthening Capabilities, but also because the types of missions the post-Lisbon EU aspires to undertake are themselves expanded under the terms of the Treaty. Article 28B refers to: 'joint disarmament operations, humanitarian and rescue tasks, military advice and assistance tasks, conflict prevention and peacekeeping tasks, [and] tasks of combat forces undertaken for crisis management, including peace-making and post-conflict stabilization.' There are other CSDP elements in the Lisbon Treaty, such as a Solidarity Clause and a Mutual Assistance Clause which we need not rehearse here. We will address the role of the European External Action Service (EEAS) below and it is more fully analysed in Chapter 5.

The CSDP Balance Sheet since Lisbon

The period since the ratification of Lisbon has been overwhelmingly marked by the economic crisis, which has effectively dominated the EU agenda. There has been precious little time to devote to other issues. The crisis itself and its attendant budget cuts and austerity measures have led to significant reductions in the defence budgets of the member states over the past few years. Between 2009 and 2010, 20 EU member states reduced their defence spending (many of them significantly), while only seven increased it slightly (the only state to have increased spending by a significant amount was Poland – from \$7,297m to \$8,273m). The net result was a reduction in the combined defence spending of the EU-27 from \$276,784m in 2009 to \$254,886m in 2010. At the same time, the United States and virtually all other major military powers increased their defence spending. In 2009, the EU-27 spent 42 per cent of the US defence budget. In 2010, they spent only 37 per cent as much as the Americans. In 2009, the EU expenditure on defence amounted to the same sum as that of the next seven military powers outside of NATO *combined* (China, Japan, Russia, Saudi Arabia, India, Brazil and South Korea). In 2010, they spent the same as only the next five players (China, Japan, Saudi Arabia, Russia and India). This is still an enormous sum of money. The problem is that much of it is wasted in fruitless duplication. Moreover, three countries alone (France, UK and Germany) spend over 60 per cent of the total. If the fourth major power (Italy) is included, those countries cover almost 70 per cent of the collective EU 'defence budget'. The remaining EU member states average out at \$3,440m each. That is less than the defence budget of Thailand. Authoritative voices have been raised warning that the EU is approaching a crisis of 'demilitarisation' which would prevent it from being an actor at all in the security field (Mölling 2011; Witney 2011).

For 20 years, enormous efforts were devoted to building up military and civilian capacity for engaging in international crisis management, to rationalising, pooling and sharing assets (Howorth 2007). Between 2003 and 2009, the EU launched no fewer than 27 overseas missions (Isis 2012). Some of them were purely military, some purely civilian, some civ-mil, but all designed to shore up stability in regional crisis zones (Engberg 2011). However, after Lisbon, these missions appeared to dry up. A small training mission for Somali security forces was launched in January 2010. Two years later, several new initiatives were announced: reinforcement of naval patrols off the Horn of Africa; Security Sector Reform and border-control in South Sudan; support for regional counter-terrorism in the Sahel. But many felt that the drive behind CSDP had disappeared.

The High Representative, Catherine Ashton, is formally responsible for CSDP, but after her appointment in 2009 she was initially preoccupied with establishing the European External Action Service (EEAS) (Carta 2012; Graesli 2011; Hannay 2011; Missiroli 2010). The service is now up and running. It was launched with ultra-discretion and no fanfare, on 1 December 2010. It features an impressive team of top diplomats, headed by the former French ambassador to the United States, Pierre Vimont, and seconded by the long-time Brussels insider, David O'Sullivan. Establishing this service within one year, and seeing off the rival claims of the Commission and the Parliament, was no mean accomplishment and was largely credited to Ashton's perseverance and bargaining skills. There is still a long way to go before the EEAS can be seen as a major force on the world stage, but the first step has been taken (Barysch et al. 2011; Lehne 2011; Vogel 2012). The energy devoted to this task persuaded Ashton's critics to hold their fire over the seeming stagnation of CSDP. After the EEAS was launched, the honeymoon ended. Critics were not impressed when, in a speech in Budapest in February 2011, Ashton stressed that the EU 'cannot deploy gunboats or bombers' and argued that its strength '*lies, paradoxically in its inability to throw its weight around*' (Ashton 2011b; my emphasis). The speech was interpreted by one analyst as an attempt 'to usurp the work of her predecessor [Javier Solana – JH], who sought for over a decade to carefully build up the European Union's credibility and authority as a "global power"' (Rogers 2011). It is widely recognised that Ashton does not care much for defence and security policy and generally considers that this should be the responsibility of NATO. One of her functions is to chair the meetings of the Ministers of Defence, a function which she also performs as Head of the European Defence Agency (EDA) – whose Steering Board is made up of the EU Ministers of Defence. However, she has also been widely criticised for her neglect of these meetings (Gros-Verheyde 2011).

Since the summer of 2011, and in the wake of the Libyan crisis which I shall analyse shortly, several EU countries have sought to pour new-found energy into CSDP. In the context of the 'Weimar Triangle' (military cooperation between France, Germany and Poland), there have been a series of initiatives in this direction, including the re-launch of proposals for an EU Operational Headquarters (OHQ) (Adebahr 2011). The Belgian and Dutch navies formed a single integrated command in the 1990s. In 2010, the European Air Transport Command (EATC) was established at Eindhoven Airbase in the Netherlands. It offers a joint set of assets to the air transport fleets of France, Germany, the Netherlands and Belgium. The European defence ministers, meeting in Ghent on 9 December 2010, agreed to examine ways of categorising defence assets under three heads: those that, for reasons of strategic imperative, would remain under national control but could be made more interoperable at EU level; those that could offer potential for pooling; and those that could be re-examined on the basis of role- and task-sharing. The Conclusions of the Polish presidency (July–December 2011) were interpreted as constituting a serious re-launch of CSDP (Ochmann 2012; O'Donnell 2012; Pflimlin 2011). In particular, the European Defence Agency, under its new dynamic head Claude-France Arnould, has kick-started a dozen major procurement projects, all of which were endorsed by the EU's defence ministers on 30 November (EDA 2011). It remains to be seen how, and how far, CSDP will progress. What is clear is that the status quo is unsustainable. Either the project makes substantial progress, or it will begin to unravel. In a major study, General Jean-Paul Perruche, the former Director General of the EU's Military Staff, concluded that the time was ripe to re-launch CSDP in the context of a rebalanced NATO (Perruche 2011). Either the Europeans agree to develop the necessary instruments to underpin their global strategic ambitions; or they agree to become a continental-sized Switzerland. That debate is now engaged. It was given considerable stimulus by the Libyan crisis in spring 2011.

Libya and the 'Existential Crisis' of CSDP

The 2011 military intervention in Libya, *Operation Unified Protector*, appears to represent a paradigm shift in European and transatlantic security arrangements. The US decision to 'lead from behind' (Krauthammer 2011; Lizza 2011; Sanger 2011), in effect to oblige the Europeans at least *to give the appearance* of assuming primary responsibility for a crisis management operation in their own backyard, was a significant turning point. The valedictory oration by US Defence Secretary Robert Gates in Brussels on 10 June 2011, at which he spoke of a 'dim, if not dismal future for the transatlantic alliance' when the new generation of US leaders who did not grow up during the Cold War would be unlikely to 'consider the return on America's investment in NATO worth the cost' (Gates 2011), also signalled a clear and significant shift in US policy. For reasons of domestic budgetary unsustainability (Mandelbaum 2010), as well as post-Afghanistan and post-Iraq strategic review (Barnett 2009; Pfaff 2010), the United States is no longer able to spend without thinking on security and defence – neither for itself, nor for its allies. A recent estimate sees the US defence budget shrinking by between $600 billion and $900 billion over the next decade (Valasek et al. 2011). The implicit downgrading of the European security relationship was confirmed in January 2012 with the publication of the Defense Department's *Strategic Guidance* paper announcing that the United States will henceforth prioritise the Asia-Pacific and Middle East regions (DoD 2012). These shifts pose a major challenge to the Europeans.

In many ways, the Libyan crisis was the archetypical scenario for which the CSDP had been preparing to assume leadership for 20 years – a medium intensity military intervention in the EU's immediate neighbourhood, either *with* access to NATO assets (Berlin Plus) or autonomously. The 'fit' between the Libyan case and the ideal-type hypothetical CSDP mission can hardly be overstated. Yet CSDP was not even considered as a potential lead agency. Key member states such as Germany and Poland, as well as a majority of the other members, were *opposed* to any European military intervention (see Chapter 4 in this volume). The High Representative espoused the thinking of these reluctant Europeans and effectively ruled out any military involvement by the EU as such in the Libyan operation. This led some commentators to speak of an 'existential crisis' for CSDP (Menon 2011). Faced with what amounted to a 'collective defection' over Libya, faced with Secretary Gates's strident warnings that the Europeans must do far more to share the allied security burden, faced with the US strategic tilt to the Pacific, and faced with the concurrent crisis of sovereign debt, and with uncertainty over the very future of the euro, EU member states in 2012 were being forced to re-examine the nature and extent of their commitment to CSDP (Biscop 2012; Open Letter 2011; Valasek 2011a). They were, as one leading commentator noted, in effect grappling with the following basic question: 'Either Europeans will develop the security and defence identity they have advertised for so long, so Europe can have its own credible voice in a world not only run by soft power, or, given the expense and difficulties of defeating even Libya, they will simply stop trying. The jury is out, but the verdict is important' (Erlanger 2011). Either way, this would amount to a paradigm shift.

NATO: 'European Hero' of the Hour or Spent Force?

What of NATO in all this? If there is a dominant perception about the Libyan operation, it is probably that it represents a clear success story for NATO, one for which the alliance can justifiably allow itself a 'victory lap' (Daalder and Stavridis 2012). In fact, the picture is far more complex than this. First, we should not be misled by the US notion of 'leading from behind'. While it is true that, of the 9,658 *strike sorties* flown between the beginning of hostilities on 19 March and the fall of Tripoli in late August, 85 per cent were flown by Europeans (50 per cent of those being by the French and the British), the United States nevertheless played an indispensable role in the mission. Libyan air defences were taken down in three days by overwhelming US assets. After this initial onslaught, the United States pulled back most of its air assets, but still continued to provide around 50 per cent of the combat support aircraft, the bulk of the strategic intelligence, real-time targeting guidance, crucial stocks of ammunition, and 75 per cent of the mission's aerial refuelling. The command chain, despite the symbolic presence, as overall commander of *Operation Unified Protector*, of *Canadian* Lt. Gen. Charles Bouchard, passed essentially via US flag officers.

Critics of the NATO mission have been as numerous as its cheerleaders. It took the 'strongest and most significant defence alliance the world has ever seen' (Obama) almost six months to 'defeat' a rag-tag Libyan army in open desert country. The major military nations of Europe, battling budget cuts and shrinking capacity, almost ran out of munitions and had to purchase them *in extremis* from the United States. Italy had to withdraw its aircraft-carrier at the height of the air campaign because of government cuts. Two-thirds of the member states of the EU and half the members of NATO opted not to be involved at all. And while the operational control may have come through SHAPE,[1] the political control seems to have been assured by an informal trilateral partnership between Paris, London and Washington, a partnership which, as early as 15 April, redefined the mission as regime change rather than the 'Responsibility to Protect' (Obama et al. 2011). All these factors pose major questions about the future of NATO. There were, in addition, numerous operational, logistical and resourcing problems which meant that the operation lasted far longer than initially anticipated and led to a highly sobering internal NATO evaluation which carried serious implications for future operations – and particularly for a hypothetical operation against Syria (Johnson and Mueen 2012; Schmitt 2012). Critics of both the mission itself and the way it was carried out were as numerous as supporters and many an analyst predicted that the Libyan operation could be NATO's very last (Applebaum 2011; Bacevich 2011; Kaplan 2011; Metz 2011; Rachman 2011). The most recent debate about NATO's future stems directly from the Libyan conflict.

That debate has in reality been running unchecked since the fall of the Berlin Wall (Rupp 2006; Rynning 2005). Constanze Stelzenmüller (2011) noted wryly after the Gates summation in June 2011, that NATO has *always* been a two-tier alliance: 'What Katherine Hepburn said of Fred Astaire and Ginger Rogers – "She gave him sex, he gave her class" – was just as true for NATO: the Americans gave us clout, we Europeans gave them cover.' The constraints of the Cold War and bipolarity dictated tight solidarity between all alliance members in all parts of the globe. NATO was truly an *alliance* as traditionally understood. Yet post-1989, in the absence of any existential nuclear or other type of threat, and in a multipolar world, regional crises impact NATO's member state interests in very different ways. There is little likelihood of unanimity on anything, particularly at great distances from Europe (Jung 2012). The 'alliance' has become a mechanism for generating

---

1   Supreme Headquarters Allied Powers in Europe, located north of the Belgian city of Mons.

coalitions of the willing. Donald Rumsfeld was (for once) correct: 'the mission determines the coalition'. NATO's most recent attempt at self-definition, the 2010 *New Strategic Concept*, is in reality neither new, nor strategic. Nor is it even a concept. It is a document which contains something fairly vague for everybody but nothing very precise for anybody. Although NATO's Prague summit in 2002 declared that distinctions between 'in area' and 'out of area' were no longer valid and that the alliance could operate throughout the world, and although this precept has been implemented in Afghanistan, there is henceforth very little prospect of European forces signing up to support US grand strategy around the globe. The US drive for a 'Global Alliance' or for a 'League of Democracies' never found favour with Europeans and has probably been administered the *coup de grâce* by the experience of Afghanistan, which, however strong the official spin may be, is almost certain to be judged by history as a military and political failure. Washington is, in any case, more comfortable with multiple bilateralisms than with ever more complicated formal alliances, as the 2011 agreement with Australia and the constant quest for new partnerships indicate. NATO's Chicago summit in May 2012 formally kept all options on the table, but ongoing questions about the real nature and purpose of NATO are unlikely to be resolved any time soon. NATO itself needs a radical re-think.

Conclusion: The Future of CSDP and NATO

As for CSDP, assuming, in the wake of Libya, that it continues to make progress, its cooperation with NATO remains more crucial than ever. It is only through the NATO framework that CSDP can actually achieve operational effectiveness and, eventually, autonomy. That suggests three things. First, it implies that the Alliance should return to Europe – including its entire periphery. It should be explicitly re-designated as a mechanism for guaranteeing regional stability in the European area and its neighbourhood. That stability, unlike during the Cold War, will not be secured through a balance of nuclear forces or through existential deterrence, but through the development of a serious capacity for regional crisis management. Collective security will complement collective defence. Second, it means that NATO and CSDP must refrain from seeing one another as rivals in a beauty contest or as contenders for a functional or spatial division of labour. The sterile quarrels over duplication in general and HQs in particular must be transcended. In a world of shrinking resources, it must be recognised that *European* forces and capacity, whether deployed via NATO or CSDP, are all drawn from the same pool. At the level of procurement, the dynamics of pooling and sharing should be concentrated in the EU. It makes no sense to have two separate processes, one operating within NATO ('smart defence') and another within the EU. There is very little chance that mere coordination of national means would suffice to meet European requirements. Shared sovereignty is only meaningful if accompanied by policy convergence and shared security and strategic objectives – in other words, a process of political integration. Pooling and sharing have political, economic, industrial and operational implications. The EU is a global political project, whereas NATO deals 'merely' with security. The EU is also the framework within which Europe generates common interests. Logically, therefore, it is the place where these interests can best be harmonised at the level of the defence industrial base. There is no question that this European procurement process should be conducted in tight liaison with NATO, but the EU framework is indispensable. The role of the EDA should be central and Allied Command Transformation (ACT) should be transformed into an agency which ensures liaison with the US defence industrial base. Third, there must gradually and progressively be an institutional and political merger between CSDP and NATO. This sounds radical, but in reality the structures of CSDP were modelled on those of NATO and the permanent representatives to the two military committees are, for the most part, the same individuals. Enhanced cooperation will, over time, lead to integration. This chapter is not the place to go into the details. The key issue is the direction in which the two entities should be moving. The US position over Libya indicates a way forward.

Operational leadership must increasingly be assumed by the Europeans. This will require serious restraint on the part of Washington and extreme seriousness of purpose on the part of the Europeans. CSDP must acquire operational autonomy *through and within* NATO and the Americans must learn to take a genuine back-seat. Progressively the balance within the Alliance must shift to one in which the Europeans are doing the vast majority of the heavy-lifting in their own backyard, and the Americans are acting largely as force enablers. There should be a return to the original structures of the 1949 Treaty. There is no reason why SACEUR[2] could not be a European flag officer. The European caucus within NATO, far from being taboo, should become the cornerstone of the Alliance. Europeans must stop believing that NATO cannot work without US leadership. However, this proposal also depends critically on US willingness to accept regional leadership by the Europeans as well as European willingness to assume that leadership. If either element is absent, then the entire experiment with European security and defence, whether CSDP or an enhanced NATO, will fail.

This recalibration of the CSDP–NATO relationship may look strangely familiar. It recalls the experiment with the European Security and Defence Identity (ESDI) of the mid-1990s. This was the initial attempt to square the circles of European military incapacity, American political disengagement, and actual regional turbulence which constituted the transatlantic response to the Balkan crises. But there is one huge difference. ESDI was predicated on continuing US primacy and American leadership of an alliance in which Europeans would simply play a more functional and operational, but subordinate, role. It was informed by Washington-imposed conditionality (Albright's '3 Ds'). The United States would retain a 'right of first refusal'. The present proposal, by contrast, is for an arrangement whereby

---

2 Supreme Allied Commander Europe – to date, always an American general or admiral.

the Europeans will be encouraged to take over leadership in order to allow the Americans to disengage properly. It is, therefore, in this sense, the direct opposite of ESDI. This is not an exercise in institutional tinkering. It is the most effective way in which Europe as a consequential security actor can actually emerge. The alternative, for Europeans, is to give up and simply submit to whatever a rapidly changing world delivers. That is no alternative.

PART II
After the Lisbon Treaty: The Common Foreign Security Policy and the European External Action Service

Chapter 4

The European External Action Service: Can a New Institution Improve the Coherence of the EU Foreign Policy?

Christian Lequesne

Introduction

The Treaty of Lisbon created the post of High Representative of the Union for Foreign Affairs and Security Policy (HR/VP). Furthermore, Article 27 of the Treaty of Lisbon states that the High Representative 'shall be assisted by a European External Action Service (EEAS). This service shall work in cooperation with the diplomatic services of the member states and shall comprise officials from relevant departments of the General Secretariat of the Council and of the Commission as well as staff seconded from national diplomatic services of the member states. The organization and functioning of the European External Action Service shall be established by a decision of the Council'. This Decision was approved by the EU Council on 26 July 2010.[1]

The establishment of a permanent secretariat, separate from the existing European Union (EU) institutions, to better coordinate the interests of the member states is not a new idea in the field of EU foreign policy, and particularly of Common Foreign and Security Policy (CFSP). In 1972, French President Pompidou already proposed an autonomous 'thinking secretariat', based in Paris, to be responsible for the then European Political Cooperation (EPC) set up outside the existing treaties in 1970 (Glaesner 1994). The integrationist countries of the Benelux opposed the proposal, because they saw a strong challenge for the Commission's powers. Fifteen years later, on 1 July 1987, the Single European Act established the first permanent EPC Secretariat. It was located inside the Secretariat General (SG) of the Council, with a budget provided partly by the Commission and partly by the member states. The EPC Secretariat was served by a small staff and played a limited role vis-à-vis the member states but also the Commission (Nuttall 1992). The EPC Secretariat disappeared in 1992 when the Treaty of Maastricht transformed the EPC into the CFSP. The coordination of the

---

1 EU Council (2010) Council Decision 2010/417/EU of 26 July 2010 establishing the organization and functioning of the EEAS, Official Journal of the European Union, L. 201, 3 August 2010.

then 'second pillar' of the Treaty was again devoted to the member states rotating presidencies in connection with the SG of the Council. The latter got an increased role when the Treaty of Amsterdam decided, in December 1999, that the Secretary General of the Council, Javier Solana, became also the High Representative for Foreign Affairs and Security Policy.

The Convention on the Future of Europe launched again, in February 2002, the idea of a permanent secretariat. The Treaty establishing a Constitution for Europe proposed an EEAS to assist the new European Minister of Foreign Affairs who should also become the Vice-President of the Commission responsible for all aspects of the EU foreign policy. The rejection of the Constitutional Treaty after the negative referendums in France and the Netherlands, in 2005, did not change the perspective to set up a permanent secretariat. The proposal on the EEAS remained the same in the Treaty of Lisbon, except that it was not to serve a European Minister for Foreign Affairs anymore, but a High Representative for Foreign Affairs and Security Policy/Vice-President of the Commission (HR/VP) under the British insistence to avoid the term 'minister'. Catherine Ashton, the appointed HR/VP, started her job on 1 December 2009 and the EEAS its activity, a month later, on 1 January 2010.

This chapter will analyse the EEAS as a bureaucratic institution set up to reduce transaction costs between the multiple actors of the EU foreign policy-making.[2] It will consider the three policy functions that the EEAS assumes: the coordination (both horizontal and vertical) of interests, the circulation of information and the production of new ideas.

Building More Coherence

The literature on EU foreign policy often emphasizes the vital need for coordination in a multi-actors polity. This literature is very often normative and concludes that the many transaction costs between the actors are at the root of a lack of coherence or consistency, which implies a lack of effectiveness of the EU foreign policy (Duke 2006). As Christopher Bickerton points out, this kind of assertion 'equates effectiveness with the institutional centralization typical of modern nation-states' (Bickerton 2011: 172–3) To complete Bickerton's relevant remark, one might add that a large part of the literature largely mythologizes the centrality of states in the shaping of foreign policies. Comparative studies show that states face regular imperatives of fragmentation between the ministries of foreign affairs and other central ministries, as well as between foreign ministries and subnational governments, especially in federal states such as Canada (Nossal, Roussel and Paquin 2007).

---

2   The term 'institution' is used in this chapter as a concept of political science and not in the sense of the Treaty on the EU that does not recognize the EEAS as an institution of the EU.

The EEAS is at the centre of a coordination function that runs along two axes: horizontally, between the EU member states and the EU institutions that have competences and expertise in the development of EU foreign policy (particularly the Commission); and vertically, between the 27 EU member states which have not relinquished their own national foreign policies.

The *horizontal coordination* between the EEAS and the Commission is the one that involves the most bureaucratic transactions. For example, aid programmes are managed within the European Commission by DEVCO as well as other DGs or services (such as ECHO or FPI), each of these having their own staff in EU Delegations. The policies in cooperation and humanitarian aid must often be coordinated with other aspects of foreign policy, in particular the CFSP, headed by the EEAS. This coordination does not come naturally due to the competition and differentiation that oppose the different actors. Stefan Keukeleire and Arnout Justaert have demonstrated in the case of Congo and Kosovo that 'each EU actor often concentrates on the realization of individual projects without taking into consideration the general scope of the required structural reforms. In the case of policy reforms in Congo, the problematic relationship between the CSDP missions and the Union Delegation resulted in a context where the required coordination was either limited or totally absent' (Keukeleire and Justaert 2012).

This example is just one among many. It demonstrates how the EEAS, which is supposed to ensure horizontal coordination, does not always succeed in facing the Commission DGs. EEAS and Commission officials are thus led to invent new institutional procedures to overcome distrust. The Executive Secretary General of the EEAS and the General Director of DEVCO are working for instance on the establishment of common procedures, aimed at making the working relationships between their officials more fluid. These efforts for a better coordination are politically backed by the HR/VP Catherine Ashton and by the Commissioner Andris Piebalgs in charge of development policy.[3]

The EEAS is also confronted with bureaucratic infighting to ensure the vertical coordination with member states. It has, however, more institutional procedures to ensure that vertical coordination, confirming institutionalist analyses, according to which procedures reduce transaction costs in bureaucratic bargains between multiple actors (Guess and Farnham 2011). The main resource available to the EEAS is the permanent chairmanship of the Council committees in charge of EU foreign policy. Since the entry into force of the Lisbon Treaty, EEAS officials have taken the place of the rotating presidencies at the head of most of the committees and working groups, as the HR/VP chairs all the sessions of the Council on Foreign Affairs, Development, and Defence issues.

In the field of CFSP, the presidency of an influential committee as the Political Security Council (PSC) now belongs to an official of the EEAS, the Swedish diplomat Olof Skoog. This institutional innovation places the EEAS officials at the heart of vertical coordination, which enables them to provide more continuity

---

3   Interview, French Permanent Representation to the EU, 22 February 2012.

than the rotating presidencies in the past. Member states officials accept the legitimacy of the EEAS permanent chairpersons in Brussels without too much resistance.[4] In the EU Delegations, the Heads of Delegation and their staff also chair coordination meetings between the EU and member states. Because it is institutionalized, the task is well accepted by the bilateral ambassadors, even if they may express some complaints about the low diplomatic skills of some Heads of Mission. There are however specific topics that some member states still refuse to discuss in meetings chaired by the EU Delegations, considering that they must remain within the jurisdiction of rotating presidencies. This is the case for consular cooperation. The British government, through the Foreign Office, is opposed to an Europeanization of consular protection – such as the evacuation of civilians in times of crisis – to avoid operations it does not want to pay for. All meetings related to consular protection therefore remain chaired by the rotating presidencies of the Council, and not by the EEAS, either in Brussels or in the Delegations.[5]

The *vertical coordination* with member states is more difficult within international organizations than on the matter of bilateral diplomacy. A relevant example is the United Nations (UN) system where the EU is not represented in different ways within the specialized institutions. At the World Trade Organization, the EU has the same membership status as its individual member states. Since May 2011, the EU is an observer to the UN General Assembly, while the 27 states are full members.[6] At the UN Security Council, the EU has no representation as such, although the HR/VP is invited to address EU positions, as provided in Article 34 of the Treaty on European Union (Marchesi 2008: 24–6). It is therefore up to the EU Delegations in New York, Geneva and Vienna to chair the committees that coordinate the positions of 27 member states. In New York, the EU Delegation has therefore replaced, since the Lisbon Treaty, the Commission Delegation and the Liaison Office of the EU Council. It organizes some 1,300 meetings a year to reconcile the positions of the member states. Overall, there is a high coherence of the positions of the EU member states at the UN General Assembly. Disagreements are more numerous at the UN Security Council, where interests may diverge on sensitive cases. In June 2011, Germany (non-permanent member) abstained on Resolution 1973, creating a 'no fly zone' and calling for an immediate ceasefire in Libya, while France and the United Kingdom (permanent members) voted for it. Similarly, in October 2011, the vote about the application of Palestine to permanent membership in the UNESCO gave rise to a complete lack of coherence between EU members. France voted yes, Italy and the United Kingdom abstained, and Germany finally voted against (*Le Monde*, 31 October

---

4   Interviews, French and Swedish Permanent Representations to the EU, 22 February 2012.

5   Interviews EU Delegation in a third country, 2 November 2011; French Permanent Representation to the EU, 22 February 2012.

6   The EU status of observer at the General Assembly is the result of UN Resolution A/65/276 adopted on 3 May 2011.

2011). The enhanced coordination under the permanent presidency of the HR/VP and the EEAS has failed, in these cases, to reconcile the conflicting positions between large member states: the national rationale has prevailed. But besides these grand bargains, there is a majority of issues of far less sensitivity where the EEAS facilitates the coordination of member states' foreign policies, with a logic that remains bureaucratic.

The establishment of the EEAS has also forced the 27 member states to think more about how their positions appear in the statements of the international organizations. Once again, a search for procedure comes after a conflict. The United Kingdom has indeed blocked in 2011 more than 80 EU declarations at the UN and the OSCE, on the ground that the EU position was mentioned only 'on behalf of the European Union'. Following this conflict, the EU Foreign Affairs Council defined on 22 October 2011 the cases in which the EU position can be expressed either 'on behalf of the EU', or 'on behalf of the EU and its Member States'. The Council Declaration foresees that the choice of these provisions belongs, first, to the EU Heads of Delegation. There are supposed to refer to the central structure of the EEAS in consultation with the Commission, only if a conflict happens at the local coordination level.[7]

The function of coordination builder – horizontal and vertical – is a primary task for the EEAS. It is not very visible, but produces effects in the bureaucratic phase of the EU foreign policy-making. Beyond policy routine (because foreign policy is also about routine), the EEAS has nevertheless no real power to influence the coordination when the issues are highly controversial between the member states. If you consider that a kind of classic separation still exists between 'politics' and 'bureaucracy' in the making of foreign policy, the EEAS is able to influence the second but not the first.

An Information Provider

The ability to circulate information through various networks is an essential function of modern diplomacy (Berridge 2010). Through its headquarters in Brussels, and its network of Delegations, the EEAS is expected to disseminate information to all EU institutions and member states on the activities of third countries and international organizations. The various stakeholders within EU foreign policy do not see the same added value in the information provided by the EEAS. For the European institutions (Commission, EP), the 140 Delegations are a useful source of information on third states' diplomacies and negotiations in international organizations. It is the same for the ministries of foreign affairs of the smaller member states like Estonia and Luxembourg, which have a limited network of bilateral embassies worldwide. However, the big member states like

---

7   EU Council (2011) Note du Secrétariat Général sur les declarations de l'UE dans les organisations internationales, N° 15901/11, 24 Octobre.

the United Kingdom, Germany and France, which have an extensive network of bilateral embassies, are much less sensitive to the flow of information from the EU Delegations.

Political reporting practices are not yet stabilized within the EEAS. First, the central structures are still struggling to produce regular documents and debriefing for the meetings. EU Delegations learn to do their share of political reporting, as this task was underdeveloped in the former Commission Delegations, except in the major posts such as Washington or Ankara. In this respect, the arrival within the EEAS of national diplomats, used to writing synthetic telegrams on the political situation of a state or a negotiation, is changing the practices. A member of the Corporate Board of the EEAS, a national diplomat himself, points out: 'I see right away by its style whether a report is written by an official from a national department, or whether it is written by an official from the Commission. The first delivers a concise analysis of the political situation in the country of accreditation, while the second will attempt to do so.'[8]

In addition, the EEAS has not yet found a system that allows compatibility in the circulation of reports with the computer systems of the European institutions and the 27 ministries of foreign affairs. In spring 2012, the establishment of a system of encrypted email allowing the secure flow between the various actors remains a topic on the EEAS agenda. These difficulties highlight the constraints characterizing a foreign policy-making with multiple actors who had not been used to routinely exchange their positions.[9]

The function of information provider therefore remains subject to the widespread practice of political reporting. This requirement can be called a 'diplomatization' of an EU institution with new practices modelled on national diplomacies. There is a huge body of literature and case studies about the Europeanization of EU member states policies, even of foreign policies (Wong 2006). In the case of information providing, we can observe quite the opposite process. It is the practices of the European actors which have to adapt to the practices of the member states diplomacies. It is a good example to be cautious about the use and abuse of 'Europeanization' as an unidirectionale transfer of rules and practices from the EU to the member states. It is much more relevant to consider that interactions exist between the EU institutions and the member states institutions and that the influences of one model to the other are working both ways.

Producing Ideas

Since the 1990s, IR scholars have focused more on the special status of ideas in the making of foreign policies. As Judith Goldstein and Robert Keohane write,

---

8   Interviews, EEAS Brussels, 26 April 2011.

9   With the exception of the COREU system in the field of CFSP (see Bicchi and Carta 2011).

'even if we accept the rationality premise, actions taken by human beings depend on substantive quality of available ideas, since such ideas help to clarify principal and conceptions of causal relationships, and to coordinate individual behavior' (Goldstein and Keohane 1993: 5). One of the questions linked to the creation of the EEAS is its ability to produce original ideas on EU foreign policy, which appear an added value compared to what the national ministries of foreign affairs and the Commission produce. Expectations within national ministries of foreign affairs regarding the production of ideas by the EEAS are stressed in all interviews. There is a clear link between ideas and legitimization. Examples show that the EEAS Directorates have been able to generate their own ideas on several specific issues. Under the Polish presidency in 2011, the idea of a road map for the neighbourhood policy was launched within the Europe and Central Asia Directorate of the EEAS. Similarly, it is within the Crisis Management and Planning Department that the idea of creating a Regional Maritime Capacity in the Horn of Africa was born in 2012. Member states accepted these proposals.[10] On the other hand, the EEAS has not established itself as the producer of global strategic ideas on the future of the EU foreign policy. One issue that will arise on the agenda will nevertheless be the possible writing by the EEAS of a general report on the security of Europe, similar to that produced in 2003 by Javier Solana. Again, the foreign ministries of some big member states, such as the Quai d'Orsay and the Foreign Office, are not favourable to it, fearing that such an exercise could generate ideas they might not share. No doubt then that there is a contradiction between the intense necessity of compromising in the EU and the possibility to deliver a strategic meta-view of what the EU foreign policy should be.

Finally, the ideas produced by the EEAS are ignored by public opinion in the EU member states. Whereas the HR/VP is the source of numerous press releases, regularly answering questions to the European Parliament either in plenary or before the Foreign Affairs Committee, she is not present in the debates in member states. The linguistic fragmentation of the European public space makes the presence through speeches difficult in general. In addition, the major governments of the member states, which have diplomacies of global ambition, do not want it. Clearly, there is a lack of discursive dimension attached to the production of the ideas generated by the EEAS. This makes a difference between the HR/VP and the national ministries of foreign affairs, which often find a way of spreading their ideas through a discursive activity in their national public spaces. Despite the existence of a HR/VP and an EEAS, the foreign policy of the EU is characterized by a weakness of public discourse from Brussels, while all comparative analyses show that the discourse is an essential dimension to the legitimization of states' foreign policies within the democratic polities (Smouts 1999: 5–15).

---

10   Interviews, EEAS, 21 and 22 February 2012.

Conclusion

The EEAS is the outcome of a series of political compromises between the EU institutions and the member states rather than the result of a grand design. The creation of the EEAS (which is not the topic of this chapter) can be analysed with the model of bureaucratic politics (Allison and Zelikow 1999). The EEAS's staff members, coming from different administrative cultures, are still in the process of establishing new practices and in search of their own identity.

The EEAS contributes to the coherence of EU foreign policy only within the limits of what is allowed to a bureaucratic body. Its ability to influence the member states' interests through coordination remains limited when politics takes the lead in the debates. The EEAS does not validate then completely the neo-realist model that will assert that the member states dominate every phase of the foreign policy-making. The EEAS can play a role when the process implies the diplomatic bureaucracies. But as the process reaches the level of the ministers or the commissioners, the EEAS is not able to produce any added value in terms of coherence.

The EEAS does have a certain capacity to produce new ideas for the EU foreign policy that can influence the member states and the Commission. However, this capacity is not strategic, in the sense of producing a meta-project of what the EU foreign policy should be. The production of ideas is very sectorial and limited to specific dossiers.

The functional potentialities of the EEAS are not absent in the fields of coordination, information providing and production of strategic ideas, but with clear limits. There is one question for further research: to what extend do these potentialities depend or not on the profile of the HR/VP? Should the member states appoint a personality with a higher political profile than Catherine Ashton, would the EEAS acquire more functional potentialities as politics and strategy are concerned? The answer to that question is not obvious, because the high transaction costs between the various stakeholders of the EU foreign policy can also limit structurally the role of the EEAS, whatever the leadership of the HP/VP is.

Chapter 5

The EEAS and EU Executive Actors within the Foreign Policy-Cycle

Caterina Carta

Abstract

The Treaty of Lisbon provoked a massive reorganization in the field of external relations at the executive and administrative level. Instead of simplifying the institutional structure, this overall reorganization crowded even further the 'leadership table' (Nugent and Rhinard 2011: 13). Within the EU, with different intensity of cooperation, conflict and contamination, a variety of governmental actors share policy responsibilities in the making of foreign policy. This chapter aims to explore the role of executive actors which concur to the EU foreign-policy making by locating them in a simplified policy-cycle model. It is here suggested that this heuristic devise offers a streamlined analytical grid to order a wide cornucopia of actors, processes and political dynamics. The policy-cycle model serves as an simplified device to detect the position of bureaucratic and administrative actors in the policy process; the set of formal and informal procedures that order their interactions; and 'the cumulative effects of the various actors, forces, and institutions that interact in the policy process and therefore shape its outcome(s)' (Werner and Wegrich 2007: 50). In order to introduce EU executive actors' interaction in the making of foreign policy, this chapter presents a simplified cycle based on four main stages: 1) policy initiative; 2) policy formulation; 3) decision-making; and 4) implementation.

Introduction

The Treaty of Lisbon provoked a massive reorganization in the field of external relations at the executive and administrative level (Carta 2012; Duke 2009; Missiroli 2010). Instead of simplifying the institutional structure, this overall reorganization crowded even further the 'leadership table' (Nugent and Rhinard 2011: 13). Within the EU, with different intensity of cooperation, conflict and contamination, a variety of governmental actors share policy responsibilities in the making of foreign policy. This chapter aims to explore the role of executive actors which concur to the EU foreign-policy making by locating them in a simplified policy-cycle model. It is here suggested that this heuristic device offers a streamlined analytical grid to order a wide cornucopia of actors, processes and political dynamics. The chapter, therefore, complements Chapters 1, 2 and 4 in this volume, by highlighting the institutional, organizational and bureaucratic constraints to the tuning of a common voice.

The policy-cycle model[1] serves as a simplified device to detect the position of bureaucratic and administrative actors in the policy process; the set of formal and informal procedures that order their interactions; and 'the cumulative effects of the various actors, forces, and institutions that interact in the policy process and therefore shape its outcome(s)' (Werner and Wegrich 2007: 50).

In order to introduce EU executive actors' interaction in the making of foreign policy, this chapter presents a simplified cycle based on four main stages: 1) policy initiative; 2) policy formulation; 3) decision-making; and 4) implementation. In presenting the stage of decision-making, the chapter mainly focuses on new arrangements in the Council of Ministers. The Council of the EU and the European Parliament (EP) share legislative competences in the setting up of 'low' policy measures. With a legislative involvement that now reaches 90 per cent of the EU policy competences, recent analysis of the role of the EP has remarkably increased with the entry into force of the Lisbon Treaty (Peters et al. 2010; Raube 2012). While acknowledging the growing importance of both the EP in policy-making, and of the European Court of Justice (ECJ, Hillion 2009; Jørgensen and Wessel 2011), this chapter refers to other analyses for a closer examination of their role. The chapter relies on 30 interviews conducted in the European External Action Service (EEAS), the Foreign Policy Instrument Service (FPI) and the Commission.

EU Foreign Policy at the Executive Level – Main Actors and Competences

The Lisbon Treaty maintained a definition of foreign policy as an artificially divided policy domain. Thus, so-called first pillar competences are still managed under the Community method, and second pillar competences follow an intergovernmental method of policy-making. In that the Lisbon Treaty maintained a markedly institutional approach, 'to streamline foreign policy by combining external action across the pillar system of divergent competences created by the Maastricht Treaty' (Laatikainen 2010: 476).

At the executive level, within the EU, the management of foreign policy issues is entrusted to three sets of institutional actors who intervene in the building up of foreign policy measures on the ground of attributed competences. These sets of actors are: 1) the European Council and the Council of the EU,[2] which

---

1   Among the proponents of the model see: Lasswell (1956) and May and Wildavsky (1978); among its critics see Lindblom (1959), Kingdon (2003), Sabatier (1991) and Everett (2003).

2   The European Council cannot be considered as an executive actor. It is here included for the important functions it performs in terms of both political lead and external

negotiate common positions in Common Foreign and Security Policy (CFSP) and ultimately decide on all common decisions; 2) the Commission, which has the right of initiative in so-called low foreign policy competences such as trade and development; 3) the High Representative-Vice President of the Commission (HR/VP) in charge of traditional foreign policy dossiers; assisted by the European External Action Service (EEAS). In addition to these, the rotating presidency – which, with the exception of the European Council and the Foreign Affairs Council (FAC) still applies to all Council configurations which refers to the General Affairs Council (GAC) – maintains a margin of policy initiative, and is illustrative of the central role that the member states play in the making of all common policies.

The role of all actors in the process is ultimately decided by the attribution of competences, even if, as will be argued, contamination and a dynamic flow of information permeate all policy fields. Four sets of competences converge in the EU external policy field: exclusive EU powers, where the member states are no longer allowed to act autonomously; collective foreign policy actions, which are pursued through the intergovernmental method of policy-making; and mixed competences, where both the Union and the member states share competences. Finally, there are competences of exclusive pertinence of the member states. These competences define the role of all actors throughout the policy process and the scope of their intervention.

Table 5.1 Competences attributed to the institutional actors of the EU's foreign policy

Executive actors converging in the process of foreign policy-making	Attributions of competences
The European Council	Role of political impetus and political lead
The Council of the European Union	Executive and legislative body, intervening in all EU measures.
The Commission	Power of initiative, policy formulation and policy implementation of common measures in first pillar and mixed competences
High Representative-Vice President of the Commission (HR/VP); assisted the European External Action Service (EEAS)	Power of initiative, policy formulation in second pillar competences (for implementation it avails of the Foreign Policy Instrument (FPI, see below))
The member states	Still competences of exclusive pertinence of the member states

representation. The Council of the European Union is not only an executive actor; it performs also legislative functions.

In organizational terms, the system does not differ dramatically from the organization of foreign policy at the national level, where the Ministry of Foreign Affairs (MFA) liaises and coordinates with several specialized ministries dealing with both external affairs (development, trade) and domestic policy-sectors of international impact. In this light, the EEAS works as a MFA – with functions of foreign-policy impetus and coordination – while the different Commission's Directorates General (DG) are in charge of specialized dossiers.

From an organizational point of view the EEAS is structured as a MFA, within the limits of the EU foreign policy system. The HR/VP directs the EEAS, along with an executive 'Secretariat' composed of an executive secretary general, a chief operating officer and two deputy secretary generals for political affairs and for inter-institutional affairs respectively. Below this level of hierarchy, a corporate board is responsible for the EEAS's policy coordination, strategic planning and the legal underpinning of its activities. It also ensures smooth relations with the European and national parliaments. As in a MFA, below the board level – together with directorates dealing with administration and finance; audit and inspection – a number of managing directorates deal with the bulk of traditional foreign-policy activities performed collectively by the EU. As is the case in other MFAs, the organization of the managing directorates reflects two main organizational criteria: the geographic and the thematic/horizontal. The new organizational chart reflects an enhanced role in foreign and security policy, with departments like the newly established Crisis Management and Planning Directorate (CMPD), the Civilian Planning and Conduct Capability (CPCC), the Military Staff (EUMS) and the Joint Situation Centre (SitCen).

From an organizational point of view, within the Commission, four Directorates General (DG) contribute systematically to the making of external policies, in analogy of what ministries of international trade or cooperation and development do at the national level. The DG for Development and Cooperation-EuropeAid (DEVCO), DG Enlargement (DG ELARG), DG International Cooperation, Humanitarian Aid and Crisis Response (ECHO) and DG Trade share competences to deal with specific macro policy-areas.

Post-Lisbon arrangements changed the composition of the RELEX family: former DG RELEX has been absorbed by the EEAS (together with some units from DG AIDCO and DEVCO); and a merger occurred between former DG DEVCO and AIDCO, which previously were separated (Carta 2012). Coordination among these DGs, and between these and the EEAS, is ensured by the Commissioners' Group on External Relations and the Commission Secretariat General. The Commissioners' Group on External Relations intervenes systematically in the making of common policies, together with the President of the Commission and the DG for Economic and Monetary Affairs (DG ECOFIN). Consistency between different first and second pillar competences is ensured by the presence of the HR/VP in the Commissioners' Group on External Relations.

Locating EU Executive Actors Throughout the Policy-Cycle

The Stage of Political Initiative: A New Actor in Town

Before the Lisbon Treaty, three main actors contributed to varying extents to define external and foreign-policy initiatives: the European Council in CFSP matters, the European Commission in so-called 'low politics' and the rotating Presidency. Under current arrangements, the stage of initiative is scattered between the European Council, the European Commission and the HR/VP. At the higher level of inter-state coordination, the European Council steers the conduct of the EU foreign and external policy. The Commission and the EEAS contribute, in their respective fields of competence, to set up the agenda of the EU. As will be argued, the rotating Presidency maintains a role in initiating policies.

The European Council has increased its leading role which virtually encompasses all policy fields. Article 15 TEU posits that its role is one of providing 'the Union with the necessary impetus for its development and [shall] define the general political directions and priorities thereof'. As was noted, the broad mandate of the European Council potentially allows it to promote initiatives across the entire spectrum of the Union's external action (Wouters et al. 2008). In light of its role of impetus, the President of the European Council is now in charge for two and a half years. The institutionalization of the European Council adds increased institutional complexity to the institutional balance (Monar 2010). It potentially creates both an overlap of functions with the new figure of HR/VP (Missiroli 2010) and a possible incursion in the Commission's functions of strategy-setting and coordination prerogatives.

The rotating Presidency still maintains both its willingness and potential to have a say in determining policy priorities at the EU level, by pushing new policy initiatives (Tallberg 2006). To begin with, the rotating Presidencies throughout the first two years contributed massively to shape the rules of procedures regimenting the EU's institutional machinery: from arrangements within the Council to arrangements in the Delegations. In the new institutional framework, the rotating Presidency still holds the chair of the GAC and, at a lower level of hierarchy, the COREPER II[3] and horizontal Working Groups (such as the Trade Policy Committee). The degree of entrepreneurship of the rotating Presidency in performing its role of agenda-setter varies widely among the member states. For example – during the semester inaugurated in July 2011 – the Polish Presidency assumed a proactive stance. *Inter alia*, the Polish Presidency sponsored the European Endowment for Democracy (EED), a private foundation under Belgian law which would add flexibility to finance democracy assistance projects

---

3   'Coreper I, consists of the deputy permanent representatives, deals with technical matters; Coreper II, consists of the ambassadors, deals with political, commercial, economic or institutional matters' http://europa.eu/newsroom/calendar/event/290057/coreper-ii-coreper-i.

(Kostanyan and Nasieniak 2012). Thanks to 'the Polish connection' within both the Commission and the EEAS, the Presidency launched in 2011 an Ad-Hoc Task Force with both EEAS and Commission's officials, in order to frame the proposal to submit to the Council (interview with an EEAS official, June 2012). Both the establishment of the task force and the EED met the lukewarm reaction of the member states. Yet the initiative shows the potential of the new architecture and the possibility of the Presidencies to gather different expertise from both the EEAS and the Commission to promote new initiatives.

The Lisbon Treaty complicated the script of the stage of policy initiative, by adding another player, the EEAS, to the process. The institutional location of both the HR/VP and the EEAS is at the crossroads between the Council and the Commission. On the one hand, the HR/VP takes part in the meetings of the European Council and can propose foreign policy initiatives. Under her Commission's hat, the HR/VP takes part in and, in absence of the President of the Commission, chairs the work of the Group of RELEX Commissioners. The hybrid position of the HR/VP, therefore, represents an attempt to exert coherence in a fragmented policy field (Duke 2009). It has been argued that the HR/VP has a double-hatted position, in reality her mandate conveyed four different and very engaging tasks: 1) setting up and directing the EEAS; 2) proposing foreign policy initiatives; 3) chairing the newly established Foreign Affairs Council (FAC); and 4) chairing the proceedings of and exerting coherence in the Group of RELEX Commissioners. With this incredible workload, the current HR/VP apparently decided to focus less on her role of Vice-President to focus decisively on the more foreign policy oriented components of her task (interview, March 2012; interviews, June 2012). As follows, the Commission's Secretary General consistently took on the task of guaranteeing both intra- and inter-institutional coordination.

The Commission maintains its power of setting the agenda in its own areas of responsibility. With the exception of CFSP, the Commission participates in the making of external policies through different portfolios of expertise: not only through the RELEX family but through 'domestic' policies with an important foreign policy component (i.e. environment, energy, agriculture). The field of intervention of the Commission, therefore, varies wide across the policy field. For instance, DG Trade drafts the mandates for international trade negotiations, which are lately agreed upon by the Council of Ministers. The importance of such initiatives is self-evident. As the Commission is not an unified actor, it needs to ensure that all its services frame their policy proposals in the most cooperative way as possible in order to perform effectively its powers (Daviter 2007). We will see this in more detail in the section on policy formulation.

Considering the presence of different and balanced sources of political initiatives, all actors need to be able to sense the general climate surrounding a policy proposal. The ability to gather consensus around policy options determines the climate of support of ostracism surrounding a policy measure and eventually its probability of success.

The Stage of Policy Formulation: Further Compartmentalization

In terms of drafting of common positions and decisions, the EEAS and the Commission DGs contribute, depending on the allocation of competences, to the preparation of policy outcomes. As with the difficulty of disentangling 'high' and 'low' components of policies, a given measure flows from desk to desk before being presented to the Council for adoption. Considering the allocation of policy competences between the EEAS and the Commission's services, several coordination mechanisms have been progressively put into place.

The necessity to guarantee a viable coordination of all EU services dealing with external relations is not new for the EU. The Commission has always faced the necessity of ensuring consistency between the interlinked activities of six DGs (Carta 2012). In order to do so, the Commission relied on a series of inter-service agreements among all DGs of the so-called RELEX family. Along different sectoral specializations, all DGs have historically developed their own organizational identity (Abélès et al. 1993), routines (Ongaro 2010), sense of mission and ideas of Europe (Carta 2011). The Commission itself, therefore, is not a unitary actor. Fragmentation impacts all aspects of its institutional life, in creating tremendous potential for conflict (Christiansen 1997), due to the national composition of each DG, the sectoral and political approaches implied, the exposure to interest groups, to quote but a few elements (Hooghe 2001).

The reorganization and the subsequent establishment of the EEAS added complexity to an already fragmented picture. The creation of the new institutional body, separated from the Commission, was surrounded by a high degree of acrimony (Spence 2012). Entire units or individual civil servants were relocated from the Commission to the new Service with few indications of their new mandate and they needed to make sense of the new system with little indication how to proceed. The inter-institutional division of labour was created in the making, and a high degree of uncertainty surrounded and still surrounds different aspects of policy coordination.

In this context, Lisbon Treaty provisions imposed a highly formalized division of competence between the Commission and EEAS. However, informality in defining the patterns of the reform is characteristic of the process. At all stages of the policy process, all actors involved need to liaise, both formally and informally, in order to guarantee an adequate cross-fertilization of policy initiatives.

The example of multilateral dossiers is telling of the necessity to engineer a sound system of coordination among all actors involved. To deal with multilateral affairs, an apposite Managing Directorate was created. This includes four units: multilateral relations and global governance (which also chairs the CONUN Working Group within the Council); Human Rights and Democracy (which chairs the COHOM WG – for more detail see Smith's (2006) comments on the working of the WG); Conflict Prevention and Security Policy; and Non Proliferation and Disarmament (which chairs the COARM, CONOP, CODUN WGs). Depending on policy dossiers and the nature of competences, these EEAS units liaise with homologous units within the Commission, which often have a Directorate or units dealing with multilateral issues. Accordingly, for trade issues, which mostly fall under the EU's exclusive competences, DG Trade relies on the Directorate F which is in charge of coordinating multilateral trade issues. Within DG DEVCO, different units deal with the Delegations to the Food and Agriculture Organization (FAO) in Rome; or the Delegations in Paris and the United States. Within the Commission not all relevant competences for multilateral dossiers fall under the remit of the so-called RELEX family.

In the drafting of common measures, all actors need carefully to individuate their homologous units in different Services, in order to be sure that they are framing a policy measure which takes on board all expertise. Accordingly, if homologous units have good relations and a good attitude towards cooperation, interaction goes smoothly, also in terms of informal factors. While pursuing the goal of rationalizing the management of both first and second pillar competences, the establishment of the EEAS imposed a further compartmentalization to the overall EU's policy-making. Due to this complication of the organizational script, the system can work only if sustained by an intensive load of coordination among all parties involved in the process of foreign-policy making and diplomatic representation.

The Stage of Decision-Making: Complicating the Script

Within the Council, the abolition of the rotating Presidency for the European Council and for the newly established Foreign Affairs Council (FAC) provoked a major reorganization of the Council structure (Vanhoonacker et al. 2011). The reorganization of the Presidency of the Council was pursued through a plural arrangement for different Council configurations due to a triple organization of functions:

1. the new permanent Presidency of the European Council, the main organ for political orientation in foreign and security matters (article 22.1 TEU);
2. the Chair provided by the High Representative to the newly established Foreign Affairs Council (FAC); and
3. the rotating Presidency, which still chairs all other Council configurations.

At lower level of hierarchy, geographical WGs are chaired by the EEAS and are afferent to the FAC and to the Political and Security Committee (PSC). So-called horizontal WGs – like the Trade Policy Committee (TPC), the Group of RELEX Counsellors, or development – follow the organizational line of the General Affairs Council (GAC) and the COREPER II, and are chaired by the rotating Presidency. The Lisbon Treaty, therefore, slightly complicated the division of labour between institutions, by introducing a complicated structure of EU presidencies. Accordingly, a massive institutional and bureaucratic reorganization took place in the Council as well.

Within the Council, both WG afferents to the COREPER II and to the PSC work synergistically to adopt the policy measures. The capacity of all actors to liaise is, therefore, telling of the way in which different proposals percolate in the making of common decisions. The presidencies of the different WGs are in charge of managing the flow of information from one WG to the other.

On arrival at the Council, the same policy proposal is discussed in several Council configurations. At the higher level, inter-institutional coordination is ensured by the involvement of competent Commissioners at the FAC, and decision-making follows swinging dynamics, with a different intervention of the EU Parliament depending on competences. Coordination between Council configurations is ensured through both informal and formal channels of information sharing. As easily understandable, high and low policy dimensions are not easy to disentangle, so an intense work of coordination between the EEAS and Commission's services needs to be guaranteed prior, during and after the meetings.

The proceedings in the Council of Ministers are generally coordinated by the HR/VP and the EEAS independently by the chairing system in place. In that, the EEAS took on the responsibilities previously held by the Council Secretariat General (CSG) in the preparation of meetings. In a far reduced format, the CSG is still in charge of more logistic aspects of coordination, i.e. making sure that documents are circulated in all WGs, that the room is set up for meetings and so forth.

According to current working arrangements on inter-service coordination, the EEAS, sided by the relevant Commission's services, ensures that the Commission is adequately represented in all WGs' proceedings. The Commission, therefore, is duly involved in the drafting of relevant Council Conclusions and statements. Usually, a member of DG DEVCO makes sure that relevant DGs' units are adequately represented when their dossiers of competence are discussed in the Council. So, for instance, in the Council Group Maghreb-Mashrek (MaMa), often a member of DG AGRI, DG Mare or DG Trade are invited to debrief on relevant policy dossiers.

With the sudden explosion of the Arab Spring, the MaMa Working Group constituted a testing ground for the newly established system of decision-making.[4] In a snapshot, at the lower level of hierarchy, the MaMa worked on setting the ground for an agreement on the measures to be adopted. Then, the same dossier was transferred to other horizontal DGs (i.e. the Trade Committee) to be finalized and then adopted, generally by COREPER II. Reportedly, no issue was so contentious to go through the ministers in the FAC: all positions were agreed upon at lower levels of hierarchy. Equally, no major disagreement among the member states was reported, with the possible exception on issuing sanctions to Syrian president Assad (interview, 4 April 2012). In the recollection of those days, members of the MaMa refer to a situation in which rules on coordination were done in the making, under

---

4   As reported by a member of the Group: 'we were driven by the events ... All of the sudden, it was all "conclusions and sanctions; conclusions and sanctions"' (interview, 4 April 2012).

extremely stringent time constraints, while the system was not yet in shape. The EEAS proposed the bulk of policy measures to adopt, under the stimulus of the member states. Thus, reportedly, the member states, usually one of the 'big three', proposed to issue sanctions; the geographic WG, under the chair of the EEAS, reached the compromise on what kind of sanctions and against whom should have been issued; and the Relex Counsellors crafted sanctions, with the support of both the EEAS and the Commission. The system of coordination was, reportedly, ensured by a four-edged mechanism: 1) the liaison role of the CSG; 2) information coming from colleagues of the rotating presidencies, who made sure that the interested WGs were progressing in a coordinated way; 3) the member of the EEAS dealing with sanctions, who was attending both groups; 4) contacts with the Commission, both through the DEVCO representative in the WG and informal contacts with the Commission's horizontal desks, interested in the decisions to adopt.

Within the Council, in the management of policy dossiers, a pillarized logic still supervises the inter-institutional and organizational division of competences among interested EU institutions and Services. The establishment of the EEAS, as argued, was meant to bridge foreign policy and external policies related competences while maintaining the division of competences mainly unaltered. In terms of executive coordination at the EU level, current arrangements, therefore, introduced further complexity to the overall EU architecture to deal with external affairs.

The Stage of Implementation: A Money Box for CFSP

In EU terminology, beyond financing, implementation of an instrument refers to the process of contracting, managing, monitoring and evaluating different projects and programmes. This definition reveals the importance of this policy stage and the potential for transformation from original policy decisions. This also reveals that implementation is done both in Brussels and in the Delegations in third countries on the one hand and on the other hand in International Organizations. This stage adds therefore vertical complexity to the process. As interviewees revealed, also at this stage, all policy actors maintain their own sectoral sense of affiliation. Competing and partially overlapping competences, as based on a distinctive attribution of functional and political responsibility pave the ways for inter-institutional conflicts, competing visions and potential policy-misfits.

Table 5.2 Division of labour between the Commission and the EEAS for macro-policy areas

	Overall responsibility	Financial responsibility	Operational management	In coordination with
CFSP	HR/VP; EEAS	FPI – Commission	EEAS	EU Council/ COM
Enlargement	Commission	Commissioner for ELARG	DG DEVCO	EEAS/DEVCO
Neighbourhood	Commissioner for ELARG and the ENPI	DEVCO under the responsibility of the Commissioner for ELARG	DG DEVCO/ EEAS	EEAS, DEVCO and other Commission's services
Development	DG DEVCO	DEVCO	DG DEVCO	EEAS and other Commission's services
International trade	DG Trade – Commission	DG Trade – Commission	DG Trade – Commission	EEAS and other Commission's services
Humanitarian assistance and crisis response	DG ECHO	DG ECHO	DG ECHO	DG Home Affairs; DEVCO; EEAS

In the Headquarters, in terms of implementation of common measures, an intense work of coordination between the EEAS and Commission's services is required, considering that operational responsibility of common measures is alternatively attributed to the EEAS or different Commission's DGs. In matters of financial responsibility, article 17.1 TEU provides that the Commission shall 'execute the budget and manage programmes'. Therefore, while operational responsibilities of common measures are alternatively entrusted either to the Commission services or to the EEAS, the financial responsibility for implementing operational expenditure is performed exclusively by the Commission. In practical terms, this means that the EEAS is tied to the Commission for any measure for which it holds operational responsibility.

The EEAS needs to rely on a 'money box' if it wants to plan things through. To make up this awkward situation, a new Service serving specifically foreign policy measures has been created: the Foreign Policy Instrument Service (FPI). As with the overall divisions of competences between the EEAS and the Commission's Services, as a general rule, the HR/VP (and the EEAS at lower level of hierarchy) is politically responsible for CFSP related measures; while different Commissioners (and, at the lower level of hierarchy, DGs) are responsible for external policy measures. Art. 9 of the EEAS Council Decision introduced the respective responsibilities of the EEAS and the Commission's services on the preparation of programming documents; Country/Regional budget allocations and strategy papers; and the multi-annual programming documents. Regardless of policy responsibilities over financial instruments of external action, it is up to the Commission to adopt all common measures, either through the competent units within the DGs or through the FPI.

Article 9.6 of the EEAS Decision states that the FPI is 'co-located' with the EEAS. The FPI holds a similarly hybrid character to the EEAS. It is organically part of the Commission, but it is functionally linked to the EEAS. Therefore, to finance foreign policy measures, the FPI follows the directions of the EEAS, but is financially accountable to the Commission. The Service merged together different units from former DG RELEX dealing with financing CFSP operations and thematic budget lines, such as the European Instrument for Democracy and Human Right (EIDHR) and the IfS (the Instruments for Stability). The unit has a simple organizational chart, composed of a director, and has four main units: FPI-1 in charge of budget, finance and relations with other institutions; FPI-2 in charge of stability instruments operations (crisis response and peace-building); FPI-3 in charge of CFSP operations; and FPI-4 in charge of Public Diplomacy and European Interests: election observation.[5]

In order to ensure sound coordination of policy and financial responsibilities, a complicate system of inter-service consultation has been set up. The EEAS, DG DEVCO and the Commissioner for ELARG are jointly responsible for the global financial share allocated to all regions of the world; for the preparation of Country and Regional Strategy Papers and for the National and Regional Indicative Programmes. An inter-service consultation mechanism is, therefore, in place for the management of most financial instruments. All financial instruments, if required, are then scrutinized by the Council through the apposite comitology[6]

---

5   Commission Decision, SEC(2010) 1307 final, 27/10/2010.

6   'Comitology has developed into a standard operating procedure in the EU system. When the EU legislators delegate decision-making power to the Commission, a comitology procedure is usually installed as a control mechanism. This system enables the member states to keep track of delegated powers and to intervene in selected cases. The system consists of 200–300 committees of member state representatives that monitor the Commission according to procedures leaving the Commission varying degrees of autonomy' (Blom-Hansen 2011: 607).

procedures. Relevant Committees follow the Commission's proposal at all stages. Although extremely complex, the reorganization of the services was meant to proceed to a simplification of a complex landscape of thematic and geographic instruments for the delivery of external assistance.[7]

Table 5.3 Political and financial responsibility in the implementation of the EU foreign policy instruments

Instrument	Policy responsibility	In coordination with	Financial responsibility
IPA	ELARG	Consultation with EEAS; DG REGIO; DG EMPL; DG AGRI; DG BUDG	ELARG
Humanitarian Aid and external aspects of Civil Protection	DG ECHO	Consultation with the EEAS; relevant Commission's services; DG BUDG	ECHO
ENPI	Commissioner for Enlargement and the European Neighbourhood Policy/DEVCO	Proposal jointly prepared by the EEAS; DG ELARG; DG DEVCO; DG BUDG	DG DEVCO
EDF/DCI	DG DEVCO	EEAS; DEV; ELARG; DG BUDG	DEVCO
Macro-financial Assistance	DG ECOFIN	EEAS; DEV; ELARG; DG BUDG	DG ECOFIN
ICI	EEAS	FPI	FPI
Instrument for Stability	EEAS	FPI	FPI
CFSP actions	EEAS	FPI/relevant Commission's services	FPI
Nuclear Safety Instrument and EIDHR	EEAS	DEVCO/relevant Commission's services	DEVCO
EOM	EEAS	FPI	FPI
Communication and Public Diplomacy	DG Communication (DG COMM)	Relevant Commission's Service; EEAS/FPI; DG BUDG	Commission (different DGs); FPI

7   House of Lords – Documents considered by the Committee on 12 January 2011 – EU External Action: the Instrument for Stability – www.publications.parliament.uk/pa/ cm201011/cmselect/cmeuleg/428-xii/42819.htm.

The procedures put into place for the European Development Fund (EDF) give a hint of the complexity of the process. For a start, this instrument was traditionally a *domain reservée* of DG DEV. Responsibility in the management of the funds for development for ACP countries profoundly contributed to shaping the sectoral institutional ethos of the DG (Dimier 2003). Throughout the politics of reform undertaken for upgrading and improving the disbursement of funds to development, DG DEVCO remained in charge of the management of the EDF despite the creation of AIDCO and the process of rationalization of disbursement of aid (Carta 2012). While still under control of DEVCO, the planning and allocation of funds now is shared with the EEAS. DEVCO holds for the Commission financial responsibility for the preparation of the EDF/DCI and frames, in collaboration with the EEAS, the Commission's Decision dealing with these financial instruments to be adopted by the Council. Importantly, the process of implementation involves consistently the Delegations, which coordinate with member states' embassies on the spot.

As mentioned, the HR/VP is responsible for the implementation of CFSP budget, the crisis response and peace-building components of the Instrument for Stability (IfS), the Instrument for Cooperation with Industrialized Countries (ICI), communication and public diplomacy actions and election observation missions under the European Instrument for Democracy and Human Rights (EIDHR). In addition to these general competences, DG ECOFIN is responsible for macro-financial assistance, which explains its presence within the Commissioners' Group on External Relations. The Commission exercises the task of financing external policy measures, while the financing of foreign policy measures is entrusted, as mentioned, to the FPI.

For instance, the Instrument for Stability (IfS) 'constitutes a short-term component, crisis response with "assistance in response to situations of crisis or emerging crisis", and a long-term component, with "assistance in the context of stable conditions for cooperation"' (European Parliament and Council Regulation, 2006,[8] articles 3 and 4, quoted in Lavallée 2011: 377). In 2007, the instrument has replaced a plethora of instruments in the fields of drugs, mines, uprooted people, crisis management, rehabilitation and reconstruction.[9] Although conceived as a civilian instrument of crisis response complementing CSDP missions, the overall idea underlying the IfS is one of ensuring a synergic and comprehensive response to crisis, which links security and development. The deployment of this instrument requires, at all levels, an intense load of coordination between all European actors. In the first place, as is the case of the EDF described above, a decision to deploy the instrument requires a vertical cooperation between the Delegations

---

8   European Parliament and Council Regulation (EC) No. 1717/2006 of 15 November 2006 on establishing an instrument for stability. *Official Journal of the European Union*, L327/ 1-L327/11.

9   For more information on the IfS, visit the website of DEVCO: http://ec.europa.eu/europeaid/how/finance/ifs_en.htm.

and Headquarters, both in the EEAS and in the FPI (interview, 7 March 2012). In preparing the draft of the Decision, the EEAS and FPI, after having heard from the Delegation on the ground, proceed, where necessary, to consultation with other Commission services, for instance in DEVCO. Finally, the IfS is submitted to comitology scrutiny in the PSC and CIVICOM WG (Lavallée 2011: 378).

To complicate the picture, two financial instruments remain excluded by article 9 of the decision establishing the organization and functioning of the EEAS: the Instrument for Pre-Accession (IPA)[10] and Humanitarian Aid (ECHO) and external aspects of civil protection. These two instruments are entirely under the responsibility of the Commission. In the case of the IPA, DG ELARG liaises with other relevant Commission's Service – like DG Region (DG REGIO); DG Employment (EMPL) and DG Agriculture (DG AGRI) – due to respective portfolios of responsibility. Humanitarian aid and external aspects of civil protection are managed by DG ECHO, which consults the EEAS and other Commission services through the inter-service consultation process. In this area, ECHO also provides for secretariat and chairs to the relevant Council Committees.

Current arrangements, therefore, create a double line of political and financial responsibilities, whereas the Commission – through its services or through the IFP – maintains the financial responsibility of all actions and the EEAS holds, in certain areas, political responsibility. This stage further reveals the limits imposed to a unified approach to foreign policy whereas, to make up to the misfits of a fragmented policy field, a complex work of institutional engineering needed to be set up to guarantee to the EU the ability to act on the international scene. The EU Delegations are fully involved in this stage and work in a synergic way with all EU services. Further empirical research could highlight the dynamics of multiple lines of both mandates and information sharing between the multiple-edged Headquarters and the Delegations on the ground (Carta forthcoming, 2013). The stage of implementation highlights that the EEAS is not the only hybrid body created under the Lisbon template. This stage, therefore, constitutes a fertile ground for empirical research. A focus on implementation could clarify how policy decisions are transposed into policy measures and explore the potential for transformation that this transposition brings with it.

---

10   The Commissioner for Enlargement and Neighbourhood Policy holds the policy responsibility for the European Neighbourhood Policy Instrument (ENPI). In order to frame the ENPI, the Commissioner relies on the geographical and thematic desks of the EEAS and DEVCO, which are not, therefore, in DG ELARG. The Commissioner for Enlargement also holds responsibility for the preparation of all programming documents, which are jointly prepared by DG DEV and the EEAS. As for other regional programmes, DG DEV is responsible to ensure the overall coherence of the ENPI with global and sectorial development policy objectives. The ENPI is then implemented by DG DEVCO.

Conclusions

Locating executive actors throughout the foreign policy cycle helps to make sense of both the position of executive actors in particular instances of the process of policy-making and of the fluid adaptation of the Lisbon Treaty. The adventurous journey of all institutions interested in foreign policy is a well acknowledged feature of this process. Personal factors and bureaucratic turf-battles, the creation of new institutions and a quite unstructured plan on how to reform the system added complexity to an already complicated system of external relations.

The policy-cycle approach reveals its heuristic value as a tool to detect formal attribution of competences and the way in which executive actors are forced to interact in the making of external policy measures. The policy-cycle approach, however, does not deny the continuous flow of contacts that intervenes among all actors and the existence of a dynamic relation among them.

To recap briefly this complexity, at the level of political initiative, different actors intervene to different extents to give impetus to the EU's external action. Both the enmeshed character of policy dossiers and a partially overlapping attribution of competences require an intense coordination both at the level of initiative and at the level of policy formulation. At this stage, coordination is needed to ensure that a given policy initiative will not turn out to be a fiasco.

At the stage of policy formulation, the parallel regime of low and high foreign policy-making and the entry on stage of a new actor, the EEAS, require an intense load of coordination to guarantee that all expertise, ideas and competences are taken on board in final policy outcomes. A high degree of formal and informal coordination is required. Depending on the attribution of competences continuous emails, phone calls, meetings between individual civil servants from both the Commission and the EEAS services beat time of the framing of common measures. Informality, therefore, sustains the formulation of policy measures and reveals that the degree of personal discretion (i.e. willingness to communicate, share information and to respect the attribution of competences) accounts for the timely and feasible delivery of policy proposals.

At the stage of decision-making, different decision-making styles alternate. The fact that discussions on the same dossiers are scattered across different venues highlights the potential for policy misfit. Beyond inter-institutional agreements, a high degree of discretion contributes to shaping the final outcome of the policy process. As interviewees witness, much coordination occurs informally and is sustained by a variable blend of personal relations and individual initiative. The occurrence, timing and venue of all actors' intervention in the policy process is formally determined by the nature of competences. In this fashion, horizontal dossiers – such as development or trade issues – refer to the GAC; while foreign policy dossiers to the FAC. In the former case, the policy-making in these areas generally mirrors the community style of decision-making. In the latter case, the prevalent style of decision-making is intergovernmental and the policy measures assumed do not have a legislative character. As some interviewees reveal, the maintenance of a pillarized logic of decision-making potentially allows the member states to try to discuss some policy competences in the FAC rather than in the GAC, by drifting away policy decisions from the rule of QMV to unanimity.

At the stage of policy implementation, the distinction between political and financial responsibility makes for separate, yet concurrent, implementation systems. All services involved in the stage of implementation need to coordinate and liaise constantly also in the stage of implementation of common measures both in the Headquarters and in the Delegations. As follows, different organizational units intervene systematically in the implementation and financing of common measures.

Currently, political analysis can depict in which cases and in which areas the system is sustained or disrupted by the high level of personal discretion. In time, institutional enactment will tell us more about the feasibility of the overall institutional system. The theoretical contributions from both public policy and bureaucratic approaches to foreign policy remind us that also at the national level the process of foreign policy-making is cut across by 'compromise, conflict and confusion' (Allison and Zelikow 1971). For as much of a strange beast as it can appear, the EU, then, is far from being an isolated example of foreign policy complexity.

Chapter 6

The Challenge of Coherence and Consistency in EU Foreign Policy

Hartmut Mayer

Abstract

This chapter specifically focuses on the conceptual challenge of coherence and consistency in EU foreign policy. It analyses the legal, institutional and political improvements through the Lisbon Treaty. Conceptually, it offers a five-tier understanding of coherence that includes *vertical, horizontal, inter-pillar, rhetorical, strategic* and *external engagement*. The chapter then argues that a comprehensive understanding of coherence might also steer more prudent policies. In the current crisis, the inherent tensions of internal and external coherence in foreign policy are likely to last. Hence, the chapter asks whether the EU would generally be better served if it distanced itself from normative calls and retreated from idealistic symbols back to concrete effectiveness and pragmatic actions. Complete coherence might even be contrary to nature for foreign policy actors. Recognizing the inevitable might make the EU a more credible and effective global player.

Introduction

When looking for the most repetitive story in the study of the European Union, the 'lack of coherence and consistency' in Europe's external relations alongside the 'capabilities–expectations gap' (Hill 1993) must be the most serious contender. Ever since the inception through European Political Co-operation (EPC) in 1970, the lack of 'cohesion, coherence and consistency' topped the chart of complaints about the nature and ineffectiveness of Europe's common foreign policy. The other persistent tales have been on 'unfulfilled promises' and on the growing gap between rhetoric and reality. These themes are all interrelated. However, many analysts have singled out the lack of legal and procedural coherence and consistency as a crucial cause for ineffectiveness, malfunctioning and poorly coordinated joint action over the last 40 years.

Europe after the Lisbon Treaty is in danger of fulfilling once again those familiar storylines. The Treaty was supposed to put a strong emphasis on finally managing the lack of coherence by fundamentally changing the institutional set-up of EU foreign policy. The extent to which this can succeed is the topic of the entire book. This specific chapter debates the conceptual challenge of coherence and consistency in EU foreign policy per se. It acknowledges that the Treaty of Lisbon had specific and admirable aims. Nevertheless, it argues that its unique timing and its surrounding circumstances once again will restrict Lisbon to another set of promising prototypes and blueprints. By no means does it provide the refined end product that would be capable of addressing the perpetual problem of coherence in EU external affairs.

The chapter provides several reflections and contributions to the wider and long-standing debate. At a conceptual level, it analyses the different pillars, spheres and meanings of coherence and consistency in EU foreign policy. It includes a theoretical and a legal examination. Anticipating that the inherent structural tensions of vertical, horizontal, internal and external coherence remain hard to overcome, it then asks whether the EU would generally be better served if it could distance itself from the overriding normative calls for coherence and consistency. It discusses whether common expressions such as 'unity', 'consistency', 'speaking with one voice' or 'acting as a whole' might in fact be fundamentally flawed and whether Europe has fallen into a self-inflicted rhetorical trap. The chapter will finally suggest that Europe might want to modify its unattainable ideal-types. Outside observers increasingly perceive the obsession with institutional coherence as a very self-centred technocratic trade. It has often been the root cause of inefficient institutional turf wars that normally bind far too much of Europe's energy. As an alternative, one should consider whether EU foreign policy should shift from idealistic symbols and identities to concrete substance and delivery. Foreign policy successes would then be measured by real contributions to solving security and other global problems – even if achieved at the expense of full formal coherence and consistency.

Conceptualizing the Challenge of Coherence and Consistency

Even after 40 years of academic analysis over cohesion, coherence and consistence in EU foreign policy, there remains significant disagreement among the experts about its fundamental concepts. While the meanings of 'coherence' remain the subject of ongoing debates, the failures and unfulfilled aspirations of EPC and CFSP have always been blamed on the 'lack of cohesion/coherence/consistency'. This has been done unfortunately without a full analysis of what actually causes these shortcomings exactly. It is therefore worth reflecting about the political, legal and institutional complexity surrounding coherence before assessing the post-Lisbon real environment later in the chapter. Reality must be the starting point for all discussions on the subject (see Chapter 2 in this volume).

Leaving linguistic problems of translating the French word 'cohérence' into the various European languages and their respective meanings aside,[1] some conceptual clarification is necessary. In a recent landmark piece Carmen Gebhard (Gebhard 2011) has provided a comprehensive analysis of the long-standing debate on 'coherence' and offered an excellent conceptual framework that guides and inspires our reflections here. She distinguishes between 'types of coherence' (vertical, horizontal, internal, external), 'faces of coherence' (banal, malign, benign) and 'means of enhancing coherence' (legal remedies, institutional reforms, political initiatives) (Gebhard 2011). While there is significant intellectual overlap with the works of Gebhard (2011), Nuttall (2000, 2005), or Missiroli (2001) to name a few, I would suggest a conceptualization and operationalization of five typologies of coherence in EU foreign policy, i.e. *vertical, horizontal, strategic, narrative* and *external engagement* coherence.

In plain language, a fully coherent and consistent EU foreign policy would consist of a tension-free and transparent interaction between all the agents that contribute to the EU's multi-level foreign policy formation. It would include harmony on values, substance, aims and processes of individual policies. This ideal-type quality would rest on at least five crucial pillars and conditions: *first*, there must be substantial agreement between the foreign policies of all member states and the common foreign policy of the EU including full compliance with agreed positions (*vertical coherence*). *Second*, at the level of the EU there must be concentration at Community and Union level with smooth coordination between the supranational and the intergovernmental spheres and competences of external relations. Hence, ideally intra- and inter-institutional battles over policy formation and authority should be absent. It would require a clear and undisputed allocation of competences between the various pillars and institutions of the EU (*horizontal or inter-pillar coherence*). *Third*, the general direction and purpose of all EU external policies must be free of contradictions. Similar or overlapping policies would follow the same principles, values and aims. Policy consistency should manifest itself in strategic (policy goals, objectives and general political agendas) (see Chapter 3 in this volume) as well as procedural coherence (*Strategic coherence*). *Fourth*, there should be coherence between the rhetoric, i.e. what the EU aims and claims to do; and its real action, i.e. what the EU actually does in EU foreign policy. For example, the EU has consistently portrayed itself as the number one leader in global climate change. However, a close examination of its influence in the global climate change regime formation

---

1 The French word 'cohérence' is commonly translated into 'consistency' (not coherence!) in English, 'Kohärenz' in German, coherencia in Spanish and coerenza in Italian. Furthermore the English word 'consistency' has then been translated into the equivalents of 'continuity' in Dutch, Swedish and Danish. The linguistic differences are important: something can be more or less coherent, but not more or less consistent. It is either consistent or not. Continuity has a different tone altogether (see Gebhard 2011; Missiroli 2001).

does not really back such claims. Or a different example: the EU aims to apply human rights provisions in trade agreement consistently but, in reality, different trade agreements have seen different interpretations of such rights. The gap between the EU's rhetoric and action has left much to be desired over the years (Mayer 2008a) (*Narrative coherence*). *Fifth*, one needs to stress that the EU's foreign policy no longer depends on European interests and visions alone. The outside world determines the scope and nature of common European foreign policy more than ever before. EU foreign policy can only flourish when developed through a mutually constitutive engagement with external powers. When the EU represents itself in international organizations, engages in strategic partnerships or addresses global problems as a signatory to an international treaty, its policy formation and effectiveness depends at least as much on what other players think (Chaban et al. 2006; Lucarelli and Fioramonti 2010) and do as what the EU itself intends to achieve. It is by no means Europe alone that 'diffuses ideas' (Börzel and Risse 2009b). Europe receives and adopts norms and ideas at the same time as it defines, sends and promotes them. In today's world, European foreign policy can no longer be seen as purely European but as a function of mutual engagement between Europe and the non-European world. This is particularly true with regard to Europe's various strategic partnerships (see Chapters 9, 10, 11 and 12 in this volume). As a result, coherence requires consistent and respectful exchange with external partners who decisively shape and define Europe's room for action and a mature, reliable and respectful dialogue with the non-European world (Mayer 2008b) (*External engagement coherence*).

Complete coherence in these five domains would amount to a desirable but largely unrealistic and unattainable state of affairs. If understood and operationalized correctly, this verdict must not be as fundamentally problematic as portrayed in most political and academic circles. For example, it is similar to the GATT or the WTO that never fulfilled the ideal aspiration of 'free trade' but always contributed to gradual trade liberalization, i.e. achieving 'freer trade rather than free trade'. Hence, further harmonization and 'more coherence' should remain on the EU's agenda and will always be one of the benchmarks when assessing the EU as an actor in international affairs. However, 'coherence' as an ultimate goal or a simple real or rhetorical litmus test for assessing success in EU foreign policy is counterproductive. Other global actors, such as the United States, China or Russia, are no more consistent or coherent in their approach to new foreign policy challenges. For example, the internal US debate on appropriate responses to the Libyan crisis in 2011 displayed as much diversity as the European (see Chapter 7 in this volume). Differences within the US administration, however, never undermine the identity of the actor itself as it does in the case of the multi-layered actor EU. In the case of China, the apparent coherence (not consistency!) could be as much of a concern to global governance as Europe's apparent lack of coherence.

As the reflections above have indicated, a mature understanding and acceptance of limited coherence might enlighten policy actors, in particular in Brussels. The worst of the three faces of coherence are the malign 'turf battles', coherence as a mere function of internal institutional power struggles. As there have been many, the Lisbon Treaty intended to clarify some of the most pressing issues.

The Legal Impact of the Lisbon Treaty: Causing and/or Curing Incoherence?

When analysing the Treaty's role in improving coherence, historical path-dependency is a fruitful point of departure. The problems are as old as EC/EU external policy. Due to the dual structure between the EC and EPC from the 1970s onwards, EU foreign policy was born with a complex coordination and harmonization handicap that was clearly deepened and perpetuated over time. The Single European Act (1986) which integrated the EPC procedures into the community framework stipulated that 'the external policies of the EC and the policies agreed in EPC must be consistent' and allocated 'special responsibility for ensuring that such consistency is sought and maintained' (SEA, Title III, article 30) in an undefined way to both, the Council Presidency and the Commission, 'each within its own sphere of competence' (SEA, Title III, article 30). This historical compromise was the legal origin of a complex bifurcation and institutional rivalry that characterizes the process and profile of EU foreign policy until today (Gebhard 2011: 104).

Every treaty reform since the Single European Act in 1986 intended to improve the insufficient standards of procedural coherence and consistency and the dysfunctional division between economic, political and defence aspects within EU foreign policy which clearly negatively affected the EU's presence on the world stage. However, neither the innovations of the Maastricht Treaty, nor the revisions in Amsterdam and Nice provided the solution for the fundamental dualist logic. The respective treaty changes offered no more than just another insufficient base for the growing tensions between member states and EU institutions, between the EU institutions themselves and between the separate logics of different policy fields. The only consistency one could detect was ongoing complexity.

The New Legal Foundations of EU External Affairs

The Lisbon Treaty was seen as a golden opportunity to fix the existing arrangements for external representation and design the institutional foundation for a more effective foreign policy. Turning the EU into a more vertically and horizontally coherent actor was one of the main goals of the Lisbon Treaty. The desire for real and full vertical coherence is most explicitly expressed and confirmed in what can be described as a 'dream ticket'-article, namely article 24.3 (formerly article 11.2 of the Nice Treaty). It reads:

> The Member States shall support the Union's external and security policy actively and unreservedly in a spirit of loyalty and mutual solidarity and shall

comply with the Union's action in this area. The Member States shall work together to enhance and to develop their mutual political solidarity. They shall refrain from any action, which is contrary to the interests of the Union or likely to impair its effectives as a cohesive force in international relations.

In addition to legally manifesting idealistic wish lists, the Treaty of Lisbon does clarify and upgrade important aspects of vertical and horizontal coherence without being able to overcome the inherent inconsistencies of a complex hybrid system.

In international law, the Lisbon Treaty formally confers legal personality upon the EU which in theory is a big step towards a more cohesive actor. The combination of article 1, saying that the EU replaces and succeeds the European Commission (TEU, article 1), and article 47, stating that the 'EU will exercise all the rights and all the obligations of the European Community' including succession of all the previous international agreements whilst 'continuing to exercise existing rights of the EU', is a strong expression of the desire to streamline a previously much more diverse actor. This certainly removes legal uncertainties and enhances the capacity of the EU to raise its status in external forums but it has no automatic effect in doing so (Emerson et al. 2011: 22). In a recent account which refers to the EU Commission's database of treaties, the EU is party to 249 multilateral and 649 bilateral treaties (Emerson et al. 2001: 3), each signed at different times with different purposes. The EU is now formally the legal successor to all which by no means amounts to a real change of the status quo of such agreements. Although the Treaty has newly clarified some of the confusion, it certainly has not disentangled it. Two aspects of external affairs continue to be inconsistent and often incoherent. First, the EU has inherited the Commission's old and different types of status in multilateral organizations and treaty regimes. The EU is in the various regimes, either:

1. member and contracting partner;
2. 'virtual member' or 'enhanced observer', i.e. a functional participant without formal status or voting rights;
3. mere observer (Emerson et al. 2001: 3–4).

It plays such roles usually alongside the member states and with inbuilt rivalries over presence and influence. Only the 'dreams' of article 24.3 would imagine full loyalty by member states towards the EU in such forums, in particular when the room for manoeuvre is determined by these external institutions rather by the Europeans themselves. The UN General Assembly, the WTO or the World Financial Institutions, the IMF and the World Bank, provide a few strong examples which should not be debated in much detail here.

The second major problem that undermines desires for vertical and horizontal coherence and keeps puzzling external partners are the confusing divisions of competences between the EU and member states in most policy fields (see also Chapter 4 in this volume). For outside observers and treaty partners, the overlapping competence between the EU institutions and the member states in different policy areas has always been a major source of confusion. According to the so-called Lisbon Treaty (TEU and TFEU), there are 'exclusive EU competencies', various types of 'shared competencies' including 'parallel competences' and 'co-ordination competences' and areas where the EU can only take 'supplementary actions' to the member states.

The Treaty on the Functioning of the European Union (TFEU) clearly defines such areas. According to article 2.4 (TFEU) 'Common foreign and security, including the progressive framing of a common defence policy, in accordance with the provisions of the Treaty of the European Union' remains a 'shared – or effectively parallel – competence'.

Hence, EU foreign and defence policy will always be a hybrid with the normal inconsistencies that naturally result from such a structure. Other aspects of external affairs are regulated in various treaty provisions. Article 3 of the TFEU mentions the *exclusive EU competences*, i.e. 'trade, competition and monetary policies' as well as the 'conservation of marine biological resources'. Article 4 lists *shared competences* in core domains. These are: *internal market, energy, cohesion (economic, social and territorial, transport, agriculture, fisheries, freedom-justice-security, environment, consumer protection, and aspects of social and public health (art. 4.2))*. *Parallel competences*, a secondary category defined in article 4.3-4, concern *research and development policies* where member states have more substantial competence. Article 5 provides for *coordination competence* between the EU and member states. It is a loose sub-category of shared competences and includes certain 'economic and employment policies'. Article 6 then grants the EU *supplementary action competence* in areas where predominant competence rests with member states, i.e. 'industry, culture, tourism, education, civil protection and public health'.

This complex list, even if simplified when compared with previous treaties, clearly makes lawyers busy and citizens dizzy, creates more or less enjoyable battlegrounds for civil servants but severe headaches for businessmen and most other professions. Furthermore, these complexities have a real impact when it comes to representation of member states and the EU in external international organizations. It would go beyond the scope of this chapter to discuss these in detail.[2] However, as internal inconsistencies transcend into incoherent external affairs, the internal complexity of the EU which is manifested in the new treaties again will always be the major obstacle to the desired external coherence. One can improve harmonization but can never reach harmony.

An attempt in this direction and, as such, a clear virtue of the Lisbon Treaty is Article 21 (TEU). At very length, it provides a list of normative principles and objectives that should guide and unite the EU and its member states in the formulation of external policies. Although some of its underlying theoretical

---

2   Emerson et al. have created an impressive four-page diagram listing the various policy areas and the resulting representation problems in various international organizations.

assumptions will continue to be questioned in foreign policy circles in Brussels and national capitals, in particular as the word 'power' does not appear once in the article, but it might at least provide the content and substantive glue for what I call 'narrative coherence', 'strategic coherence' and 'external engagement coherence' in the conceptual typology above.

Article 21 (TEU) prescribes that the Union's action should seek to advance in the wider world 'democracy, the rule of law, the universality and indivisibility of human rights and fundamental freedoms, respect for human dignity, the principles of equality and solidarity and respect for the principles of United Nations Charter' (art. 21.1). In order to do so, the EU should seek global partnerships with countries, international, regional and global institutions. Art. 21.2 stipulates that the EU should 'work for a high degree of co-operation in all fields of international relations' and achieve the following objectives:

1. safeguard its own (21.2a) 'values', 'interests', 'independence' and 'integrity';
2. consolidate and support (21.2b) 'democracy' and 'the rule of law' and 'human rights';
3. preserve (21.2c) 'peace' and 'security' in accordance with the UN and the Helsinki accords;
4. foster (21.2.d) 'sustainable economic, social and environmental development' giving priority to 'eradicating poverty';
5. encourage (21.2.e) the 'integration of all countries into the world ecnonomy';
6. preserve and improve (21.2.f) the 'quality of the environment and the sustainable management of global natural resources';
7. assist (21.2g) in cases of 'natural or man-made disasters';
8. and promote (21.2.h) 'an international system based in stronger multilateral cooperation and good global governance'.

Article 21.3 then famously calls on the Union for the tall order to 'ensure *consistency* between the different areas of its external action and between these and its other policies'.

The values and principles enshrined in this key article are hardly contested, but as always, the proof remains in the pudding. In theory, all these objectives are supposed to be implemented by the newly strengthened institutional set-up.

Institutional Innovations

As other contributors to this volume focus very specifically on the European External Action Service (EEAS) (see Chapters 4 and 5) and the duties and present performance of the New High Representative (see Chapters 2, 3 and 4), judgements on these issues should be limited to a minimum here. As far as contributions to coherence and consistency are concerned the new institutions clearly had a suboptimal start. They have not eliminated outside perceptions of growing disunity about the nature of the new service. Formally founded in December 2010 the EEAS officially began operating in January 2011. Ongoing negotiations over the budget and the staffing of the service as well as inter-institutional disagreements and infighting have been recounted, staff morale has reportedly been varied both in Brussels as well as in external delegations abroad. There were also some signs of back-tracking among members over an effective support for the new external affairs provisions of the Lisbon Treaty (Emerson et al. 2011) One can detect serious danger that further disagreements on budgets and staffing will continue. This will then absorb further energies away from substantive questions of EU foreign policy. To sum up, what we have seen so far is not conducive to fostering unity and coherence in EU foreign policy. As the process is still young, one should refrain from overdramatic judgements at this point in time and should not draw ultimate conclusions from the unconvincing start. From a normative perspective it should be evident that if the EU wishes to seek coherence in foreign policy in the long run, a much better diplomatic corps needs to emerge. The status quo is by no means sufficient at all, but the larger questions will all boil down to political will and confidence.

Generally speaking, the legal foundations and institutions of EU external affairs have always been ambivalent and confusing. New treaties usually tried to repair the ills which the previous treaties had created. In a twisted way, the legal foundations have both been the root causes as well as the prescribed medicine and treatment for the EU's lack of coherence in external affairs. However, the law only expresses the difficult compromises reached between the political wills of the member states and the European institutions. Any legal provision and institutional innovation of the Lisbon Treaty is only as strong as the political will and leadership behind it. This is where Europe's real challenges currently lie.

The European Crisis and the Post-Lisbon Treaty Global Realities: What are the Consequences for Foreign Policy Coherence?

Despite the institutional innovations of the Lisbon Treaty that increase coherence and upgrade, rationalize and concentrate the EU's external representation in an unprecedented way, it is actually more than uncertain whether EU foreign policy will actually progress in the foreseeable future. As a result of the financial crisis and the generally multidimensional shifts in global order (Hurrell 2007, and see Chapter 1 in this volume), the EU has reached a turning point.

Four defining features should be highlighted before deliberating whether coherence and consistency are really necessary preconditions for effective foreign policy.

First, the Treaty of Lisbon was supposed to legally address the challenge of vertical (i.e. coordination between member states and the EU foreign policies) and horizontal (i.e. internal coordination between EU policies and institutions) coherence. While confirming the principles of horizontal and vertical coherence in articles 21 and 24 respectively, it nevertheless fails to draw a conclusive picture. The treaties read together still leave room for further legal disputes: for example as the accompanying Declarations 13 and 14 of the CFSP provisions of the Treaty seem to stress once again member states' sovereignty in foreign affairs.

Second, the Treaty's institutional innovations raise high expectations that an effective European Diplomacy could finally emerge. The initially much celebrated idea of a European External Action Service (EEAS) and the strengthened capacity of the new High Representative (HR) who is supposed to lead the EEAS, coordinate as Commission Vice-President all areas of EU external relations, chair the Foreign Affairs Council, were bold steps indeed. In practice, the first years in operation have however shown that the designated 'wonder children' EEAS and High Representative had, to say it mildly, more than the normal teething problems. However, as the evolution of the EEAS and the HR are currently at the very beginning premature judgements would be inappropriate as a base for political advice.

Third, the signature and ratification process of the Lisbon Treaty was more than ever embedded in a widespread 'unite or fail' narrative. More strongly than before have senior politicians and Commission representatives claimed that Europe would no longer be taken seriously in the new multipolar world if it did not speak as a unit and if it did not conduct a coherent and consistent common foreign policy.

Fourth and most decisively, the fundamental crisis of the Economic and Monetary Union as a result of the financial turmoil seriously threatens to derail the entire historical project of European unification. It has and will continue to overshadow all attempts of improving cohesion in EU foreign policy which today seems a somewhat marginalized concern in light of the cracking larger economic foundations.

As a consequence of these four overriding features, one must conclude that the prospects for achieving a truly coherent and consistent EU foreign policy remain as slim after the Lisbon Treaty as they always have been before. The legal basis for foreign policy coherence remains somewhat ambivalent although there are objective improvements. The construction of the new institutions has so far revealed disunity rather than convincing harmonization. The gaps between 'rhetoric and action' and 'expectations and capacity' in EU foreign policy are by no means closing. In the non-European world, the respect for and patience with Europe's common foreign policy efforts is gradually withering. And finally, the overall interest in the matter even within Europe itself is currently sharply declining in light of the much bigger questions raised by Europe's general financial, political and identity crisis (Habermas 2012; Piris 2012).

How then should Europe respond to this unsatisfactory and unpromising state of affairs?

Referring back to conceptual distinctions and Gebhard's different means for improving coherence, it seems 'political initiatives' (or lack of) would trump all 'legal remedies' and 'institutional innovations' of the Lisbon Treaty. The impetus for change must come from politics as the legal and institutional mechanisms have been exhausted for the moment. Further treaty changes will be necessary in the future but the time is not yet ripe. Unfortunately, currently the overriding political picture seems more than weak. The essential crisis that includes doubts over the general economic competitiveness and prosperity of Europe, fundamental democratic legitimacy in member states and existential trust in national political leaders will overshadow any progress on the EU's common foreign policy coherence.

It is, unfortunately, a marginalized issue at the moment.

There can be little doubt that crisis management mode since 2008 has shifted the centre of policy-making away from the Brussels based EU institutions to other actors, first and foremost national capitals (see Chapter 4 in this volume) in and outside Europe, the ECB, the IMF, banks and financial markets. It remains to be seen whether this emphasis will have a lasting impact on a re-nationalization of foreign policy or a general decline in interest in military and defence affairs (see Chapter 3 in this volume).

Objectively, politicians and electorates should realize that the crisis, the dramatic shifts in global power and the revival of hegemonic thinking in various corners of the multipolar world all call for more Europe in foreign affairs rather than for less. Declining domestic defence budgets and large agreements over the general values of Europe's role in the world clearly suggest pooling of resources and acting jointly whenever and wherever possible. Acknowledging that the legal and institutional means have been exhausted, the emphasis needs to be on a shift of narrative. As Bickerton (2011) has analysed brilliantly, one of the central features of EU foreign policy has been that it shifted its emphasis from external effectiveness to internal identity, used the claim for external cohesion as an instrument for teleological institution building. Elsewhere I have criticized the Eurocentric naval-gazing in the past decade and called for a new narrative for Europe in a Non-European World (Mayer 2008b).

When applied to the problem of coherence and consistency, the answer to the question of whether we can afford to continue with the 'one voice, one unit' narrative is normatively unsatisfactory but practically unavoidable. The obsessive desire for cohesion is a European debate for Europeans. For all others outside Europe effectiveness always trumps cohesion. Hence, the EU must revert to stressing practical effectiveness rather than lofty identities. Recognizing that vertical, horizontal, inter-pillar and inter-institutional coherence and consistency are unachievable still leaves a lot of room for enhancing 'narrative coherence', 'strategic coherence' and 'external engagement coherence'.

The new mega-narrative of Europe in a non-European world would abandon simplistic 'one voice' straitjackets. It would stop assessing EU action by its internal cohesion but rather by concrete achievements in practical action. It would nevertheless emphasize and work towards the overriding values expressed in article 21 TEU. However, it would be more modest about its capacity and limits. It would be open to admitting that different member states and different EU institutions might have individual interpretations when applying these principles. All in all, some more 'unity in diversity' will be a possibly sufficient state of affairs for Europe. The new mega-narrative of Europe in a Non-European World would label naïve and obsessive claims for consistency as misleading. Global responsibility and effective external contributions to global public goods are better avenues than sticking to unreachable and internally driven priorities for cohesion. More cohesion and more consistency for the EU are legitimate goals but currently of a secondary order. A much more modest narrative and practical incremental achievements in joint action seem the only realistic way forward in times of severe stagnation in EU foreign policy.

Conclusion

As the above analysis has shown, at no time in the long history of progress towards a more coherent foreign policy have the significant innovations provided by the Lisbon Treaty been brought to life in more difficult global circumstances. Similar to the EPC, the Single European Act, Maastricht and the treaties of Amsterdam and Nice, Lisbon does initiate further enhancement of coherence in European foreign policy. Nevertheless, it is bound to fail to achieve its ambitious goals once again. Whilst previous treaty revisions also had obvious shortcomings, they were normally concluded in a more favourable spirit of general optimism about the European project. EPC began its life in the positive climate of East-West détente. The Single European Act became a catalyst for improving the common market. Maastricht was signed in the context of Western pride about the peaceful ending of the Cold War to which European integration had so significantly contributed. Amsterdam and Nice promised to prepare for the big wave of enlargement for the completion of the common European house that Europe's founding fathers had envisaged. In contrast, the Lisbon Treaty lacks any sign of surrounding enthusiasm. It was signed after a decade of lost economic competitiveness at the global stage and a long-drawn out negotiation marathon that saw severe political and institutional setbacks ever since the Constitutional Convention. With the Lisbon Treaty there was a bigger clash between desires and realities from the very start, and there was already a sense of exhaustion even before the new institution began to operate. And then, even worse, the real financial and political crisis hit.

In times of severe political and economic uncertainty it is not only traders in financial markets and politicians who might occasionally overreact. Also academic analysts tend to amplify views and fuse analysis with intellectual crusades. Being aware of such danger one needs to give the new institutions in foreign policy, the EEAS and the High Representative, time to find their footing before offering a considered judgement. Nevertheless, with its internal tensions and contradictions, the EU's external relations might for the foreseeable future remain as incoherent as they have ever been.

Europe's engagement with the rest of the world, more moderate targets for common action, a less ambitious rhetoric and small steps towards concrete successes in managing global problems might be all one can and should ask for.

Europe's obsessive desire for coherence and consistence might never stand the tests of practice anyway. Quoting some of the most incisive intellectuals on 'consistency' might not deliver solutions for one of the EU's most long-standing dilemmas but it provides at least some comfort. For bad or for worse, it might in fact be true that 'foolish consistency is the hobgoblin of little minds' (Ralph Waldo Emerson, *Self-Reliance*, 1841), that 'consistency is the enemy of enterprise, just as symmetry is the enemy of art' (George Bernard Shaw, 1991) and that, ultimately, 'consistency is contrary to nature, contrary to life. The only completely consistent people are the dead' (Aldous Huxley).[3]

Long live EU foreign policy.

---

3   Quotes found on longer list of classic reflections on 'consistency' provided by wikiquotes.

PART III
Assessing CFSP and the EU's External Relations in Action: Near and Far Abroad

Chapter 7

The European Neighbourhood Policy and the Challenge of the Mediterranean Southern Rim

Richard Gillespie

Abstract

This assessment of the European Union's response to the Arab Spring takes account both of the internal financial, political and institutional difficulties experienced by the EU post-Lisbon Treaty and of the complexity of the challenge posed by the recent Arab insurrections, whose outcomes have been far from uniform across the southern rim of the Mediterranean. Surprised by the events, the EU has responded primarily by using and developing the European Neighbourhood Policy and by mainstreaming support for democratization in its relations with Mediterranean (though not Gulf) Arab partners. Having engaged in a partnership with authoritarian Arab regimes in the past, it has been challenged severely by the pace of change in some Arab countries and the bitterness and persistence of internal conflict in others. The performance of the European Union is analysed here against four criteria. Leadership and strategy are seen to have been lacking; the discourse has become more consistent over time; and the legitimacy of the response still hangs in the balance. The reputation of the EU in southern countries undergoing reform is affected by the recentness of democratic prioritization and the limitations of the support given thus far, which does not amount to a fundamental reconsideration of Euro-Mediterranean structural relationships as sought by Arab partners.

Introduction

The European Neighbourhood Policy (ENP) has been the fundamental vehicle of response of the EU to the challenges posed by the so-called 'Arab Spring'.[1] This has been a result of the pressures on European policy-makers to respond quickly to fast-moving events in its southern neighbourhood. At the outset of the Tunisian uprising in December 2010, there was simply no other regional framework fit for

---

1   This chapter draws upon interviews with EU officials in March 2011 and January 2012.

purpose. The Union for the Mediterranean (UfM), created in 2008 and weighed down by dysfunctional institutions, had not got off the ground; and in any case had focused on large-scale technical projects while effectively taking democratization off the Euro-Mediterranean agenda (Bicchi and Gillespie 2012; Gillespie 2011a). Compounding its lack of impact was the stigma of having Egyptian president Hosni Mubarak occupy its southern co-presidency right up to his fall from power. The UfM had effectively replaced the Euro-Mediterranean Partnership (EMP), also known as the Barcelona Process, leaving scattered remnants in isolated areas of activity, such as inter-cultural dialogue and inter-parliamentary collaboration.

Despite this sorry state of fragmentation, there was no mood in the EU to innovate at the multilateral level when faced with the new challenges arising along the southern rim of the Mediterranean. France had invested so heavily and Sarkozy so personally in the UfM that a reform initiative would have been perceived then as a rebuff; meanwhile, potential alternative policy entrepreneurs such as Spain were preoccupied with financial crises and in no state to offer leadership.

In contrast, the bilaterally-based ENP was already six months into a policy review by December 2010. As the events in the Arab world unfolded, it seemed logical simply to revisit the emerging proposals and add new emphases in response to the prospect of regime change in the south. Thus the first communication to be considered by EU institutions, calling for 'A Partnership for Democracy and Shared Prosperity with the Southern Mediterranean' in March 2011 (European Commission/High Representative 2011a) was largely ENP in substance. Less than a page was devoted to 'regional and sub-regional implications', acknowledging the UfM's failure to deliver and making a bland mention of the need to reform it. This document, primarily drafted by Commission officials, received a broad welcome but was questioned on various grounds, including its use of the term 'partnership' and references to mobility partnerships and enhanced market access for southern agricultural and fisheries products (Commission interview, 22 March 2011).

More positively received within the Council was the ENP revision document, approved in May, entitled 'A New Response to a Changing Neighbourhood'. What some scholars have called the 'New ENP' or the 'ENP-plus' is an enhancement that was envisaged already when the policy was launched in 2004. Its emphasis on 'more for more' (and implicitly 'less for less') represented a response to criticisms of the original ENP's approach to conditionality rather than a specific response to the Arab Spring. Though the latter did inspire the EU to sharpen the ENP emphasis on 'differentiation' in dealing with individual neighbours, it is important to note that the revised ENP was directed towards the whole neighbourhood, southern and eastern. The idea of placing more emphasis on democracy had been intimated already by the commissioner for enlargement and neighbourhood, Štefan Füle, in October 2010 (Colombo and Tocci 2012: 84).

Owing to the pressure of events and the circumstances in which the policy response was organized, neither of these documents contained analysis of the nature of the challenge posed by the upheaval in the Arab countries, nor a strategic discussion of EU interests. A formalized discussion of such matters would have risked exacerbating the disunity surrounding CFSP. Nonetheless, the nature of the challenge is the first thing that needs to be established in any evaluation of the European response. This chapter will commence with an overview of the context before summarizing EU responses and will proceed to assess performance on the basis of four criteria – leadership, capacity for strategic action, consistency of discourse and legitimacy – proposed by Mario Telò's background (2012).

Nature of the Challenge

The outbreak of popular protest leading to attempts to achieve regime change in much of the Arab world came as a complete surprise to EU actors and observers, despite numerous warnings that the old authoritarian regimes were no guarantee of stability. It came at a time when CFSP had been losing momentum for years and the Lisbon Treaty, rather than making a positive difference, had added (initially at least) to intergovernmentalism in Europe by provoking fresh disputes, particularly over the role of the High Representative (HR) for Foreign and Security Policy/ Vice-President of the Commission and the structuring of the new European External Action Service (EEAS). Thus there was great uncertainty and disputation over how EU foreign policy should be led, with a variety of high-level actors feeling entitled to pronounce – and indeed coming under public pressure to do so – amid massive media coverage of events in North Africa.

The financial crisis placed evident constraints on the EU's ability to mobilize additional funds to support political change in its southern neighbourhood. Anyone hoping for a 'Marshall Plan' was bound to find its offer niggardly by comparison. Apart from the volume of material support, the crisis had left European foreign policy actors preoccupied with their own continent where policy became driven by narrow geo-economic considerations (Martiningui and Youngs 2011; Youngs 2011). Yet it is arguable that the main shortcomings of Europe's response were not those associated with resources. The EU was able to refocus existing lines of finance and even mobilize additional funding, mainly through European financial institutions. Where it proved most disappointing was in its capacity to act politically, as will be illustrated below.

Any discussion of shortcomings needs to consider the dimensions of the challenges emanating from the southern Mediterranean, which were both complex and formidable. The Arab Spring has not brought an inexorable tide of political change throughout the area, assisted by the collapse of an empire as in Central and Eastern Europe and producing similar outcomes in each country over a short period of time. Indeed, an already fragmented Mediterranean area has become more politically differentiated. Compared with the Eastern experience, moreover, a lack of accession prospects left the EU with less effective policy instruments with which to exert influence. Furthermore, the EU's southern neighbourhood was attracting a greater range of external actors than 20 years earlier: by now Turkey had a regional role in the eastern Mediterranean, Gulf states were showing more interest in North Africa and, with the Arab Spring as a catalyst, the League of Arab States at last seemed to be acquiring a capacity for regional diplomacy. From further afield, Russia and China also were to come into the picture, especially over Syria.

In terms of internal contestation over regime change, some uprisings took longer than others to achieve breakthroughs, while elsewhere authoritarian regimes have remained in power. Thus, rather than being able to react to a wave of successful regime change across a whole region, the EU has been trying to respond to constantly 'evolving realities'.[2] However, many European actors have been slow to grasp the contrasts in national situations. Western responses in general have been informed by perceptions of 'transitions' to which external experiences may have something to contribute, yet time has shown that the patterns seen in Tunisia and Egypt (rapid overthrow of the ruler followed by transitions, more complicated in the latter than in the former country) are not the norm and in several cases prolonged social violence has ensued (Heydemann 2012: 24). A further contrast exists between countries that are attempting a process of reform 'from above' (Morocco, Jordan) and those that have seen revolutions involving the deposition of a ruler.

The notion of different 'rhythms' of regime change in the southern neighbourhood, used by former Spanish foreign minister Trinidad Jiménez to justify her country's engagement with the Syrian regime long after other EU states had broken with it,[3] had as its dubious premise the notion that all Arab countries were at different stages of 'democratization' processes. In reality, the EU was faced with some situations in which rulers attempted to hang on to power doggedly through a massive use of repression and with external assistance – as exemplified by Syria, where there was also the prospect of conflict becoming regionalized through spill-over.

ENP Support for Arab Spring

EU responses to the events in the Arab world can be judged at different levels, in terms of political positioning, material aid aspects and actual interventions that go beyond diplomacy. At the start of the Arab Spring, the European reaction needed to be immediate, consistent and substantial, but also to show recognition of its significance and empathy with those seeking to achieve change. The EU, however, has not shown itself capable – in terms of coherence and leadership – to produce such a response and its early reactions caused confusion. While cautious, 'moderate' messages may have been understandable while power still lay in the balance in Tunisia, the EU gave the impression to North Africans that it did not

---

2   Štefan Füle, 'One Year after the Arab Spring', Committee on Foreign Affairs, European Parliament, 24 January 2012, SPEECH/12/33.

3   *El País* (Madrid), 6 March 2011.

know which side to back, whereas verbal US support for the uprising came much more quickly. Colouring perceptions of the EU role was the individual response of France, whose leaders offered security equipment to the embattled Ben Ali regime while blocking European condemnation of regime violence against the people (Driss 2012: 100–1; Heydemann 2012: 22).

Eventually, when support was expressed, it failed to capture the historic dimensions of what was happening, to express real regret for European partnerships with the old rulers of North Africa or to promise an exceptional level of commitment in order to open a new chapter in Euro-Arab relations. Getting Tunisia 'right' was especially important because it was in the vanguard and represented, in European perceptions, a country with relatively strong prospects of democratization. While some speeches by EU leaders were more uplifting than others, the High Representative often sounded as if she were addressing fellow officials in Brussels and did not even present the basic European offer of 'money, mobility and markets' particularly well. Local expectations may have been unrealistically high, but the announcement by Catherine Ashton in Tunis in February 2011 of initial support of just €17 million in emergency aid and €258 million by the end of 2013 produced local disappointment and was publicly ridiculed by one Tunisian minister (Driss 2012: 101; Eurobusiness.com 15 February 2011; Euractiv.com 18 February 2011).

The EU has been able to offer a modest increase in funding for the Mediterranean southern rim countries, without any European belt-tightening. Apart from the reallocation of aid expenditure, most of the revised package has come from extending the scope of EIB and EBRD operations southwards. The main elements of ENP enhancement in the year following the Tunisian rising may be summarized as follows:[4]

1. An addition to the EU budget of €1.2 billion in ENP funding in general for 2011–13.
2. €350 million for the SPRING programme adopted in September 2011, for southern neighbours undergoing transition 'to strengthen their emerging democratic institutions, to protect deep and sustainable democracy and to improve inclusive growth and job creation'.
3. A €1 billion addition to EIB funds for the southern neighbourhood and extension of the EBRD lending mandate to the same area, potentially for another €2.5 billion.
4. A new Civil Society Facility with €22 million for 2011–12 to be shared equally between South (especially Tunisia, Libya, Egypt) and East, one priority being to enhance women's rights. Involvement of civil society organizations in political dialogue and in EU neighbourhood activities.
5. A European Endowment for Democracy (EED) to be created by the end of 2012 with the aim of assisting political institutional development at

---

4 Štefan Füle, 'One Year after the Arab Spring', Committee on Foreign Affairs, European Parliament, 24 January 2012, SPEECH/12/33.

grassroots level, where necessary expeditiously, implying a structure with some autonomy from EU institutions.

6. Cooperation with the Council of Europe through a €4.8 million programme to support the building of political institutions, starting in Tunisia and Morocco.
7. Facilitation of 'progressive and deep economic integration with the EU internal market' by negotiating 'deep and comprehensive free trade areas', initially with Egypt, Jordan, Morocco and Tunisia.
8. As a step towards this, bilateral agreements to liberalize trade in agricultural products (approved by the European Parliament for Morocco in February 2012; Tunisia next in line).
9. Dialogues with Tunisia and Morocco on migration, mobility and security, leading to mobility partnerships from October 2011. Additional Erasmus Mundi grants to fund academic exchanges.

Most of these elements represent continuity with existing ENP provision, the only real innovation, though with origins predating the Arab Spring, being the EED. In places, this enhanced effort has had an impact on the ground, especially in Tunisia (early balance of payments assistance, an EU presence in the elections, engagement with civil society, etc.). However, the EU's readiness to respond to change in the Arab world faces internal dissension over the structural aspects of Euro-Mediterranean relations. Having spoken about trade liberalization in agriculture for decades, the EU remains deeply divided over the issue. The agreement with Morocco was approved by the European Parliament with a rather modest majority (369-225 with 31 abstentions);[5] and with certain member states having resisting strongly at first, the prospects of more general trade concessions to southern Mediterranean neighbours remain uncertain. Morocco and Tunisia may end up as exceptionally privileged.

A further crucial test is posed by the misnamed 'mobility partnerships'. Of the three 'M's, (money, market, mobility) mobility is the one that holds most appeal for young North Africans, eager for opportunities to work or study abroad at a time when youth unemployment in Arab countries has been double the world level, at around 30 per cent in 2005–6 (Murphy 2012: 9). Yet in practice the EU appears to be more discriminating with its actual market and mobility offers than it is with money. For the moment, enhanced mobility is only in prospect for Morocco and Tunisia, the former with an existing record of cooperation with the EU in migration management and the latter with only a small population (just under 11 million). Despite the talk of fostering people-to-people contact, the EU framing of cooperation links mobility and migration essentially to security. Officially, mobility partnerships are intended to 'help develop comprehensive and balanced cooperation in the management of regular migration, irregular migration,

---

5   ENPI News, 16 February 2012.

readmission, visa, international protection, borders and security matters'.[6] Although opportunities to study abroad have increased and visa-free travel for business may be following, the greater emphasis has been on preventing irregular migration to Europe, with mobility partners expected to play an enhanced role in policing northward migration, in return for limited concessions for their own nationals. As Colombo and Tocci (2012: 91) observe, the limited mobility on offer may not provide sufficient incentive for southern parties to really take on the costs associated with readmission and border controls. Driss (2012: 108) goes further in his critique, referring to the proposed trade-off as 'one-way conditionality'.

Overall, it is important to note the increased emphasis on differentiation and conditionality. The title of the March 2011 Commission/High Representative document implied a political partnership only with countries genuinely seeking to democratize. This implied putting some Mediterranean polities into a grey category while including and excluding others. The ENP logic, however, remains one of keeping doors open, even to countries that showed initial disinterest (Algeria) or failed to qualify in the past (Libya), unless repression becomes so extreme that any degree of partnership proves unsustainable (Syria). The Algerian case may provide some vindication for the ENP in that finally, though influenced more by the Arab Spring than by the EU offer, a more positive attitude towards the Neighbourhood Policy emerged in Algiers in 2011,[7] followed by unprecedented European (and other international) observation of the Algerian parliamentary elections in May 2012.[8]

What has changed has been the preparedness to use negative conditionality in the form of withdrawing support or applying sanctions when faced with regimes that forcibly resist pressures for political change from popular movements. This has been accompanied by a new interest in establishing bona fides with opposition forces before they come to power and some relaxation of the EU's traditional concern about Islamist movements, further reassurance having come from constructive early exchanges with electorally-successful Islamist parties in Tunisia and Morocco.

Differentiation is certainly a precondition for effectiveness in a more politically fragmented Mediterranean, but it does not guarantee equal effectiveness in different situations. The EU was internally divided over its reaction to regime massacres in Syria, where wider international and regional considerations came strongly into the equation. It seemed to be even more uncertain about policy towards Egypt, at least until the election of Mohamed Morsi in June 2012. Here the EU was faced with a still powerful army with which it had no leverage; meanwhile it had little ability

---

6 Štefan Füle, 'One Year after the Arab Spring', Committee on Foreign Affairs, European Parliament, 24 January 2012, SPEECH/12/33.

7 EEAS interview, January 2012.

8 Visiting Algeria in March 2012, Füle expressed 'full support' for Algeria's official reform process and promised additional allocations under the SPRING programme in the hope of encouraging a transition from above (ENPI News, 20 March 2012).

to court emerging elites by means of economic assistance, given the vastness of the national development challenges compared with those of Tunisia. In view of these considerations, one can understand why some EU officials had advocated concentrating support on Tunisia, hoping that democratization there would make it an inspiration for other southern Mediterranean countries.

Assessing Performance

The experience of early EU responses to the Arab Spring has provided little reassurance that the EU may be regaining momentum towards a more effective foreign policy. At most it has managed to harness existing resources at a time of persisting intergovernmentalism and financial crisis, with the EEAS still in its infancy. Eventual improvements should not be ruled out. However, the weakness of the European response to political transition and ongoing confrontation in Arab countries has proved costly to the EU's reputation already. While the EU's responses have been based largely on the ENP – a policy envisaging the Mediterranean space as a European neighbourhood – the reality is that actors for change there have been asserting their own identities and demands and calling for more balanced North–South relationships.

The limitations of the EU response to the Arab Spring are evident against all of the four criteria being used here to evaluate performance.

Leadership

First, leadership has been lacking, especially during the early weeks following the Tunisian rising. Notwithstanding the existence of a High Representative under the Lisbon Treaty, EU responses were subject to laborious internal negotiations and complicated by initial fuzziness regarding the roles of the political figures heading the EEAS. The most consistent voice in addressing the Arab Spring was that of a foreign policy professional, Štefan Füle, yet at the end of the day, he was only a Commissioner, one voice among several in the EU and its member states, including that of a High Representative with no previous track record in foreign policy or of holding elected political office. At times, other EU representatives tried to go further in terms of critical political dialogue with Mediterranean southern rim's governments, notably Jerzy Buzek, president of the European Parliament. Joining in the EU congratulations of Morocco for the outcome of elections in November 2011, he urged its authorities to put citizens at the centre of reform and suggested that electoral participation would have been higher if there had been 'a swifter and more inclusive democratic transition'.[9] In contrast, Füle was to express the EU's

---

9   ENPI News, 28 November 2011.

'full support' for the Algerian 'reform process' based on a transition from above, even ahead of the parliamentary elections in May 2012.[10]

More generally, disagreements over the methodology and organization of democracy promotion and support have been evident in ENP discussions concerning the planned European Endowment for Democracy, arising from a Polish rotating Presidency proposal. Lukewarm attitudes on the part of the Commission and High Representative seemed implicit in scant references to it in pronouncements made by Ashton and Füle, and a minority of member states also expressed reservations.[11] Some Commission officials felt that the existing European Initiative for Democracy and Human Rights (EIDHR) could be reformed to serve the same purpose and that the proposed EED would end up relying heavily on Commission funding, given the disappointing level of contributions pledged by member states.[12]

The more fundamental deficits in leadership, however, came from autonomous member state initiatives, as national leaders became impatient with lethargic responses from Brussels to situations demanding urgency. France, in particular, with special domestic political interest as well as Mediterranean influence at stake in the aftermath of the Arab Spring, acted autonomously on two occasions: in March 2011, by ignoring the Schengen agreement and treating asylum seekers as illegal immigrants when migrants from Tunisia reached Lampedusa in substantial numbers and Italy facilitated their onward journey to France (Driss 2012: 102); and in responding to incipient civil war in Libya and Colonel Qaddafi's brutal response to insurgency. With Germany opposed to military intervention and other member states insisting on difficult preconditions, it was France, and not the EU, that called the conference in Paris on 19 March 2011 to consider such a response, and France and Britain that proceeded to push for intervention by means of a coalition of the willing, reliant on NATO/US support. President Obama made it clear that he expected the EU to take responsibility for its own backyard, yet was presented initially with further evidence of European intergovernmental division (and not least French–German disunity), combined with what one commentator has called an 'opportunistic quest for influence' on the part of France (Mikail 2011).

A Strategic Approach?

There is little evidence of strategy to be found in EU responses to the Arab Spring. More clearly these have been marked by improvisation and, at a time of austerity, by substantial resort to existing policy provision (Gillespie 2012: 212–15). EU activity has been criticized for lacking a vision of what it would like the southern Mediterranean to look like in the future (Youngs 2011: 3). The policy documents cited above were notable for the absence of 'self-criticism and political, strategic thinking' (Soler i Lecha and Viilup 2011: 5). Some veterans of EU Mediterranean

10   ENPI News, 20 March 2012.
11   Global Europe Morning Brief, 1 December 2011.
12   European Commission interview, 13 January 2012.

policy hark back to the days of former external relations commissioner Chris Patten, 20 years ago, for anything of that sort.[13]

The EU has even been inconsistent in defining the Euro-Mediterranean space in which it wishes to build a partnership, as shown by the contrasts in geographical scope between the EMP, UfM and ENP. Perplexity regarding EU objectives is often expressed in the South. North Africans are well aware of the EU's normative discourse but often call for a more honest and transparent expression of EU interests.[14]

Debate in the EU about European interests remains inconclusive, hampering the development of strategic behaviour. Senior representatives acknowledge that Europe is 'continuously struggling to keep its values and interests as close as possible in dealing with Southern neighbourhood' (*sic*).[15] They have identified two key objectives: to support partners who undertake reforms towards 'deep democracy, rule of law and human rights' and 'inclusive economic and social development'; and 'to develop a partnership with societies alongside our relations with governments'.[16] However, over conditionality there is internal divergence over two questions: how far reformist southern partners are expected to actually deliver before being 'rewarded', and whether negative forms of conditionality really serve European interests. Critics see the ENP as being 'trapped in the logic of enlargement' and maintain that the EU is seriously underestimating the costs to Mediterranean neighbours of entering into securitized mobility partnerships (Colombo and Tocci 2012: 90–1), especially in view of the upheavals that some countries have gone through.

Further curbing the potential for strategic action, the early years under the Lisbon Treaty have seen unclear systems of line-management now that the EEAS exists alongside the externally-oriented directorates of the Commission. With the latter's position in EU Mediterranean policy returning to pre-eminence as a result of such heavy recent reliance on the ENP, officials within DG Development and Cooperation have been likened to a parallel diplomatic service. Within the EEAS one hears complaints about the 'chequebook mentality' of Commission officials and the 'unsuitability' of many of their own personnel – especially those nominated recently by Eastern member states who lack the ethos of recruits coming from the Brussels policy community.[17] While some internal criticism may reflect the personal grievances of officials who lost out under the implementation of the Lisbon Treaty, it is clear that external relations remains a domain of EU activity lacking in cohesion and streamlining.

---

13   Interview with EEAS officials, 12 January 2012.

14   Interviews with diplomats from three Arab countries, Brussels, March 2010.

15   Štefan Füle, 'One Year after the Arab Spring', Committee on Foreign Affairs, European Parliament, 24 January 2012, SPEECH/12/33.

16   Ibid.

17   Personal interviews, Brussels, January 2012.

The specific case of the Mediterranean is no exception and the failings are particularly marked insofar as the UfM is concerned. Even when in February 2012, after two years of arguments, agreement was reached that the EU would replace France in the northern part of its co-presidency,[18] the actual arrangement involved having no less than five different configurations in representation of the EU: the HR at foreign ministers level, the HR and Commission representative for ministerial meetings on matters of exclusive EU competence (e.g. trade), the rotating President of the Council of Ministers for ministerial meetings on matters of member-state competence, the Commission in 'full cooperation' with the rotating Presidency for meetings dealing with mixed competence issues, and the EEAS for meetings of senior officials.[19]

A Consistent Discourse?

Consistency in EU pronouncements on developments has grown since the start of the Arab Spring. Early on, the call for a 'Partnership for Democracy and Shared Prosperity' in March 2011 had the purpose of initiating a policy discussion and thus there was bound to be some modification of policy emphases, at least until the more definitive ENP revision document was approved two months later. One must remember also that the earlier of these documents addressed the challenges of the southern Mediterranean whereas the later one was concerned with the neighbourhood as a whole.

That said, there continue to be underlying incoherencies in the EU's Mediterranean policy, dating back to the origins of the Barcelona Process. The logics underlying this policy have been variously interpreted by academics (Attinà 2003; Solingen and Şenses Ozyrt 2006) as being driven either by security considerations or by neo-liberal economic thinking. Discourse analysis of EU pronouncements since the start of the Arab insurrections continues to reflect this divergence. Thus, while Hollis (2012) and Driss (2012) primarily see evidence of security motivation in EU responses to the Arab Spring, and Colombo and Tocci (2012) perceive a shifting emphasis towards democracy promotion still accompanied by security concerns, Reynaert (2011) finds promotion of a market-based economy as fundamental to the EU positions on civil society, the functioning of the state and democracy promotion.

The original Barcelona Process was ambitiously wide-ranging in scope. Different logics, in some tension with one another, were encapsulated in its differentiated three (later four) 'basket' approach (a political and security partnership, an economic and financial partnership, a partnership in social, cultural and human affairs and eventually justice and home affairs). While the replacement of the EMP by the UfM in 2008 brought concentration on the second of these areas,

---

18 Established in the name of co-ownership, this is the key respect in which the UfM differs from the Eastern Partnership.

19 Global Europe Morning Brief, 1 March 2012.

a broader agenda has been evident once more in EU responses to the Arab Spring – although, with Euro-Mediterranean relations lacking support from a functioning multilateral framework, the components have lacked overall coordination and integration (between the UfM, Commission programmes, Parliamentary Assembly, Anna Lindh Foundation for the Dialogue between Cultures, etc.). With such a range of activity and actors, there is inevitably much potential for tension within the European discourse relating to the southern Mediterranean. This could be exacerbated, for example, if radical Islamist agendas were to prevail eventually in countries such as Egypt or Algeria. The EU's current insistence on respecting the outcome of elections[20] (in contrast to its position on Algeria two decades ago) might then be difficult to reconcile with the increased European emphasis now being placed on the rights of women.

Legitimacy

The legitimacy of EU policy in the southern Mediterranean might reasonably be expected to be enhanced by some aspects of its response to the Arab Spring. First, the focus on democracy is now much more central to overall European activity in the region. In a sense, the EU's normative discourse has been 'validated' by the way in which Arab mass movements have embraced notions of democracy that are commonly held in Europe. Second, EU efforts to incorporate civil society representatives into cooperation activity and dialogue may help give legitimacy to European initiatives. Third, even when military action came into discussion as a result of the Libyan crisis, those European leaders who pressed for intervention took care to obtain a green light from the League of Arab States before moving to deployment.

Yet, one cannot expect a scenario of enhanced EU legitimacy to unfold simply as a consequence of such considerations. It may not be enough to try to appear to be making a new start, when there is such substantial continuity in the ENP fundamentals of European policy and in security concerns. The EU has done little to express regret for its traditional relationship with authoritarian rulers. As recently as 2007, Nicolas Sarkozy was trying to promote his Mediterranean Union proposal by making speeches in North Africa celebrating the colonial relationship with France (Rubio Plo 2008: 4).

Moreover, the prospect of deriving fresh legitimacy from current EU support for democratization in the South may well suffer from southern disappointment with the level of European material support. This is not simply a matter of new governments coming to power with inflated expectations of aid: it is a matter also of civil society being disappointed with European actors, especially in those North African countries where EU policy is lacking impact on the ground. Egyptian NGOs have lamented the EU's failure to react more strongly to regime attacks on them since the fall of Mubarak. Indeed, receipt of European aid has become

---

20   For example, Füle's speech in Munich, reported in ENPI News, 3 February 2012.

something of a stigma in Egypt, leading some organizations to seek alternative sources of support. European influence may indeed be declining in civil society as other sources of support are found elsewhere. Finally, legitimacy may be impaired as a result of ultimately unsuccessful attempts to support regime change, as risked happening in Syria.

Conclusion

Any assessment of EU responses to the Arab Spring must be somewhat provisional, given that we are analysing such recent and ongoing events. One needs to be wary of placing too much reliance simply on policy documents and statements, though these have certainly attracted monopolized much of the scrutiny thus far, given that actions on the ground inevitably require more time to research. Both discourse and practical activity need to be considered in any overall judgements.

The evidence offered here suggests that *leadership* and *strategy* have been the main EU weaknesses, sorely lacking in EU responses to the turbulent events in the Arab world; *discourse* has been more consistent, but perhaps at too superficial a level; and *legitimacy* may still be in the balance.

There remain issues concerning the policy framework. The EU has relied to a great extent on the ENP as its vehicle of response. Yet is the ENP enough? Future consideration of how to maintain and enhance European influence in the southern Mediterranean will need to focus on the challenge of coordinating all aspects of EU Mediterranean policy through an integrated framework, if synergies are to be exploited. Moreover, the web of bilateral North–South relationships encompassed in the ENP may face criticism from elected south Mediterranean authorities as a form of divide and rule. To the extent that politically transformed Arab countries may improve their own coordination, one can expect demands from the South for a new multilateral framework that the EU would need to respond to.

Chapter 8

Inter-Regionalism as a Coherent and Intelligible Instrument in the EU Foreign Policy Toolbox: A Comparative Assessment

Frederik Ponjaert

Abstract

As the European level's impact on the international stage has grown, a commensurate body of literature and commentary has emerged seeking to describe and assess such a novel kind of macro-regional actor. Interest in the external action capabilities of the European regional edifice has only increased as its distinctive brand of regional governance through deep institutional cooperation gained new significance in the face of rapidly mounting global systemic interdependencies. When interacting with its near and far abroad the EU deploys a set of specific policy tools which reflect both its political goals as well as the inherent opportunities and limits of its *sui generis* type of polity. With this distinctive toolbox, inter-regional partnerships occupy a crucial and symptomatic position. Treaty after treaty, as a structural feature of the EU's external action, inter-regional initiatives have echoed each of the advances (and lemons) associated with the EU's ever more complex foreign policy machinery. The comparative analysis of the growing number of inter-regional initiatives launched by the EU confirms the ever growing scope of the EU's external action and the concomitant 'capability–expectation gap' this came to cultivate. As an answer to this dilemma the TEU/TFEU introduced a series of institutional changes focused on enhancing both the legitimacy and efficiency of the Union's external action. However, the same comparative exercises shows that these reforms have not meant a qualitative jump, but rather a deepening of prevailing tendencies within the EU's inter-regionalism: (1) strong constituency with the EU's overall political goals; (2) an inter-regional narrative dominated by Eurocentric tendencies which foster regular inconsistencies; (3) a marginally improved horizontal policy coherence within each interregional platform through bureaucratic streamlining but at the costs of higher inward looking-ness; and finally a de facto division of labour between the members of the emerging three-headed foreign policy leadership. Group-to-group relations thus increasingly echo one of these agendas: economic (global) governance within the PEC, enhanced actorness for the EU within the offices of the HR/EEAS and the preservation of its key supranational prerogatives within the EC.

Introduction

Repeatedly the international environment has acted as a further catalyst for the European institutions' decade-old endogenously-driven evolution towards joining the ranks of fully-fledged established international actors. Over the course of its first five decades of existence, the EC/EU slowly emerged as an idiosyncratic yet universally recognized international actor in its own right. However, this remarkable emergence of a macro-regional grouping as an institutionalized and widely acknowledged global partner did not occur without highlighting certain challenges or shortcomings. The challenges facing the EU's external action are consistently either cast in terms of its inadequate external actorness (e.g. Cooper et al. 2007: 1); or in light of an ill-managed 'Expectations–Capability Gap' (Hill 1993).

Be it in terms of the limitations facing the EU's external actorness – i.e. the recognition of its regioness, purposefulness and distinctive presence of its actions (Hettne 2007: 110); or the disconnect between the expectations the EU fosters and the competences it brings to bear (Hill 1998: 18–38); the crucial challenge facing the EU as a diplomatic actor is the assessment of the ultimate efficiency and legitimacy of the foreign policy outcomes born from its unique 'dialectic process between endogenous and exogenous [macro-regional] forces' (Hettne 2007: 111). Accordingly, as the EU's foreign policy machinery has grown – both in scope and complexity, challenges to its effectiveness or legitimacy have mainly crystallized around questions pertaining to the perceived lack of coherence and/or intelligibility of its foreign policy's underlying dialectic.

Bearing these two features in mind – i.e. coherence and intelligibility – this chapter will seek to contribute towards this book's overall assessment of the legitimacy and efficiency of the EU's Foreign Policy and Diplomatic Action in light of the changes wrought by the Lisbon Treaty (TEU/TFEU); it will comparatively examining one of the EC/EU's most recurring and distinctive foreign policy platforms: inter-regional relations.

As the EC/EU became ever more active in a growing number of fields and arenas, it developed a wide array of foreign policy relations (FPRs). Accordingly, the EU's external policies have become ever more tailored towards their specific target constituencies: (1) enlargement logics when dealing with the perceived core of Europe; (2) stabilization and partnership mechanisms in the EU's so-called neighbourhood or near-abroad (see Chapter 7 in this volume); (3) bilateralism with regards to strategically significant states, notably emergent global powers (see Chapters 9, 10, 11 and 12 in this volume); and (4) inter-regionalism with respect to other regional groupings; be it within the framework of its neighbourhood policy when dealing with its near abroad (Ponjaert and Bardaro forthcoming; Seidelmann 2009) or as a stand alone policy platform in its far abroad (Santander and Ponjaert 2009).

When considering the EU's far abroad over 'the last decade[s] interregional cooperation in particular has become an important component of EU foreign policy and external relations. This foreign policy doctrine is deeply rooted in the

European Commission and has [consistently] been expressed by leading politicians and policy-makers. The policy is realized through a large number of inter-regional arrangements with other regions around the world, particularly in Africa, Asia and Latin America' (Hettne and Söderbaum 2005: 535). Macro-regional group-to-group relations are therefore understood to be both emblematic and symptomatic of the EU's expanding external action agenda. Their comparative analysis will thus shed further light on the changing coherence and intelligibility of the EU as a foreign policy actor.

Considering the distinctiveness of inter-regionalism as a necessarily marco-regional foreign policy platform which is inevitably deployed at the macro-regional/meso-level of the multi-level international system (e.g. Hänggi 2006; Ponjaert 2008), a streamlined yet workable typology of the policies supposed coherence and intelligibility is to be favoured.

On the one hand, among the numerous existing typologies of a (external) policy's coherence (Gebhard 2011; Nugent 2003: 490; Nuttall 2005):[1] the question of the EU's inter-regionalism's *internal horizontal coherence* and *external compatibility with a given target constituency* remain; whereas that of its *internal vertical coherence* is relatively moot considering there are strictly speaking no directly competing policy initiatives at the member state (MS) level. On the other hand, the intelligibility or consistency of the EU's inter-regional agenda is reflected in its discursive and strategic cohesion (Börzel and Risse 2003; Schmidt 2008);[2] both of which are again uncommonly straightforward to locate within the EU's complex foreign policy framework since regional institutions, within or beyond the EU, are the only possible principled policy platforms for any inter-regional policy narrative. Accordingly, the following chapter will assess both the – *horizontal and external* – coherence and the – *strategic and discursive* – consistency of the EU's inter-regional foreign policy initiatives over time and with regards to different target regions.

The EU amidst other Regional Groupings: Lone Wolf or Pack Animal?

Have inter-regional initiatives over time effectively left the EU isolated on the international stage? Or have they proven to be valuable platforms able to forward the EU's external agenda? As the number of regional groupings has consistently continued to rise over the past decades (see Figure 8.1), the EC/EU foreign policy machinery has had to assess and react to this evolution. Inter-regionalism has thus emerged as a structural and distinctive feature of the EC/EU's standing foreign policy toolbox. The strategic underpinnings, prevailing narratives and institutional

---

1   For further detail on the discussions regarding the coherence of the EU's external action please see Chapter 6 in this volume.

2   For further detail regarding the discursive and strategic consistency within the EU's emerging foreign policy machinery please consider both Chapters 4 and 5 in this volume.

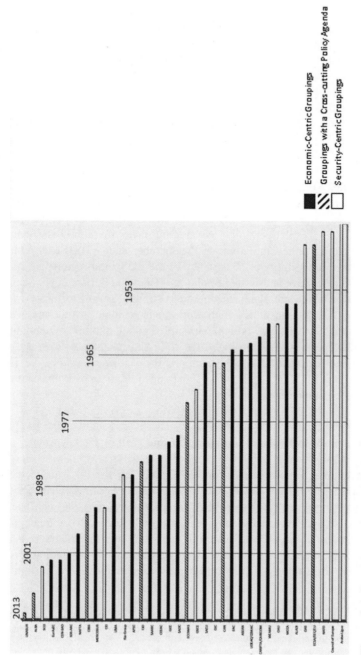

Figure 8.1 Genealogy of Existing Regional Groupings

Table 8.1 Chronological list of inter-regional relations entertained by the EEC/EU

		Period	Wave	Bilateral with (strategic) state	Group-to-group with other regional organizations	Group-to-group with other regional grouping
Cold War – bipolarity	Actor-specific inter-regionalism	1970s		EEC-Canada (1976) EEC-PRC (1978)	EEC-ASEAN (1972/8)	EEC-ACP (1975)
		1980s	US-centric regionalism	EEC-PRC (1985)	EEC-ASEAN (1980) EEC-CAN (1980/3) EEC-SICA (1983) EEC-SADC (1986) EEC-Rio Group (1987) EEC-GCC (1988)	
Hastened globalization – unipolar moment	New inter-regionalism geared towards systemic challenges	1989–97	First wave of new regionalism	EU-Canada (1990/6) EU-Japan (1991) EU-Chile (1996) EU-RoK (1996)	EU-CAN (1992/6) EU-SAARC (1994/6) EU-SICA (1996) EU- MERCOSUR +2 (1992/95)	EU-ARF (1993) Euromed (1995) ASEM (1996)
		1997–2007	Second wave of new regionalism	EU-PRC (1998) EU-USA (1998) EU-Mexico (1998/2000) EU-India (2000) EU-Indonesia (2000) EU-Japan (2001)	EU-MERCOSUR+2 (1998) EU-ECOWAS (2000)	ASEM (1998/2000/2/4/6) EU-LAC (1999) EU-ACP (2000)
Strained global governance – heightened multipolarity	Complex hybrid	2007–	Competitive regionalism	[EPA] EU-RoK (2010) EU-Japan (2011)	[EPA] EU-CARICOM (2007)	EU-MERCOSUR (2007) EU-AU (2007) UfM (2008) ASEM (2008/10/12) EU-LAC (2010)

set-ups associated with said agenda will provide valuable insights into some of the endogenous dynamics shaping the EU's foreign policy dialectic.

A Component of the EU's Strategic Response to Structural Challenges

Quite soon after the initial steps towards a European region-wide attempt at external action, the European Commission (EC) sought to bank on its specific trade and development competences to start sketching the initial contours of an inter-regional agenda. Before the end of the 1970s the first set of trade and/or development-centric interregional agreements were launched and signed by the EC. In 1975 partnership between a standing regional organization such as the EEC and an ad hoc purpose-built African-Caribbean-Pacific Countries (ACP) regional grouping was ushered into existence. And in 1972/8 two standing regional organizations, the EEC and the Association of South East Asian Nations (ASEAN), were the first to agree to a partnership linking to pre-existing regional entities. Unsurprisingly, as a logical outshoot of regionalism, inter-regionalism has seen its fortunes linked to the ebb and flow of regional groupings. As such each increase in the number of regional actors has been echoed by a comparable rise in compatible forms of inter-regionalism (Doidge 2011: 1–31). Accordingly, the EC consistently developed its inter-regional agenda in accordance with the successive waves of regionalism which characterized the last 50 years (Telò 2007: 2–4).

Considering it has been a stable feature of the European Institutions' foreign policy mix; inter-regionalism – both as a strategic outlook as well as a policy platform – is a consistent and manifest component of the EU's external action.

However, if inter-regionalism has from the onset been a structural component of the EEC/EU's strategic outlook, the number of institutionalized relations – either between regional organizations or among groups of states from two or more regions – has grown exponentially since the early 1990s. 'At present, almost all regions and sub-regions are engaged in some sort of institutionalized interregional activities' (Hänggi 2006: 31). Said proliferation of inter-regional relations coincides with the collapse of the bipolar world order which in turn unleashed major economic forces – be it of globalization or regionalization – which would ultimately lead to a restructuring of the international system. The heightening of the aforementioned interdependencies – which contributed towards undermining the effective control of the nation state whilst also limiting the range of legitimate policy choices – favoured post-hegemonic foreign policy thinking geared towards governance-centric readings of the global system rooted in civilian forms of power (Telò 2005). As such, the multiplication of inter-regional initiatives supported by the EU is both a product of the more heterogeneous and fluid systemic reality its foreign policy must navigate; and a consistent feature of the EU's specific strategic response to the new global system. It is a clear and unwavering option in favour of multi-level (effective) multilateralism (Telò 2012). The repeated appeal to inter-regional foreign policy platforms is therefore both the product and expression of the EU's overall political agenda.

As such the incipient web of treaty/agreement-based inter-regional relations cultivated by the EC/EU consistently reflect Europeans' preferences for a world governed by international law and multilateral institutions rather than a mere balance of powers. 'One might say that if the U.S. was the sheriff of the liberal order, the European Union was its constitutional court' (Leonard 2012). In that spirit, group-to-group agreements are seen as open-ended platforms able to better socialize third parties into the global multilateral system, whilst also defensively buttressing the system's existing institutions and practices (Rüland 2006).

The general political strategy in favour of multilateralism has remained unchanged following the near concomitant entry into force of the TEU/TFEU and the sudden degradation of the EU's economic situation which is likely to constrain its performance in multilateral diplomacy for the better part of the Treaty's foundational years. The EU continues to push further institutionalization and multilateralization of international relations, be it from a less comfortable and more defensive position.

European diplomatic daily routine (e.g. participation in international organizations and global governance structures), as well as the occasional diplomatic brinkmanship (e.g. the relatively successful 2011 UN talks which made some progress towards a legally binding deal on carbon emissions) remain largely wedded to a multilateral strategic outlook, and inter-regional contacts are consistently exploited to buttress the wider multilateral agenda. If the office of the High Representative has shown a relatively smaller interest in such strategic multilateralism, notably through a relative marginalization of the notion of 'effective multilateralism' (Gowan 2011), the other major office created by the Lisbon Treaty – i.e. the Council Presidency – has invested heavily in the global multilateral governance agenda, and by extension in inter-regional avenues.

As such, inter-regional initiatives have enjoyed something of a revival – be it a defensive tactical one – following the introduction of the TEU/TFEU. The newly minted offices of the Council Presidency have opted to be singularly focused on the dissemination and socialization of the EU's preferred options regarding Global Economic Governance.[3] Besides these new more visible and actor-centred initiatives laden with the political ambitions of the Council Presidency; the web of system-centred group-to-group contacts largely engineered by the European Commission has prevailed. When provided with a consistent input from the Commission driven components of the EU's external action, these inter-regional partnerships have effectively continued to flourish. However, if the European

---

3   For example see the ASEM 8 – Brussels Declaration on More Effective Global Economic Governance: Towards More Effective Global Economic Governance, 5 October 2012, Brussels – see http://www.asem8.be/sites/1226.fedimbo.belgium.be/files/asem_8_-_brussels_declaration_on_more_effective_global_economic_governance.pdf; or the EU-LAC Summit Madrid Speech by Herman Van Rompuy, President of the European Council, at the closing ceremony, 18 May 2010 – see http://www.consilium.europa.eu/uedocs/cms_Data/docs/pressdata/en/ec/114523.pdf.

Commission can still claim to be a major force behind the expansion of such dynamics, it can no longer claim sole sponsorship of an increasingly heterogeneous inter-regional playing field (Hänggi 2006: 32).

Inter-regionalism has proven a stalwart component of the EU's underlying strategic goals, and has as such consistently been developed within each specific systemic context the European Institutions have had to function in. The commitment to new civilian forms of power deployed within a post-hegemonic multilateral and multi-level rules-based system remains the fundamental strategic goal of the EU. Inter-regionalism is understood as a continuation thereof. The innovation introduced by the TEU/TFEU, notably the multiplication of high level institutionalized foreign policy actors on the European stage, has not altered the fundamental strategic coherence of the EU's approach to inter-regionalism; but by way of a relative form of burden-sharing it has allowed the EU's institutions to simultaneously develop different forms of inter-regionalism in terms of causal factors – 'specific type of actor (agency) [apparently aspired to by the Council Presidency], versus the continued commitment to systemic change (structure) [on the Commission's behalf]' (Hänggi 2006: 33). If the EU's strategic commitment towards inter-regionalism has been consistent over time, the matter of its foreign policy discourse on this topic is muddled.

Self-Indulgent Narrative or Champion of Regional Cooperation?

The European institutions have a long-standing narrative regarding inter-regional relationships. However, due to its peculiar nature – which squarely positions the regional level at the centre of any such relationship, the foreign policy narrative in this area is uniquely moulded by the regional entities involved. Consequently, inter-regionalism proved a welcome and useful foreign policy theme for the European Commission as it emerged as one of the few external action areas: wherein it enjoyed a relative level of policy autonomy. From the outset, inter-regionalism was a welcome source of self-legitimization and (Eurocentric) aggrandizing; and a possible means of breaking the EC/EU's isolation on the international stage by building bridges towards other regional groupings.

As stated above, during the initial forays of the European Institutions into inter-regional foreign policy making, 'under the conditions of systemic bipolarity, interregional relations were largely confined to the European Community's (EC) so-called group-to-group dialogues with other regional organizations or groups of states' (Hänggi 2006: 32). Under the auspices of the European Commission's foreign policy initiatives, these dialogues emerged in the 1970s, and spread in the 1980s thus covering most of the European Community's far-abroad on the eve of the 1990s. These actor-centric endeavours were of little relevance to the wider global system but of great importance to its main patron: the European Commission (Regelsberger and Edwards 1990: 14). Given the fact the European Community was the most advanced regional organization, and the Commission at the time its only standing, if fragmented, foreign policy voice; this first inter-regional network was conceived of as a 'hub and spoke system' centred on Brussels and rooted in a policy narrative geared towards strengthening other regional grouping by way of 'extra-regional echoing' or mimicry (Zimmerling 1991). However, its main concern was fostering internal European coherence (Nuttall 1992: 156) and a distinctive international profile as a 'civilian power' on the international stage (Maull 1990–1).

Accordingly, initial European foreign policy discourses on inter-regionalism were very much centred on the European Commission, heavily Eurocentric in their outlook, and steeped in the self-affirming exercises the European Community was engaged in as an incipient and unprecedented type of international actor (Vanoverbeke and Ponjaert 2007). Though a major innovation in terms of foreign policy instruments, and one of the first major forays of the European Institutions into a relatively autonomous form of foreign policy, initial discourses surrounding inter-regionalism – be they academic or policy-oriented – were far removed from actual foreign policy concern. They were for the most part the product of both the EU's introspective exercise of self-definition, and the process of individuation of Europe's nascent macro-regional Polity. For the first 20 years a consistently Eurocentric narrative on inter-regionalism dominated European institutions; one which echoed the ongoing discussion on the European Community's distinctive nature as a 'civilian power' (Duchêne 1972). With regards to the Community's far abroad this was for example done by: emphasizing its preference for development-oriented relations with Latin American regional groups over US insistence on security (Crawley 2006); by vaunting the supposed transformational nature of the new EC–ACP relationship over former colonial ties (Dimier 2003); or by hypothesizing the learning benefits for supposedly less advanced regional organizations such as ASEAN (Mols 1990).

The European inter-regional foreign policy narrative underwent a substantial transformation in the wake of the end of the bipolar world; the concomitant acceleration in new regional dynamics; the rise of outward looking systemic forms of inter-regionalism; and the signature of the Maastricht Treaty which marks the advent of the EU and its three pillar structure. The 1990s thus witnessed a shift away from the European Community's previously very coherent but self-indulgent inter-regional narratives towards more complex but at times more duplicitous rhetoric.

Major new legal provisions (the second and third pillars of the EU's Maastricht Treaty structure); novel institutional arrangements (CSFP, a beefed up European Council, etc.); and a clearly stated political ambition to see the European Union play a more prominent international role all conspired in the early 1990s to fundamentally change the coherence and consistency of the EU's foreign policy. With regards to inter-regionalism this meant an explosion of new initiatives (see Table 8.1) and an increasingly ambitious inter-regional policy agenda seeking to weigh on rapidly changing diplomatic practices so as to foster a re-balancing of relative power and rule-based international relations in favour of the EU. For example, this ambitious new turn in the inter-regional discursive agenda is neatly reflected in the two founding statements which lie at the basis of the Asia-Europe Meeting (ASEM): the 1994 communication by the Commission 'Towards a New Asia Strategy' (COM 94 – 314) which details the EU's desire to see the scope of its inter-regional policies to be widened to include all aspects of international life; and the November 1994 joint political statement by Singapore and France calling for a joint EU-Asia summit clearly echoing the shared aspiration to counter-balance the perceived overweening influence of the United States in both regions (Gilson 2002). As a result, European foreign policy discourse on inter-regionalism in the 1990s evolves towards an all-encompassing narrative with transformational ambitions. However, these lofty policy statements rapidly betrayed the obvious institutional and political limits of these inter-regional platforms (Rüland 1996). The 1990s thus witnessed a growing discrepancy between the goals set out by the prevailing inter-regional discourses and the concrete actions and achievements secured. As such, inter-regional foreign policy became a poster-child for the EU's much discussed 'Expectation–Capability Gap'.

The growing confusion regarding the foreign policy discourse surrounding inter-regionalism is also reflected in the growing disagreement on the nomenclature of the growing number of cross-regional arrangements (Ponjaert 2008; Söderbaum and Van Langenhove 2005). Beyond the varying typologies – many of which were mainly sought to rehabilitate inter-regionalism through changed reference points – a growing consensus emerged over the 1990s as the dominant narrative came to identify inter-regional endeavours as heterogeneous platforms which can contribute to the management of international relations by allowing for an additional 'vehicle for this project of external relations' (Söderbaum and Van Langenhove 2005: 371). Accordingly, by the time of the introduction of the Lisbon Treaty and the crippling effects of the Eurozone crisis, the sights of most of the different components of the EU's foreign policy-making community had readjusted their expectations regarding inter-regional platforms re-framing them as policy management tools within the context of wider Global Governance dynamics.

Counter-productive dynamics within the inter-regional discourse developed within the EU have thus been addressed independently from the institutional or legal changes introduced by the Lisbon Treaty by revising the underlying political ambitions downwards. However, by addressing the challenge to the EU's foreign policy narrative on inter-regionalism solely by purging it of most of its political significance in favour of a managerial understanding, the EU's diplomatic discourse is merely trading the problem of frustration resulting from under-achievement for disinterest born from irrelevance. If after a brief period of politics without much policy, inter-regional discourse has converged with other EU foreign policy narratives by suggesting policies without politics. Changes to the EU's foreign policy machinery (legal or institutional) have made little difference to the public intelligibility and political performativity of its external action.

Overall, if structurally present and important for internal reasons, the EU's foreign policy narrative on inter-regionalism remains unreliable, fundamentally inward-looking and lacking in political ambition or drive. Recent institutional changes seem to have had little impact on this state of affairs as much of the discourse has retreated further into technocratic considerations. Internal evolutions and reactions to systemic changes have thus over time fostered a consistent and cogent interregional strategy, but its shifting inter-regional narratives have proven reliably inward-looking and disappointing. The EU's foreign policy on inter-regionalism has been steadfast over time but has neither succeeded in fostering the necessary political will, nor marshalling a constructive narrative. Having established that institutional changes, such as the introduction of major treaty changes, have had but a limited impact on the consistency of the EU's approach in these matters, the question remains if institutional and legal changes affected its horizontal coherence.

Bureaucratic Evolutions: Convergence, Adaptation and Constraint

The remaining endogenous force possibly weighing on the underlying dialectic driving the EU's foreign policy with regards to inter-regional relations are the benefits incurred from bureaucratic, legal or institutional changes formalized by way of major treaty changes.[4]

As previously discussed, up until the introduction of the TEU/TFEU most institutional changes brought with them a functional broadening of the EU's inter-regional foreign policy agenda beyond its original Commission-driven (DG Trade and DG DEVCO) focus on Trade and Aid. As a result all inter-regional arrangements set up by the EU came to include, in varying forms: a political, an economic and people-to-people pillar. This flexible, yet holistic, set-up allowed for all parties involved – both within the EU as within the partner regions – to table or quash any topic of their choice. This in turn fostered highly responsive, bottom-up dynamics which were largely tributary to the dominant foreign policy concerns formulated elsewhere. Inter-regionalism covers a group of 'nested arrangements which draw on elements from the framework of broader institutions to make them compatible while providing an element of hierarchical order' (Aggarwal 1998: 47). The contingent nature of the foreign policy agendas of inter-regional forums is therefore patently obvious as reflected in the haphazard set of topics broached at the first eight ASEM summits (see Table 8.2).

---

4   For detailed discussions regarding the recent evolutions of the EU's foreign policy bureaucracy please see Chapters 4 and 5 in this volume.

Table 8.2 Salient agenda points at the last eight ASEM meetings

	European interests	East Asian interests
ASEM 1 1996 – Bangkok	1. Profit from the **East Asian Economic Miracle** through enhanced market access 2. UN reform	1. Enhanced market access to **prevent 'fortress Europe'** 2. UN reform and balancing the United States
ASEM 2 1998 – London	1. Limiting fallout from the **East Asian Financial Crisis** 2. Value debate (*democracy and human rights*)	1. Managing the fallout from the **East Asian Financial Crisis**
ASEM 3 2000 – Seoul	1. **Institutional formats** of cooperation 2. Values debate 3. Regulatory harmonization 4. Korean Peninsula	1. **Korean Peninsula** 2. Informal formats of cooperation 3. Economic management
ASEM 4 2002 – Copenhagen	1. **Anti-terrorism** 2. **Multilateralism** 3. Values debate 4. Economic cooperation 5. Institutional cooperation formats	1. **Economic management** 2. Anti-terrorism 3. Multilateralism
ASEM 5 2004 – Hanoi	1. **Anti-terrorism** 2. Economic cooperation 3. Values debate	1. **Anti-terrorism** 2. EU enlargement 3. **ASEAN enlargement and its implications for ASEM** (*e.g. Myanmar question*)
ASEM 6 2006 – Helsinki	1. Non-proliferation 2. **Deepening of institutional cooperation formats** 3. **Values debate**	1. **Economic cooperation** 2. Non-proliferation
ASEM 7 2008 – Beijing	1. **Climate change** (i.e. 2008 Copenhagen Conference) 2. Deepening of institutional cooperation formats 3. Global governance	1. **Technology transfers** 2. Climate change (*i.e. 2008 Copenhagen Conference*) 3. Development
ASEM 8 2010 – Brussels	1. **Squaring reactions to Global Financial Crisis** 2. Global governance reform 3. **Implementing 'Lisbon Treaty'**	1. **Global institutions' rebalancing** 2. **Asian Thaw** (i.e. Japan-PRC) 3. Global growth

A further sign of contingency is the limited coherence when it comes to the preponderant bureaucratic agent on the EU side (see Table 8.3). On the whole, inter-regional platforms provide the participating foreign policy actors with a lot of policy leeway, and thus horizontal policy coherence is to be garnered from within by forceful and purposeful constituents.

Table 8.3 Salient themes and bureaucracy in inter-regional arrangements involving the EU

	Salient recurring Thematic	Seemingly dominant bureaucracy on EU side	
		Before TEU/TFEU	*After TEU/TFEU*
ASEM	Global governance	Rotating council Presidency	Council Presidency
EU-CARICOM	Trade	DG DEVCO (cf. ACP)	DG Trade
EU-MERCOSUR	Region-building (and trade)	DG RELEX	EEAS
EU-AU	Security policies	DG DEVCO (cf. ACP) & DG RELEX	EEAS (Special Envoy)
EUROMED	Neighbourhood	DG RELEX	EEAS
UfM	Global politics	/	Council (rotating) Presidency
EU-LAC	Region-building (and trade)	/	EEAS
EU-ASEAN	Trade (and region-building)	DG RELEX and DG Trade	DG Trade (blocked in 2010 in favour of bilateral EPAs)
EU-ACP	Aid and trade	DG DEVCO	DEVCO
EU-CAN	Aid and trade	DG DEVCO	DEVCO with CAN DG Trade was negotiated EPA with Peru/Colombia
EU-GCC	Trade	DG Trade	EEAS (EPA negotiations resumed by DG Trade in 2007 have advanced at a halting pace)

The gradual development of the EU's foreign policy machinery, including its inter-regional dimension, implies deeply seeded path-dependencies which explain various bureaucratic practices and accepted hierarchies. One can thus distinguish between the oldest relationships initiated either under the auspices of DG Trade or DG DEVCO. In the first case one can see despite successive institutional evolutions trade-oriented platforms remain under the relatively autonomous and supranational auspices of DG Trade, whereas the former development-oriented relationships steered by DEVCO are being doubled or supplanted by newer, broader and more strategic inter-regional dynamics initiated from within EEAS. Later arrangements, be they actor-centric or system-centric, originated mainly from within the Council and have remained in its wider purview. As a result, the Council Presidency has stood in for the horizontal coherence of more system-oriented issues (i.e. Global Economic Governance) and the EEAS hierarchy pushing for greater horizontal coherence in matters pertaining to the EU's own actorness – i.e. its capacity to act, its visibility and the recognition it receives.

The TEU/TFEU stated ambition to relieve some of the obstacles to increased horizontal coherence (between the various bureaucracies and their respective functional fields) has resulted in a partial consolidation of the EU's foreign policy approach to inter-regional arrangements but has neither produced a 'one-size fits all' policy formula nor 'a single voice' speaking for the EU on inter-regional affairs. Complexity has not so much been alleviated as it has been redistributed. A number of inter-regional and bilateral relations with the EU's far abroad have emerged as singularly re-focused on the issue of a possible EPA and thus mainly driven by the concerns of DG Trade; other partnerships have seen their agenda coalesce around a more strategic agenda open to horizontal issue linkages under the auspices of the hybrid EEAS; and finally some partnerships have remained tributary to contingent political agendas and as such are mainly within the purview of the Council Presidency (the most overtly political of all EU-level foreign policy agents).

As the innovations introduced by the TEU/TFEU are only slowly bearing their fruits – a process further delayed by the Eurozone crisis and its specific challenges – a final judgement on the TEU/TFEU's capacity to increase the EU's horizontal coherence and thus ability to call upon issue-linkages in its inter-regional contacts remains an open question. Nevertheless, at this point in the EU foreign policy machinery's moulting, one can hazard the following conjectures regarding future inter-regional relations:

1. Complexity will remain the rule, notably regarding competence distribution as both the EU machinery and third parties will have to get used to new foreign policy decision-procedures; some of which will involve a new actor – i.e. the European Parliament. If the involvement of the EP was a response to a democratic imperative, its inclusion was welcomed with wariness outside of the EU as other regional groupings and partners are well-aware of the added complications this will bring. The EP is set to act as the main

political lever geared towards increasing the policy impact of the common values listed in article 21 (TEU/TFEU). As such, the involvement of the EP created unforeseen frictions on human rights questions in such EPA negotiations between the EU and Peru/Colombia; or cranked-up familiar disagreements such as the paralysing effect of automobile-related concerns in EU-ROK EPA negotiations. As a political amplifying chamber the EP has a significant compelling but also disruptive potential as it can put forward new issues, or heighten existing questions.

2. It is likely that the top of the EU's triple-headed foreign policy pyramid will be preoccupied with staking out a coherent, strong and distinctive EU position in international affairs. If this is done abruptly or inappropriately it will backfire. Indeed, for all its capacity, bluster and heightened legal and institutional heft the EU remains a partial foreign policy actor in comparison to any major nation state. As such it is fundamentally more akin to other regional groupings. One of the first exercises in actor-centric inter-regional foreign policy piloted by the EEAS and its High Representative under the new post-Lisbon Treaty framework (September 2010) resulted in a policy miscarriage. The EU's initial attempt to secure observer status in the UN General Assembly (UNGA) failed in light of opposition mainly driven by CARICOM and other regional groupings which felt marginalized by the EU's insistence on its exceptionality. It's only after further negotiations and a small modification to the resolution allowing for the possibility of other groupings being recognized in the future that the EU was admitted as an observer to the UNGA. These learning pains remind both outside observers as well as EU foreign policy officials that in spite of endogenous improvements to its policy machinery with real improvements in horizontal coherence, the EU is increasingly tributary to exogenous forces and must thus not see its relative increase in horizontal coherence foster excessive inward-looking-ness and arrogance.

Over time and in spite of their limits, inter-regional arrangements have become a structural feature of the EU's distinctive foreign policy mix. Inter-regionalism fits seamlessly with its broader multilateral, multi-level strategic agenda and has proven useful for its internal legitimating process. Europe's foreign policy discourse on inter-regionalism also betrays a deep-seated Eurocentrism and thus risk of excessive inwardness. Inter-regional policies are not imbued with the needed political perspective to thrive and contribute to a proactive agenda-setting European foreign policy. Inter-regional policy is thus often secondary in nature allowing mainly for practices established elsewhere to be consolidated. As an additional opportunity to strengthen international cooperative management of global affairs, inter-regional arrangements call upon the EU to provide sufficiently coherent input over the various policy-fields involved in increasingly holistic policy platforms. Here the latest treaty innovations have allowed for some bureaucratic rifts to be bridged, but at the cost of ever increasing complexity. Inter-regional relations under the current EU foreign policy constellation appear to be coalescing around three transversal but distinct policy logics: Region-Building mainly driven by the EEAS; Global Politics shepherded principally through the Council Presidency; or Capacity-Building squarely steered by the specialized Commission DG, which in most cases is DG Trade dealing with EPA negotiations. In inter-regional affairs, strong strategic consistency, a still often introverted political discourse and a strengthening of actor-centric bureaucracy, have made both the EU's bark more distinct and its bite relatively incisive. Nevertheless, both global shifts towards multipolarity and internal crisis have made the imperative for the EU to find like-minded partners even more important. And though most of the EU's new foreign policy machinery is modelled on that of the nation state, the EU remains more than ever a hybrid actor which is doomed to be an (institutional) loner engaged in a constant search for resonant partners – and this is where other regional groupings remain a crucial component of the EU's foreign policy outlook.

As the importance of these other regional groupings – as possibly supportive exogenous partners – becomes ever more apparent and the EU's widening foreign policy instances have slowly built up region-specific approaches to the main comparable regional entities in its far abroad.

Making Room for Diversity: Evolving Inter-Regional Relations through Adaptation

As the EU's inter-regional foreign policy has ebbed and flowed over the past 50 years it has increasingly been exposed to the risk of navel-gazing or marginalization – be it because of a lack of political will, bureaucratic insularity or Eurocentric *hubris* – the key determinant in the future evolution of the dialectic shaping the EU's inter-regional agenda is therefore its capacity to engage its potential partners and identify appropriate foreign policy options. As described above: policy-feedback cycles, bureaucratic path dependencies and institutional innovation following the TEU/TFEU have produced roughly three clusters of inter-regional relations each with its own distinctive logic.

As its relations to its far abroad is concerned, the EU has increasingly developed: (1) a set of inter-regional arrangements with other institutionalized regional organizations with an eye on strengthening the regional order on either side through emulation; (2) a few broad arrangements aimed at nesting global preferences; and (3) a number of expert-driven relationships geared towards building up the partnership's endogenous capacity in a given field.

Encouraging Regional Polities through Emulation

As the regional organizations on either side of these relationships have matured the main common agenda point has been the mutual bolstering of regional dynamics, be it through cooperation, capacity-building, mutual learning or merely emulation.

The EU's inter-regional foreign policy toolbox in these instances is slanted towards supporting the emergence of stronger and further institutionalized regional organizations. To this effect the EU might conclude formal region-to-region agreements setting out joint partnership focused on deepening certain dimensions of a partner region. To this effect, the EU has developed a set of targeted tools, including: expert evaluation mechanisms of the challenges facing a partner organization; mutual-leaning programmes through expert exchanges; institutional strengthening through the promotion of the Rule of Law or bureaucratic capacity build-up; as well as funds specifically earmarked to support regional economic integration and trade facilitation (e.g. the mainstreaming of Regional Indicative Programmes – RIP).

The main policy tools called upon in these situations remain relatively inexpensive and are essentially financed through the EEAS's own budget. The lion's share of the inter-regional policy-making is focused on: capacity build-up both through mutual learning as well as buttressing respective regional markets. The administrative and procedural innovations introduced by the TEU/TFEU have allowed for these inter-regional relations, which in the most part had lost much steam, to come relatively unstuck and for new pluri-annual support programmes to be drawn up (i.e. Regional Indicative Programmes – RIP). It nonetheless remains to be seen how sustainable this new dynamic is seeing that the fundamental variables (i.e. political will, available budgets, strategic calculations and overriding power-balances) have remained unchanged.

The inter-regional dynamics included in this group involve a set of institutionally heterogeneous groupings; their main commonality being that they are all anchored around a tentative customs union largely influenced by the biggest member of the group. Moreover said biggest member is also a bilateral strategic partner of the EU. Accordingly, the inter-regional relations developed in these situations are mainly actor-driven and centred on geo-political and geo-economical balancing exercises with regards to a significant third party and its hinterland. As such, they have very little autonomous internal impetus (e.g. Santander 2012).

If said partnerships have at times fulfilled a secondary encouragement function to existing endogenous regional dynamics, they have mainly proven to be a bluster exercise for the larger parties involved. To that effect, besides the generalization and systemization of the principle of Regional Indicative Programmes in the EEAS's policies towards other groups, the recent strengthening of the diplomatic and public policy apparatus of the EU has made it keen to be seen and heighten its profile by 'rubbing elbows' with other powers and their regional hinterland. Recent institutional evolutions seem to have strengthened the bilateral tendencies towards key strategic partners and by knock-on effect relegated a given number of inter-regional platforms to being an echoing chamber for international positioning and even posturing.

Table 8.4 Examples of group-to-group contacts centred on region-building

	Start	Start of current round	Running policy framework	Regional indicative programme	Regional trade and aid facilities
EU-MERCOSUR	1992	2007 Re-launch of a comprehensive policy towards region-building	**Regional Strategy Paper** (2007–13) Mid-Term Regional Strategy Review (2011/12) Mid-term objective: Association Agreement	€50 million	**Stalled Trade Agenda** Association Agreement including an EPA. **Aid singularly invested in regional economic integration and social capacity building**
EU-SAARC	1994	2010 Re-launch of a Multi-Annual Indicative Programme for Asia (€400 million in total)	**Regional Strategy for Asia** (2007–13) South Asia is characterized by a low level of regional integration, and our direct cooperation with SAARC is seriously hampered: a limited number of sector-bound cooperation but direct cooperation institution-to-institution remains modest	€63 million *(shared with ASEAN and ASEM)* of which: €7.8 million invested in SAARC	**Stalled Trade Agenda** negotiations as bilateral negotiations with India take the foreground **Limited aid sums** invested in regional dimension because seen as cost-efficient way of building capacity
EU-EurAsec	No formal formalized partnership		Informal and political contacts on mutual learning and expertise exchange regarding customs unions	**No Trade Agenda** Strong calls for bilateral FTA from EurAsec (Russia) but strong silence/rebuttal from EU (DG Trade) **Targeted aid towards sub-regions** Region-building seen as efficient way of dispersing aid notably in Central Asia *(cf. special EU envoy)*	

Strengthening Global Governance through Socialization

These broad groups of countries are either the theatre of some of the globe's major challenges or count *several* of the emerging powers/strategic partners amongst their membership. These inter-regional platforms have become privileged venues to discuss global challenges as well as socialize new governance standards and practices.

The common driver amongst these inter-regional exercises is a clear policy of international burden-sharing. Burden-sharing through cooperation is thus to be fostered over time: either through direct investments in capacity-building (amongst others €7.2 billion was invested in fast-track climate change projects across Africa between 2010 and 2012 and €100 million in Asia between 2007 and 2010) or by socializing the behaviour of states through repeated interaction (Acharya 2011). These system-oriented and extroverted exercises in inter-regional foreign policy consultations mark the continuation of the broad spectrum policy discussion which characterized the second wave of inter-regionalisms (e.g. Hänggi 2006).

These policy platforms are extremely fluid, particularly receptive to exogenous imperatives, and reliant on flexible and light institutional frameworks with clearly identifiable political leadership. The EU's traditionally Eurocentric inter-regional narrative combined with its horizontally fragmented policy made it difficult for European partners to fully engage in such multifaceted endeavours without frustration building up on either side. Herein some of the improvements wrought by the TEU/TFEU have proven relatively well equipped to table and enforce its policy preference than before.

The more integrated European foreign policy machinery has been able to better shepherd multifaceted negotiation agendas and impose its preferred negotiation procedures and practices. As an example of the later, the EU imposed the President of the European Council (M.H. Van Rompuy) as the Chair of the 8th ASEM meeting in spite of opposition from several Asian partners who preferred to see a conference of Heads of State/Government presided over by a peer. It has also launched and steered the complex EU-Latin American and Caribbean dialogue which covers several other bilateral, inter-regional and strategic partnerships without major frictions and with a relatively coherent sense of direction. The EU-LAC platform has seemingly allowed the initial stages of European strategic thinking on Latin America to emerge. Finally, the growing continental dimension of the EU's Africa policy is quickly emerging as one of the key litmus tests for the expected benefits in terms of increased horizontal foreign policy coherence as said action plan includes nearly all the instruments available in the EU foreign policy toolbox (e.g. exclusive, shared, parallel, coordination and supplementary competences) and covers all the major policy areas: Peace and Security; Democratic Governance and Human Rights; Regional Economic Integration, Trade and Infrastructure; Millennium Development Goals; Climate Change; Energy; Migration, Mobility and Employment; Science, Information Society and Space.

Table 8.5 Examples of group-to-group contacts centred on governance challenges

	Start	Start of current round	Running policy framework	Regional Indicative Programme (RIP)	Trade and aid facilities
ASEM	1996	2010 Bi-annual plan approved at the 8th ASEM Summit in Brussels	**Every two years Heads of Government Meeting** fixes agenda for the coming two (*uses dedicated EEAS funds and Asia-Europe Foundation*)	€63 million (*shared with ASEAN and ASEM*) and funds made available through the Asia-Europe Foundation (ASEF)	**No internal Trade Agenda** EPAs discussed in smaller venues **Aid: human capacity-building** Funnelled through the ASEF, it focuses on inter-regional P2P exchanges
EU-LAC	2009	2009 EU communiqué: 'Global Players in a Partnership'	**2007–2013 Regional Strategy Paper** combining a variety of policy instruments and financing (*EEAS, European Investment Bank, EDF, etc.*)	€525 million for regional Integration support	**No internal Trade Agenda** EPAs discussed in smaller venues **Aid: institutional capacity-building** Funnelled through the European Commission and Latin American Institutions it focuses on institutional exchanges
EU-AU	2007	2010 Joint Tripoli Declaration	**2010–2013 2nd EU-AU Action Plan** Regional Strategy Paper combining a variety of policy instruments and financing (*EEAS, EIB, EDF, ACP funds, etc.*)	Important budget coalescing funds from a variety as most aid programmes include a RIP dimension	**No internal Trade Agenda** EPAs discussed in smaller venues **Aid: security capacity- building** Focused on 'Human Security' capacity-building funds go either to local and transnational civil society actors OR regional security forces

Accordingly, the EU's recent Lisbon Treaty reforms have given it a higher profile within the confines of the broad and open inter-regional forums as it is now better equipped to participate in complex multifaceted policy discussions, identify and press on with strategic preferences, and bring more weight to bear in the negotiations. However, if recent reforms seem to have allowed the EU's foreign policy machine to engage more readily and forcefully with transnational socialization dynamics, the question remains whether it will also prove more receptive to outside information. (For more on the EEAS as information-gatherer and possible vessel of foreign policy expertise see Chapter 4 in this volume.)

Capacity-Building through Policy Rationalization

The final set of inter-regional initiatives are mainly focused exercises aimed on one of the two traditional policy fields initially associated with inter-regionalism: trade facilitation or aid dispersal. For those inter-regional policy endeavours focused on securing some form of EPA between both regional groupings, the partnership's rhythm and agenda remains dictated by DG Trade. As a result, the exogenous partner and any other foreign policy entrepreneur within the EU are often relegated to second fiddle. The opposite experiences of the ASEAN-EU and CARICOM-EU EPA negotiations are in this symptomatic of the unchanged practices of the EU's foreign trade negotiation machinery. If DG Trade steamrolled the negotiations with CARICOM to a fruitful and desired conclusion, DG Trade unilaterally decided for tactical reasons to freeze the inter-regional negotiations with ASEAN and favour competitive bilateral negotiations in South East Asia.

Clearly focused end-goals, well established and highly routine supranational negotiation practices, a highly trained and integrated negotiation team and bureaucratic infrastructures which have remained wholly autonomous from the rest of the EU's evolving foreign policy machinery all explain why trade-centric partnerships remain despite the changes introduced by the Lisbon Treaty, a clear-cut rational bargaining exercise. A single uncertainty remains as one possible change introduced by the TEU/TFEU could upset the EU's established international trade negotiation policies and that is the inclusion of the European Parliament as ultimate arbiter of any concluded agreement. This poses a fundamental policy question to the custodians of the EU's trade negotiation strategies: should the parliament be included early on, or even throughout to heighten overall coherence; or should Parliament merely approve or reject the proposal as negotiated by the experts. At any rate, the established depolarization and depolitization of trade negotiations as presently established in the bureaucracy-driven EU trade negotiations might now be at least partially at risk.

Whether this partial introduction of electoral politics, combined with the widening of the negotiation agendas associated with Economic Partnership Agreements will lead to a convergence between the Trade and General Policy arms of the EU's foreign policy edifice is doubtful. Bureaucratic turf-wars are the most likely scenario. Conversely, those inter-regional relations more oriented

Table 8.6 Examples of group-to-group contacts centred on capacity-building

	Start	Start of current round	Running policy framework	Regional Indicative Programme (RIP)	Trade and aid facilities
EU-ACP	1975	2010 2nd Revision of Cotonou Agreement	**2010–14 Revised Cotonou Agreement** focus on insuring its conformity with WTO rules	€17,766 million between 2008 and 2013 *(through EDF and other fund)*	**Replacing PTAs by EPAs** For the central component of the ACP (preferential Trade Agreements) to subsist in light of the WTO they must be transformed into EPAs **Aid: economic capacity-building** To allow ACP countries to compete in EU and global market
EU-Ecowas/ Weamu	2000	2008 development programme	**2008–13 Regional Strategy for West Africa**	€118 million *(through EDF)*	**No internal Trade Agenda** Trade dealt with bilaterally in ACP context **Aid: Common Market capacity-building** Funds geared towards integrating the sub-regional markets to improve competitiveness and support continental regional evolution
EU-SADC	1986	2008 development programme	**2008–13 Regional Strategy for SADC**	€392 million *(through EDF)*	**No internal Trade Agenda** Trade dealt with bilaterally **Aid: Common Market capacity-building** Funds geared towards integrating the sub-regional markets to improve competitiveness and support continental regional evolution
EU-ASEAN	1972	2007 Inter-Regional EPA Negotiations	**2010 negotiations abandoned** by EU in favour of parallel bilateral negotiations with ASEAN member countries	€63 million *(shared with ASEAN and ASEM) of which:* €30 million *Invested in ASEAN*	**Trade Agenda frozen** Tactical shift on EU's part to bilateral negotiations (domino effect of other successful bilateral FTAs in the region by Japan, United States, China …) **Aid: cautious careful region-building** Institutions and civil society are both targeted in an effort to build-up regional awareness without vexing strong endogenous regional dynamics

towards development and the efficient use of the European Development Fund (EDF) have come to fall under the EEAS's strategic remit. The EEAS appears poised to take over the strategic planning of the EU's foreign aid policy, thus integrating it more deeply into its broader external action agenda.

Conclusion

Inter-regionalism has proven to be a fundamental and symptomatic characteristic of the European region's slow emergence onto the international scene as a distinct and unique type of global actor. As such, the European institutions have been formally engaged in inter-regional forums since 1972, and each reform of its foreign policy apparatus has brought with it a widening of the scope of said inter-regional partnerships, whilst simultaneously heightening their complexity.

The EC/EU's continued commitment to inter-regionalism as a part of its overarching strategic choice in favour of multi-level multilateralism reflects a high level of strategic coherence on the part of the EU's foreign policy instances, and this from the outset, long before the successive developments wrought with each new treaty. Accordingly, in spite of its fragmentation and heterogeneity the EU does seem to subscribe to a constant and consistent worldview which informs its various inter-regional actions.

But if the steadfastness of the inter-regional agenda's strategic orientation bodes well for the EU's strategic consistency, the EU's partial and self-centred inter-regional discourse reflects poorly on its underlying political ambition and seriousness. Counter-intuitively a lot of the EU discourse on inter-regionalism has remained blind to the outside world and stubbornly self-referential. The rise of new actors, the unforeseen constraints befalling Europe in crises and the continued rise of other regions have all conspired to cool the transformational ambitions of the European inter-regional policies; but the EU's inter-regionalism is still lacking a constructive and consistent narrative.

The main and most palpable innovations introduced by the Lisbon Treaty were: (1) streamlined institutional arrangements through the reform of the European Council Presidency and the creation of the High Representative at the head of a distinct diplomatic services (EEAS); (2) the strengthening of the legal underpinnings of the EU's external action by both giving it a single legal personality and more forcefully listing its normative underpinnings (art. 21); and (3) finally addressing the 'democratic deficit' challenge of the EU's external action by including the European Parliament in most final decisions. These innovations did not produce any fundamental changes in the EU's approach to inter-regionalism but it did strengthen an ongoing trend towards a certain consolidated differentiation between those policy-centred inter-regional partnerships driven by either trade or aid considerations; those broader partnerships attuned to the wider international politics; and those centred on a given actor and their relationship to their hinterland. The EU foreign policy machinery has taken stock of each new treaty – including the TEU/TFEU of Lisbon – to hone the coherence and targeted efficiency of its inter-regional actions.

A key concern, and open question, is whether the weightier and more complex European foreign policy superstructure will facilitate the region's engagement with its peer. Or, on the contrary, foster further isolation? This crucial question for EU foreign policy's future coherence with regards to the outside world in general, and its fellow regional grouping in particular, will depend largely on the sagacity of those wielding the heftier and at times more blunt levers of the EU's particular foreign policy presence. A foreign policy which would completely side-step the inter-regional dialogue and focus solely on joining the ranks of the largest nation state foreign policy actors will isolate the EU and leave it subjected to the inevitably more nimble national actors. Conversely, the EU must keep in mind and publicize that a significant part of its international heft flows from its capacity to act on par with the dominant forces in international affairs – i.e. the larger nation states. Cultivating bilateral strategic partnerships is therefore a complementary and not contradictory imperative. Time and again, reform after reform, and following successive consolidations of the EU's foreign policy machinery, the general adage that 'politics is the art of the possible' (O. Bismarck, 1867) has simply rung particularly true when considering the foreign policies of a evolving and hybrid entity such as the EU.

In conclusion, let us return to the much bandied about 'Expectation–Capability Gap' of the EU and the impact of the TEU/TFEU. For inter-regional partnerships the hybrid machinery created by the TEU/TFEU will do little to better address either the exogenous third parties' expectations, nor will it reconcile endogenous constituencies' expectations with the inter-regional reality. The same innovation will however make the expectations of the unwieldy EU-level policy-shaping community more potent; as the impact of its choices and strategic options will be felt, for better or for worse, to a far greater degree by all its partners, included the inter-regional ones.

Chapter 9

The EU Strategic Partnerships: Process and Purposes

Giovanni Grevi

Abstract

Bilateral strategic partnerships between the European Union (EU) and major global actors are an emerging feature of EU foreign policy. This chapter reviews the ongoing academic and policy debates on the concept and practice of strategic partnerships, highlighting the considerable scepticism surrounding their development. It goes on to argue that, despite their flaws, strategic partnerships are an important and multi-purpose tool in the EU foreign policy arsenal, potentially fulfilling reflexive, relational and structural goals at once. Based on this original analytical perspective, the chapter suggests that strategic partnerships are those that help pave the way from bilateral transactions to cooperation in broader mini-lateral and multilateral formats. After reviewing the performance of EU strategic partnerships at these three levels of analysis, and delivering a sobering but not dismissive picture of their output to date, the chapter addresses the connection between the EU discourse on strategic partnerships and policy-making in the post-Lisbon institutional context. It detects piecemeal progress in agenda-setting and representation but exposes a serious deficit of coordination among EU bodies and with member states, which as yet prevents the EU from devising an integrated approach to its strategic partnerships.

Introduction

The European Union (EU) has established 10 so-called 'strategic partnerships' with pivotal global actors in the attempt to confirm and redefine its role in a diverse and polycentric international system. However, it has been slow in defining the priorities that these partnerships should achieve, based on an assessment of its core interests. Besides, as the delicate post-Lisbon Treaty institutional framework took shape, the EU decision-making process failed to deliver an integrated, strategic approach to these important relationships. The relevance and credibility of strategic partnerships is challenged not only due to their modest policy output but also given the normative dissonance between the EU and unlike-minded partners, notably large emerging powers.

This chapter fleshes out the broad lines of recent debates on the concept and practice of strategic partnerships, provides an innovative framework for assessing their purpose and takes a closer look at the deficiencies, but also piecemeal progress, of EU policy-making in this domain. It argues that, despite their inadequacy so far, bilateral strategic partnerships are a critical dimension of the EU's foreign policy adjustment to a fluid global context where power shifts, different perceptions and agendas co-exist and interdependence deepens.

An innovative framework for assessing the relevance and performance of EU strategic partnerships is proposed here, highlighting that they fulfil reflexive, relational and structural purposes at once. Based on a number of interviews with EU officials, the recent practice of EU policy-making is scrutinised, detecting incremental innovation in the approach to strategic partnerships and in agenda-setting. At the same time, this investigation exposes serious shortcomings when it comes to coordination between EU bodies and among member states, which prevent crafting an effective and strategic approach to separate partnerships.

According to EU policy documents and joint statements, 10 countries are commonly included in the list of EU strategic partners, namely Brazil, Canada, China, India, Japan, Mexico, Russia, South Africa, South Korea and the United States. The overarching review carried out here does not aim to reflect the remarkable diversity of EU partners and partnerships. It goes without saying that some partnerships are more strategic than others when it comes to Europe's security and prosperity. Instead, this chapter looks at how key bilateral partnerships serve multiple purposes to enhance the EU's profile, interests and values.

Strategic Partnerships: A Contested Concept

EU relations with its strategic partners are inevitably very different in scope, depth and ambition. It is difficult to identify common criteria for selecting this particular set of countries, whether in terms of their power status, their normative affinity to the EU, or the core EU interests pursued through such partnerships (Gratius 2011). The 2003 European Security Strategy did not provide much guidance on this point. Having defined the transatlantic relationship as 'irreplaceable' and called for progress 'towards a strategic partnership' with Russia, this document stated that the EU should 'look to develop strategic partnerships with Japan, China, Canada and India'. This was not to be considered a closed list, however. Partnerships could be envisaged with all those who share the Union's interests and values 'and are prepared to act in their support'. A distinction was introduced (Renard 2011) between the essential partner (the United States), pivotal ones (the BRIC countries), natural partners (Canada, Japan and South Korea) and regional actors (Mexico and South Africa). Such a ranking exposes the two basic rationales underpinning strategic partnerships, namely the normative proximity and/or the political and economic clout of the partners.

On that basis, partnerships of choice among like-minded states, which expose a natural convergence of priorities, can be differentiated from partnerships of necessity. Under the latter, priorities may differ but seeking common ground is critically important given the potential of individual partners to foster or harm the EU's interests. The EU shares values and a vast platform of common interests with traditional allies such as the United States and Canada, as well as Japan, whereas its relations with China and Russia are mainly based on economic or energy needs. Such a distinction, however, is probably too neat to reflect real politics (Grevi 2011a). Each partnership includes an uneven mix of elective choice, inescapable necessity and also quite practical convenience, depending on the issues at stake.

Strategic partnerships can be regarded as part of the evolution of EU foreign policy from traditional Cold War alliances to inter-regional relations in the 1990s to eventual linkages with emerging powers in a multipolar context (Gratius 2011). The relationship between bilateral partnerships and the EU commitment to multilateral cooperation is often portrayed as a trade-off. However, the 2008 report on the implementation of the European Security Strategy speaks of 'partnerships for effective multilateralism', including bilateral ones, while providing no direction on how the two dimensions may reinforce each other. The question remains whether bilateral partnerships are alternatives or complements to other vectors of engagement, notably inter-regional relations with regional groupings abroad and multilateral cooperation.

The case can be made that effective strategic partnerships are those that pave the way to reconciling bilateral engagement and multilateral cooperation, strengthening both dimensions at once (Grevi 2010; Grevi and de Vasconcelos 2008). Such an approach broadly fits and informs the EU discourse on strategic partnerships. For example, as High Representative (HR) Ashton stated with reference to the BRICS countries, 'We need a more creative and joined up approach as we look at how we deal with those bilateral relationships, but also to work with that group of countries in regional and global forums'.[1]

Different views on the links between bilateral and multilateral cooperation are however important in assessing the pertinence of the very concept of strategic partnerships. The latter has been widely criticized as ill-defined, all-inclusive and relatively empty of political substance (Menotti and Vencato 2008). Some stress that this 'amorphous' concept has led 'a somewhat awkward life in EU diplomatic parlance' to the point of resulting in relative obscurity even among EU officials well into 2010 (Keukeleire et al. 2011). There have been helpful attempts at defining the basic elements of a real strategic partnership, which would include comprehensiveness, reciprocity, empathy and normative proximity, duration and the ambition to reach beyond bilateral issues. Based on this demanding benchmark, only the EU–US relationship would conceivably qualify as a strategic partnership.

---

1   C. Ashton, speech on 'EU Foreign Policy towards the BRICS and Other Emerging Powers', European Parliament, Brussels, 1 February 2012.

A different approach to the issue would consist of shifting the focus from criteria and definitions to substance and, above all, purpose. Partnerships do not become strategic by virtue of defining them as such and the practice of attributing this label to important bilateral relations has surely been inconsistent. However, putting these partnerships in a global context, strategic ones are those that accompany current power shifts with a shift towards positive-sum and not zero-sum relations among major powers (Grevi 2010). Assuming that this is an overarching, defining goal for the EU, strategic partnerships are those that help in this direction. They are essential, if imperfect, enablers of dialogue and cooperation among pivotal and increasingly interdependent powers.

The strategic value of EU partnerships need not be undermined by tactical reversals. Mixing up the two levels would amount to missing the wood for the trees. Taking the case of the often challenging EU–Russia relationship, the President of the European Council (PEC) Van Rompuy noted: 'Recognising the modernisation of Russia as a core interest for all 27 member states should be the pole star on our strategic compass.'[2] Strategic partnerships are those that are pursued consistently over time, keeping the bar straight through the ups and downs of the respective relationships.

This requires that the EU becomes better able to set its own priorities and stick to them. Such priorities can be defined in more or less transactional terms, as only consisting of the gains that the EU reaps from its partners (market access, energy supplies). They can also be related to the EU's vital interest in an open and stable international system (averting protectionism, mitigating climate change, preventing WMD proliferation, enhancing maritime security and cyber-security). A strategic approach to bilateral partnerships would encompass both profit-maximising and system-shaping goals.

Such an approach would not simply take stock of normative proximity but also consider the scope for normative convergence over time. Where the latter proves beyond reach over the short term, strategic partnerships can serve an important purpose by preventing mutual alienation. This risk cannot be neglected in a global context where countries with different worldviews and self-conceptions rub shoulders. The unintended consequences of drifting apart would be serious, whether in terms of trade protectionism, a scramble for resources, friction between spheres of influence, irresponsibility to protect and overall fragmentation of global governance. This is not about Realpolitik, but about a realistic approach to advancing EU interests and values in ways consistent with the EU identity of a civilian (but not necessarily soft) power in a polycentric world (Telò 2005).

---

2   H. Van Rompuy, speech on 'The Great Challenges of the European Union', Warsaw University, Warsaw, 17 January 2011.

Strategic Partnerships: Multiple Purposes

The relevance and effectiveness of EU strategic partnerships need to be assessed at multiple levels, avoiding narrow or stark binary approaches. A narrow approach to strategic partnerships largely focused on specific deliverables at the bilateral level, risks neglecting issue-linkages, the connections between separate partnerships as well as the implications of bilateral dealings for different levels of engagement, including multilateral frameworks. A binary approach to these critical relationships, framing them as directed to *either* maximise respective interests *or* pursue broader goals to reform the international order, does not do justice to the inevitable complexity of foreign affairs.

Real-life strategic partnerships are multi-purpose ones, pursuing *both* bilateral and multilateral objectives and shifting focus across these and other dimensions of the relationship in a fairly pragmatic way. The ability to do so represents a key benchmark of their efficacy. Testing strategic partnerships means, therefore, dissecting their multiple functions as a foreign policy tool, thereby delivering a more sophisticated picture.

Reflexive Partnerships: Putting the EU on the Map

The first function of strategic partnerships is a reflexive one, namely the self-assertion of the EU as a partner, an actor or a pole in a challenging international system. From this standpoint, the very fact of announcing a strategic partnership sets up the two parties as pivotal mutual interlocutors, upgrading their status in mutual relations and beyond.

From an EU standpoint, strategic partnerships fulfil not only a 'positional' role – setting the EU on the map as a key global player beyond trade and economic issues – but also what has been defined as an 'integrative' role (Smith 2011). Performing as a strategic partner requires the EU to improve coherence between the different instruments in its toolbox and between action at the EU and national level. In other words, setting up strategic partnerships entails, at least in principle, deepening the political cohesion of the Union and intensifying foreign policy cooperation.

The integrative implications of strategic partnerships operate both in day-to-day policy-making and at the level of perceptions. Launching these partnerships focuses minds and creates expectations, putting the credibility of the Union on the frontline and sending a message both to third countries and to EU member states. The self-assertion of the EU as a strategic partner and its recognition as one by leading global actors augment its profile. However, they also raise the stakes for the EU, if such a status is not matched by institutional performance and political substance. From this standpoint, as illustrated below, the practice of strategic partnerships exposes the relative fragility of the Union at both the institutional and political level.

The integrative potential of EU strategic partnerships remains largely to be fulfilled. The question is, of course, a political and not an institutional one. Since late 2010, the uprisings shaking the EU's Southern neighbourhood have diverted political focus and resources from the drive to upgrade strategic partnerships. Fire-fighting dominated EU foreign policy in 2011 and economic challenges marginalised broader foreign policy objectives (Martiningui and Youngs 2011).

Mutual positional goals and EU integrative aims continue to underlie strategic partnerships but, since the economic and financial crisis hit the EU in 2008, the politics have arguably shifted. Shaken by Eurozone troubles, hampered by anaemic growth and torn by political tensions, the EU is both less attractive to its partners and more in need of recognition as a cohesive, significant political actor. The terms and perception of the relationships with some large partners such as China, India and Brazil are changing. The EU is no longer mainly a supplier but increasingly a *demandeur* of political recognition, which, conversely, appears less urgent for partners whose self-confidence is rising even faster than their GDP figures.

Relational Partnerships: Economics First

Strategic partnerships serve to manage bilateral relations in the direct pursuit of the respective interests of the two parties. The conclusions of the European Council in September 2010 put the accent on this relational dimension. The document stressed that EU strategic partnerships 'provide a useful instrument for pursuing European objectives and interests' but made clear that this would only work 'if they are two way streets based on mutual interests and benefits and on the recognition that all actors have rights as well as duties'. EU leaders agreed on the need for Europe to 'promote its interests and values more assertively and in a spirit of reciprocity and mutual benefit'.

Economics remain the backbone of the partnerships' agendas, such as in the case of the EU and the United States (non-tariff barriers, regulatory convergence, transatlantic marketplace, action plan for growth and jobs), the EU and China (market access, market economy status, level playing fields, subsidies, investment agreement), the EU and India (market access, trade and investment agreement, technology transfers, energy) and the EU and Russia (energy, economic modernisation). Trade and investment, in particular, are the cornerstones of most strategic partnerships. The EU is the biggest merchandise trade partner of six of its strategic partners (Brazil, China, India, Russia, South Africa and the United States), the second largest for two of them (Canada and Mexico), the third largest for Japan and the fourth for South Korea. China will soon become the EU's largest trade partner.

The Union's trade volumes with most of its partners remain large, although they are mostly declining as a share of the respective partners' overall trade volumes. Instead, the levels of foreign investment stocks and flows between the EU and its strategic partners offer a very uneven picture. The EU absorbed 60 per cent of US foreign investment between 2000 and 2010 and its current stock of investment in the United States is about 40 per cent larger than that in all the other nine strategic partners combined. Conversely, the inward investment stock from these nine partners amounted in 2010 to only one-third of that coming from the United States. Investment from Canada in the EU was larger than that of the five BRICS together and Brazil's stock bigger than that of the other four BRICS combined. Recent data point, however, to new important trends. In particular, while starting from a low basis, Chinese investment flows in Europe tripled between 2006 and 2009 and then again between 2010 and 2011 to €7.4 billion last year. Estimates project an annual average of €15–23 billion Chinese direct investment in Europe over the next decade, which calls for a common approach at European level to maximise the benefits of such inflows (jobs) while preventing market distortions, volatility and competition among EU member states.

Following the conclusion of a free trade agreement with South Korea in 2010, trade liberalisation and the promotion of two-way investment flows are a major dimension of EU relations with Brazil (whereas negotiations with MERCOSUR are prolonged), Canada (Comprehensive Economic and Trade Agreement due for signature in 2012), India (negotiations on a Broad-based Trade and Investment Agreement at an advanced stage) and Japan (ongoing scoping exercise towards the negotiation of a comprehensive trade and investment agreement). Progress on these major strands of negotiations will be an important indicator of the effectiveness of the respective strategic partnerships. That said, prospects for concluding the envisaged FTAs with MERCOSUR and India are not encouraging, at least over the short term.

Over the last two years, negotiations on trade and investment issues have taken place within a new political context, given the impact of the sovereign debt crisis on Europe's cohesion and uncertainty over the future of the Eurozone. The EU has to perform a delicate balancing act between pursuing its trade interests and seeking financial support from China and other emerging countries with large currency reserves. These countries as well as the United States are, in turn, vulnerable to Europe's economic downturn and very critical of the Eurozone's lack of resolve to address the crisis.

Russia and China hold a considerable share of their foreign currency reserves in euros (estimated at, respectively, 40 per cent and 30 per cent of the total). It is notable that over 2011 China has diversified its currency reserves portfolio away from the US dollar (-10 per cent) and towards the euro (+7 per cent) in a contrary move to other major central banks. The BRICS countries have called for a multipolar monetary system, of which the euro would be a cornerstone, less dependent on the US dollar as the global reserve currency. That said, they have made their help conditional on additional commitments by Europeans themselves to their bailout mechanisms and to operating via multilateral channels. This position is directly related to their claims for a new round of negotiations on the revision of the distribution of quotas and votes in international financial institutions.

Following Japan – the first EU partner that provided US$60 billion in new IMF resources in April 2012 – China (US$43 billion), Russia, India and Brazil

(US$10 billion each) announced at the G20 summit in Los Cabos in June 2012 that they would contribute to strengthen the IMF firewall against contagion from the Eurozone crisis (albeit these and other funds are not specifically earmarked for Europe). While these countries accept that their economic fortunes cannot be delinked from prospects over Europe's recovery, the crisis has unquestionably dented the image of the EU as a reliable partner and tempted EU member states to turn to strategic partners for financial support instead of adopting a concerted strategy.

Structural Partnerships: Enhancing Global Governance

Strategic partnerships are important bilateral means that can be mobilised to foster international cooperation. The redistribution of power at the international level enhances the clout of a number of EU partners in formal and informal multilateral formats. Given the diverse priorities and normative outlooks of its main stakeholders, a more heterogeneous international system results in a more contested and consequently weaker multilateral order. At the same time, there is little evidence of a bloc of emerging powers countervailing established ones (assuming these broad categories make sense) or of the West being confronted by the rest across the board (Jones 2011).

Structured relations with major states, whether global or regional actors, can provide critical leverage for common action or at least to approximate respective positions on the multilateral stage. Effective strategic partnerships are those that seek to make bilateral dealings not only compatible with but also conducive to stronger multilateral cooperation. As such, they form part of a structural approach to foreign policy, shaping international relations beyond bilateral transactions. A structural foreign policy, as traditionally practised by the EU, is grounded on coherence between internal and external policies and the pursuit of specific interests through broader, sustainable frameworks of rules and cooperation (Keukeleire and MacNaughtan 2008).

Linking bilateral partnerships and multilateral cooperation faces normative hurdles. Put simply, most of its strategic partners do not share the EU's stated aim to strengthen a multilateral, rule-based order and delimit their national sovereignty in the process, taking instead a selective and instrumental approach to international cooperation.

While such a normative disconnect hampers substantial cooperation on many grounds, it does not pose an insurmountable impediment to engaging at the multilateral level. Both the EU and its strategic partners are less dogmatic and more flexible than their rhetoric would suggest. The EU talks multilateral but can act via different channels when needed. For example, it actively pursues bilateral trade deals while the Doha round is sinking, it favours differentiation in dealing with individual countries in its neighbourhood, and EU member states seek to shape or join multinational coalitions to address geopolitical crises if multilateral bodies are paralysed, as has been the case for Syria.

Conversely, the fact that most of its partners reject binding constraints on their sovereignty does not mean that they are not prepared to define new terms for cooperation at the international level, when it suits them. China and Russia have joined the WTO and both of them – as well as many other EU partners – have a strong stake in the nuclear non-proliferation regime. Climate change negotiations in Cancun and Durban have delivered sensible, if as yet inadequate, progress. While uncomfortable with their representation or standing in institutions such as the IMF and the World Bank, the BRICS have been seeking a stronger position within, and not outside, these bodies.

The EU clearly frames its partnerships as transcending the purely bilateral dimension. 'Europe and China can pave the way for global solutions and promote international peace and security across the world', stated President Van Rompuy in Beijing.[3] 'In today's world ... Europe is the United States' indispensable partner for building a multilateral world that integrates emerging powers', argued President Barroso in New York.[4] 'I see India as a vital strategic partner to meet a vast range of global and regional challenges on top of more advanced bilateral cooperation', said High Representative Ashton in New Delhi.[5]

Between 2010 and 2012, the EU has launched a high level dialogue on foreign and security issues with China and regular foreign policy consultations with India, both led by the High Representative for foreign and security policy and her counterparts. In addition, the EU holds regular consultations at ministerial level with the United States and Russia and meetings of political directors with all its major partners. More structured high level exchanges have begun to deliver some progress in dealing with transnational threats such as terrorism, piracy and cyber-crime. The EU aims to deepen the level of cooperation with its strategic partners involved in the naval operations against piracy in the Indian Ocean. For example, the EU and India have agreed in principle to cooperate in escorting the shipments of the World Food Programme to Somalia. The EU and the United States have set up a cyber-security and cyber-crime working group in 2010, followed by the decision to establish an EU–China cyber task-force and to intensify consultations on cyber issues with India this year. In the absence of a relevant multilateral framework to protect the freedom and security of the Internet, such bilateral dealings may help pave the way for future international regimes.

Strategic partnerships have been so far of limited relevance to cooperation in crisis management. Framework agreements on the participation of personnel from strategic partners in operations under the EU's Common Security and Defence Policy have been concluded with Canada and the United States and are under discussion

---

3   H. Van Rompuy, speech on 'Europe and China in an Interdependent World', Central Party School, Beijing, 17 May 2011.

4   J.M. Durao Barroso, speech on 'Post-Crisis: A Leading Global Role for Europe', Columbia University, New York, 21 September 2010.

5   C. Ashton, speech on 'EU-India Relations Post-Lisbon: Cooperation in a Changing World', India International Centre, New Delhi, 23 June 2010.

with Russia and Brazil. Enhanced consultations on EU–US cooperation in crisis management are underway. At the political level, however, EU member states are the primary actors in this context and their initiatives, or differences, entail that the EU is often not seen as a primary interlocutor, including within the UN.

That said, a review of the negotiations concerning three major geopolitical crises in 2011 shows some scope for concerted European action at the UN level to engage relevant partners, including those most uncomfortable with European positions (Gowan and Brantner 2011). UN debates on intervention in the Ivory Coast and in Libya, as well as on how to deal with the violent government repression of the uprising in Syria, exposed a varying degree of pragmatism on the part of the BRICS countries. The defence of the principle of non-interference is one variable among others in determining their position. Recent experience suggests that there is at least room for the EU to engage some of these partners on the question of responsibility to protect. The debate on 'responsibility while protecting' launched by Brazil at the UN in November 2011, following controversy over the conduct of the Libya operation, provides an important input in this context.[6]

Bilateral partnerships can be a suitable format for regular exchanges on geopolitical hotspots, such as the sensitive question of Iran's nuclear programme. The 5+1 group leading international diplomatic efforts includes of course three EU strategic partners (the United States, Russia and China). The positions of India and also Brazil (let alone Turkey) are increasingly important factors in the equation. China and Russia supported the United States and the EU in imposing sanctions on Iran in 2010 but opposed further coercive measures in 2011. The effectiveness of Western sanctions is at least in part predicated on the stance of Asian powers concerning their energy imports from Iran. Russia, China and others are part of the critical mass that can foster progress: they are walking a tightrope between their concern with WMD proliferation and their suspicion of punitive or intrusive measures sponsored by the United States and the EU.

High level dialogues and councils on issues of energy and climate change, such as those established with, among others, the United States, China and Brazil, are an important complement to laborious multilateral negotiations in this domain. Cooperation on concrete projects or sectors such as carbon capture and storage with China, clean energy technologies with the United States and China and bio-fuels with Brazil builds mutual understanding from the bottom up and, if sustained through regular consultations, can create space for innovative deals at the multilateral level. Intensive dialogue between the EU and Brazil has, for example, played a critical role to set the terms of the deal reached at the Durban conference

---

6   Letter from the Permanent Representative of Brazil to the United Nations addressed to the Secretary General and Annex, A/66/551, 9 November 2011. This initiative was followed by an informal UN General Assembly discussion on 'Responsibility while Protecting' hosted by the Minister of External Relations of Brazil on 21 February in New York.

on climate change in December 2011, including the prospect of introducing by 2015 a framework with legal force on emissions reduction applying to all emitters.

Dialogues on development cooperation have recently been upgraded with the United States and Japan but also with China and Brazil. The EU aims to develop so-called triangular cooperation on development and related issues (food security, health but also good governance and human rights) with its partners and recipient countries, notably in Africa. For example, triangular cooperation with Brazil focuses on bio-energy development in Africa. Bilateral exchanges in this domain also fit into the difficult shift towards a new development agenda with the input of old and new donors.

Because of its own experience of integration, the EU is a natural advocate of multilateral cooperation. This reputational advantage, however, can quickly turn into a political deficit if the EU and its member states do not practice what they preach. As noted above, lack of cohesion in tackling its economic crisis has diminished the EU as a strategic partner and in turn hampered its ability to work with others in the context of the G20. Likewise, EU member states resist pulling their weight and representation in Bretton Woods institutions, which affects the credibility of the Union as a partner and an agent of effective multilateralism. In these and other fields, enhancing multilateral cooperation through EU partnerships requires a high degree of internal cohesion, and joined up policy-making.

The Process: Business as Usual Plus

Strategic partnerships offer an interesting vantage point to observe the interconnection between political discourse, institution-building and policy-making. The issue of strategic partnerships climbed the EU foreign policy agenda right at the time when the Treaty of Lisbon came into force and new appointments were made to the top EU posts. Deepening these partnerships provided a rationale for progress in implementing the Lisbon Treaty reforms and a political selling point for the new EU leadership. The newly appointed President of the European Council convened an extraordinary meeting of the European Council mainly dedicated to EU foreign policy and strategic partnerships in September 2010, preceded by an informal debate at ministerial level at the Gymnich meeting in Brussels.

According to its conclusions, the European Council discussed in September 2010 'how to give new momentum to the Union's external relations, taking full advantage of the opportunities provided by the Lisbon Treaty'. Besides, leaders agreed that, 'In accordance with the Lisbon Treaty, and in line with the European Security Strategy, the EU and its Member States will act more strategically so as to bring Europe's true weight to bear internationally'. The EEAS is called upon to support all EU institutions 'concerning the strategic overview and coordination necessary to ensure the coherence of the European Union's external action as a whole'.[7]

As mandated by the summit conclusions, the HR delivered in December 2010 a first set of three reports focusing on the United States, Russia and China and sketching out the objectives of the Union over the short to medium term and some options on how to achieve them. While the EEAS was taking the first steps in the course of 2011, the elaboration of the EU approach to strategic partners continued, although in a rather unstructured way. Three more reports addressing the partnerships with Brazil, India and South Africa were delivered to the Gymnich meeting in Sopot in September last year.

There is a notable affinity between the goals pursued by institutional reform under the Lisbon Treaty and the basic requirements for running effective strategic partnerships. Doing so presupposes vision, confidence, direction, coordination and flexibility. The reforms introduced by the Lisbon Treaty are essentially about providing more continuity, coherence and agenda-setting capacity at European level, while thickening the links between EU and national diplomatic structures and initiatives.

Discrete, incremental if as yet inadequate progress can be detected in EU policy-making concerning strategic partnerships. The EEAS is laying out the building blocks of a more integrated approach to them. However, the mostly polite but decidedly unsentimental liaison of the new service with the Commission often falls short of delivering joined up policies.

Ongoing reflection on EU strategic partnerships within the EEAS suggests a shift from a focus on the 'partners' to a focus on 'partnering'. In other words, a partner-based and an issue-based approach need to co-exist and reinforce each other. The question for policy-makers is not just what can be done with individual partners but which partners can work with the EU in addressing priority issues. Emphasis on partnering in addressing concrete requirements enriches the concept of strategic partnerships beyond the bilateral dimension and helps develop a nimbler approach to international cooperation. That said, it is harder to implement in a rather segmented institutional framework.

A strong input from the top down has been and remains essential to mobilise services in the pursuit of strategic partnerships. The PEC has put the issue on the map early on and gained credit for a proactive approach to the partnerships question. The HR has complemented this drive with a prevalent focus on the foreign and security policy dimension, launching or deepening high level foreign policy dialogues with the United States, China and India. The PEC, the President of the Commission and the HR constitute the so-called new Troika replacing the rotating presidency of the EU Council vis-à-vis important external partners. On this and other dimensions of EU foreign policy, the advantage of continuity is at least in part offset by the lack of the fresh initiatives sponsored by successive presidencies. Besides, commitment at the top is as important as it is volatile, given

---

7　Conclusions of the European Council, EUCO 21/10, 16 September 2010.

the unpredictable sequence of crises and priorities absorbing the time and attention of EU leaders.

Sustained commitment at the highest political and institutional levels is decisive to better structure summit preparations and follow up. Roughly four or five months in advance of scheduled bilateral summits, inter-service meetings are convened to select priorities and delegate follow up. Considerable effort is going to improve the previously very weak capacity to monitor the implementation of summit commitments. The practice is emerging to deliver annual progress reports as well as interim ones to member states' representatives in geographic working groups. While of course not decisive to enhance coordination among member states, these reports offer at least common updated information as a shared basis for decision-making.

Coordination is a Treaty obligation for EU institutions and EU member states, an imperative for effective partnerships and a core task of the EEAS. And yet, with a view to strategic partnerships, progress on this score has been slim. The core platform for inter-service (EEAS and Commission) consultation and coordination on individual partnerships are the country teams, inherited from the pre-Lisbon Treaty era. They typically meet every three or four months, even if the launch of the EEAS and the corresponding rotation of personnel has introduced some discontinuity, and are convened and chaired by the EEAS. Some officials stress the importance of these meetings for networking and socialization with colleagues from other institutions or departments. That said, it is widely acknowledged that the EEAS hosts these meetings but does not carry the weight to set priorities and steer coordination across the various dimensions of EU external action which fall within the remit of the Commission.

Coordination by consent, or good will, may occasionally work but is not a sound premise for integrated policy-making. However, there is no legal solution to an essentially political and cultural problem. More frequent meetings of the so-called RELEX group of Commissioners, chaired by the HR, could be considered a vehicle to provide joined-up direction. At the same time, her prerogatives under CFSP leave to the HR little space for sustained investment in the coordination of external action at large.

Within the EEAS itself, the flow of information between geographic and thematic divisions is not systematic. There appears to be more than occasional disconnect between officials working on individual partners and those dealing with dossiers of relevance for respective partnerships, except in the run up to key events, as well as between the proceedings of geographic and thematic Council working groups, where a silos approach still prevails. This makes geographic groups useful for a comprehensive overview of the partnership but unsuitable to amalgamate issues, reconciling different policy strands in an integrated stance towards a strategic partner.

Cross-sectoral policy-making, a presumed by-product of Lisbon Treaty reforms, is mostly yet to materialise. This is not a challenge specific to the EU, as inter-agency competition is a familiar feature of policy-making at the national level too. Given its fragmented governance system, however, bureaucratic disconnects pose a critical vulnerability for the EU in dealings with its strategic partners. Comprehensive strategies are hard to lay out and ultimate authority is hard to locate, which hinders a flexible posture and the definition of issue-linkages and trade-offs.

Coordination between the EU and its member states in dealing with strategic partners remains loose. At the political level, the end of the rotating presidency of the EU Council in the foreign policy domain poses a problem of ownership of EU strategic partnerships among member states, which are no longer responsible for running the summits with third parties. At working level, geographic groups in the Council are the main transmission belt for regular consultation. These groups also meet at directors' level, meaning with the participation of key officials from national capitals, three or four times per year, which allows for a direct connection between senior EU and national policy-makers. Council working groups are involved in the preparations of joint bilateral commissions or committees (when the partnerships are based on partnership and association agreements or similar Community formats) and of summit meetings.

On balance, information between EU institutions and member states seems to flow better one way – towards capitals – than the other – towards Brussels. Member states, and notably the larger ones, do not share much information on respective bilateral dealings and even less so on bilateral security cooperation with strategic partners. It even proves difficult to get capitals to share the timing of respective high level meetings with relevant partners. Such information, collected in a running calendar, would allow to better connect successive meetings, as recommended by the European Council almost two years ago.

Slow, piecemeal innovation in Brussels reportedly contrasts with some progress in coordination between EU and national officials on the ground. The leadership of large EU delegations such as those in Beijing and Delhi has been renewed and top political advisers appointed coming from national diplomatic services. These and other delegations have taken a proactive approach in pursuing coordination with national missions via different meeting formats, whether with a sectoral focus (political counsellors, human rights, development) or at the level of Heads of mission. The latter quite regularly issue joint reports to Brussels and EU delegations increasingly feed into policy-making at headquarters' level, for example in the run up to summit meetings. Delegations also play an important role in the management of the increasingly frequent visits of very senior EU officials to partner countries, streamlining an important and intensifying level of interaction. Institutional practice seems paradoxically more advanced in the field than in Brussels. That said, the quest for compromise between different national postures and agenda-setting upstream poses a different order of political challenges than coordination in representation, monitoring and reporting in the field.

Conclusion

EU strategic partnerships are a work in progress and their output is very uneven, depending on the respective partner countries and policy domains. This chapter has argued that strategic partnerships transcend the purely bilateral dimension to connect multiple levels of cooperation in the pursuit of the distinctive EU normative goal of strengthening international cooperation.

Over the last 10 years, the EU has been widening the range of its strategic partnerships without a clear rationale but engagement with major global and regional players was elevated to an EU foreign policy priority in 2010. Drawing definitive conclusions on the development and efficacy of EU strategic partnerships under the post-Lisbon Treaty regime would be premature at this stage. However, an interim and non-comprehensive assessment of recent experience shows a modest, if as yet unsatisfactory, degree of progress.

At the bilateral level, strategic partnerships have grown more focused with the negotiation of several large trade and investment deals with South Korea, Canada, India and, in perspective, Japan, and the launch of an action plan for growth and jobs with the United States. The economic dimension is complemented by the establishment of high level dialogues on foreign and security affairs with China and India and of similar formats addressing climate change and energy issues with the United States and China, among others. Concrete projects and specific areas of cooperation have been identified under these frameworks.

The EU has shown a clear intent to mobilise bilateral partnerships to address global and regional issues and crises with its partners. This is part of a nimbler, if only tentative, approach to bridge normative divides and foster international cooperation by linking bilateral, mini-lateral and multilateral formats. Evidence of progress is as yet rather modest but sustained bilateral dialogues are key to building the necessary confidence and common ground to join forces, or avert clashes, on the global stage.

From an institutional standpoint, emphasis on the importance of selected partnerships has focussed minds and entailed some progress in policy-making. However, this process remains fragmented and fails to inform a sense of strategic purpose. At the political level, the financial and economic crisis has strained political cohesion within the Union, sidelined foreign policy priorities and seriously affected the EU's profile and credibility in the eyes of its strategic partners. It remains to be seen whether EU institutions and members states will mobilise sufficient political will to make of the economic crisis a political opportunity, define their core priorities and join forces to pursue them on the global stage. Strategic partnerships will be a critical test of their common resolve, or mutual estrangement. The jury is still out.

Chapter 10

The Efficacy of Post-Lisbon Treaty EU's External Actions and China–EU Strategic Partnership

Chen Zhimin

Abstract

At the time of EU's new post-Lisbon foreign policy apparatus being put into place, the relationship between the EU and China was experiencing its low point after the launching of a bilateral strategic partnership in 2004. The chapter argues that, with the uplifted focus on EU's bilateral strategic partnerships, new EU foreign policy leaders and institutions have made a series of important steps to revitalize relations with China. Such a more pragmatic China policy is also partly shaped by the economic challenges stemming from Europe's sovereign debt problem, even though the overwhelming focus on managing this internal economic crisis has distracted the EU's attention from foreign policy, including its relations with China. Nevertheless, the improved atmosphere in bilateral relations has not so far been translated into substantial achievements in the relationship in addressing the key concerns of the two sides. Furthermore, the existence of the two-level system in the EU, hence the development of two-level strategic partnerships with China, has complicated the process of partnership-building.

Introduction

The Lisbon Reform Treaty created a vastly different EU foreign policy apparatus and facilitated renewed efforts to revitalize the EU's bilateral strategic partnership strategy. This chapter will assess the efficacy of post-Lisbon Treaty EU's external actions in the context of EU–China strategic partnership building. It will investigate if a reformed EU foreign policy institution has contributed to reverting the hollowing-out of a once thriving EU–China strategic partnership before the Lisbon reform. It will also discuss the impacts of the European financial crisis on the EU's handling of its relations with China, and explore how the two-level nature of the EU foreign policy system complicates the development of this partnership.

The EU–China Strategic Partnership: The Pre-Lisbon Treaty Ups and Downs

Amid heightened concerns over American unilateralism in the wake of the American invasion of Iraq, in September 2003, the European Commission issued a new China policy paper, which stressed that 'the EU and China have an ever-greater interest to work together as strategic partners to safeguard and promote sustainable development, peace and stability'.[1] A year later, the EU and China announced the launching of a China–EU strategic partnership.

From the mid-1990s, China has initiated partnership diplomacy, aiming to form closer collaborative relations with major players around the world, but avoiding any formal security alliance. The new strategy saw its first bilateral partnership with Brazil in 1993, then with Russia in 1996, and a short-lived one with the United States in 1997. After the 1998 announcement of a China–EU 'comprehensive partnership', a further lift to a strategic partnership is anticipated as a logical development from the Chinese side. On the EU side, the EU used the expression 'strategic partnership' for the first time in its relations with Russia in 1998. The reason why the EU is a latecomer in developing strategic partnerships 'is that strategic partnerships cover two dimensions in which the EU has traditionally been quite ineffective, i.e. a strategic approach to foreign policy and bilateral relations with other powers' (Renard 2011: 7). As the EU tried to find common ground for its Common Foreign and Security Policy (CFSP) and European Security and Defence Policy (ESDP) after the bitter internal division over responses to the American military intervention in Iraq in March 2003, the European Security Strategy, drafted in June and finalized in December 2003, enlisted six EU strategic partners, which included China.[2]

The launching of China–EU strategic partnership in 2003 was of real substance. The bilateral economic relationship was booming, a wide range of sectoral dialogue mechanisms were in place, and the relationship was increasingly institutionalized with an annual China–EU summit at the top level, supported by regular meetings of ministers and senior officials. More importantly, on some real strategic matters, EU countries, particularly those who opposed the war in Iraq, like France and Germany, intended to develop closer cooperation with China with a shared interest in constraining American unilateralism under the Bush administration. The EU and China signed an agreement on cooperation in the EU's Galileo satellite navigation programme in 2003, which was seen by the United States as a rival to the American GPS system, thus not welcomed; and later that year, French President Jacques Chirac and German Chancellor Gerhard Schroeder both publicly supported a re-examination and possible lifting of the EU's arms embargo policy against China. The rapid warming of relations between the EU

---

1   European Commission, 'A Maturing Partnership – Shared Interests and Challenges in EU-China Relations' (2003). COM(2003) 533.

2   See 'A Secure Europe In A Better World: European Security Strategy', Brussels, 12 December 2003.

and China in 2003 and 2004 led observers to proclaim that a China–EU 'Axis' was in the making (Shambaugh 2004: 243–8).

However, the 'love affair' between the EU and China did not last long. As the United States faced a prolonged struggle in both Iraq and Afghanistan, the second Bush administration started to improve its relations with its European allies, thus reduced the European anxiety over a more hegemonic United States, and hence the incentive to forge closer strategic ties with China. After leadership changes in Germany (2005) and France (2007), German Chancellor Merkel and French President Sarkozy both put the United States on top in their foreign policy agenda, and embraced at a certain point a so-called values-based diplomacy, which triggered a number of political problems with China, such as more official meetings between the Dalai Lama and Chancellor Merkel and President Sarkozy. The latter event was especially annoying to the Chinese side, as President Sarkozy at the time was also presiding over the European Council. In the aftermath of this meeting, China cancelled the China–EU summit during the French presidency, which was a major setback for both China–France and China–EU relations. Moreover, China's investment and participation in the development of the EU's Galileo satellite navigation programme was seen as a symbol of the 'strategic partnership'. However, a few years later, the EU changed its mind, and in 2008 finally decided to exclude Chinese contractors in the procurement scheme for the second phase of Galileo. With that decision, some observers argued that, by the summer of 2008, the 'Sino-European techno-political linkage would be largely over' (Casarini 2009: 2). In return, China decided to launch its own Beidou satellite navigation system, and the two sides locked in a head-on competition for the same frequency (He 2009).

While the political and strategic substance of the partnership is being diluted, bilateral economic relations, which used to be seen as perfectly win-win and complementary, also became somewhat controversial. After the EU became the number one trading partner of China, the EU complained about its enlarging trade deficit with China, and stepped up its pressures on China to open its market. The 2006 Commission China policy paper labelled China as the EU's 'single most importance challenge to EU's trade policy'.[3] The change of tones and approaches in the EU's trade policy towards China led one American scholar to claim that the EU was adopting an Americanized style (Bates 2008: 276).

Lisbon Reform Treaty and its Boost for China–EU Strategic Partnership

The Lisbon Treaty created a brand new foreign policy apparatus for the EU: the EU takes over the European Community as the legal person under international law; at

---

3　European Commission, *Accompanying COM(2006) 631 final: Closer Partners, Growing Responsibilities. A Policy Paper on EU-China Trade and Investment: Competition and Partnership*, Commission working document, Brussels, 24 October 2006.

the summit level, it puts in place a permanent president of the European Council, abolishing the rotating system to ensure policy continuity; at foreign minister level, the new High Representative for Foreign Affairs and Security Policy (HR), combining the functions previously held by the High Representative, the foreign minister of the rotating presidency and the Commissioner for external relations in the European Commission, is empowered to preside over the Council of foreign ministers, lead and coordinate the external actions of the Commission, and shall be supported by an integrated European External Action Service (EEAS). The EEAS is 'a functionally autonomous body of the Union under the authority of the High Representative'[4] and modelled after national foreign ministries, has its central administration in Brussels and 140 delegations in third countries or international organizations. By the end of 2011, the EEAS had 3,611 staff, including 1,551 working in Brussels and 2,060 in delegations.[5]

Many observers deplored the fact that member states decided to install two low-profile politicians, Mr Herman Van Rompuy of Belgium and Lady Ashton of the UK, to fill the two new positions, which seemingly underused the potential offered by the treaty reforms (Patten 2009). Nevertheless, as the system starts to function, a new momentum for a more purposeful and strategic EU foreign policy is activated.

After a preparatory informal Gymnich meeting of foreign ministers chaired by Lady Ashton, a special EU Council was held in September 2010 to discuss the EU's strategic partnership, a first attempt in the EU to address the issue at the highest level. In the President's Conclusion after the meeting, the European Council stressed that the European Union and its member states should 'act more strategically so as to bring Europe's true weight to bear internationally'. In doing so, the EU has to clearly identify its strategic interests and objectives at a given moment, as well as the means to pursue them more assertively. In that context, 'the European Union's strategic partnerships with key players in the world provide a useful instrument for pursuing European objectives and interests'.[6]

While European leaders acknowledged the emergence of new players with their own worldviews and interests as an important new feature in the international environment, they seemed to set their strategic priority in relations with emerging powers on securing Europe's balanced share of the growth benefit, and ensuring the even sharing of international responsibilities by the emerging powers, in the name of 'reciprocity'. In particular, regarding the October 2010 EU–China summit, the

---

4 Council of the European Union, *Council Decision of 26 July 2010 Establishing the Organisation and Functioning of the European External Action Service*, 2010/427/EU. http://eur-lex.europa.eu/LexUriServ/LexUriServ.do?uri=OJ:L:2010:201:0030:0040:EN:PDF.

5 Report by the High Representative to the European Parliament, the Council and the Commission, 22 December 2011, para. 21. http://eeas.europa.eu/images/top_stories/2011_eeas_report_cor_+_formatting.pdf.

6 European Council. European Council conclusions on 16 September 2010. Brussels.

Conclusions called for the EU to 'actively pursue its strategic interests, including as regards the promotion of bilateral trade, market access for goods and services and investment conditions; the protection of intellectual property rights and the opening up of public procurement markets; stronger discipline in the field of export subsidies; and the dialogue on exchange rate policies'.[7] On appearance, the demands were all economic, neither political and security issues were mentioned, nor a trade-off formula was offered.

The October 2010 EU–China summit was a failure, ending up with a very short joint statement of only 11 paragraphs. One analysis of the failure was that reciprocity was applied too bluntly and without the necessary preparation that negotiation with China requires (Vaïsse et al. 2011: 28). In other words, while the EU was not prepared to lift the arms embargo, its counter-demands for granting China a market economy status (MES) were far beyond what China was willing to accept. For China, MES has been a top demand in its relations with the EU. However, according to China's WTO accession agreements, China will automatically enjoy that status by 2016. So the value of MES has been depleting year by year. China may offer some economic concessions in exchange for earlier obtainment of that status, but it seems that Europe's demands were way beyond what China was willing to accept.

Under Van Rompuy's request, Catherine Ashton presented to the December 2010 European Council meeting a first 19-page progress report on the EU's strategic partnerships, which focused on the United States, China and Russia. According to media reports, Ashton adopted a pragmatic approach with regard to China. Catherine Ashton reopened the issue of the EU's arms embargo against China, saying the current arms embargo is a 'major impediment for developing stronger EU-China co-operation on foreign policy and security matters', and the EU should 'assess its practical implication and design a way forward'. On human rights issues, although Ashton would continue to promote the EU's norms, she admitted that the EU can do little to change Chinese society. 'China will not match EU standards of human rights and rule of law for some time to come. Future convergence is best sought by concentrating on common ground.' Acknowledging widespread negative views about China in Europe, she also proposed that the EU should 'design a coherent communication strategy' to 'explain' its view of China to the European public, with 'facts about China [to] be mainstreamed at all levels of education' (Rettman 2010).

Ashton's proposal did not get off to a good start. She failed to persuade the UK and other Beijing-critical member states to lift the EU arms embargo on China. In the following meeting of EU foreign ministers, the arms embargo issue was not discussed, and apparently there was no new consensus on lifting the arms embargo (Rettman 2011).

On 12 May 2011, Catherin Ashton met in Prague with her Chinese counterpart, State Councillor Dai Bingguo, for a second EU–China strategic dialogue. China

---

7   Ibid.

and the EU had established strategic dialogue at the vice-ministerial level from 2005. After the Lisbon Treaty, both sides agreed to upgrade it into a HR–state councillor level between Ashton and Dai Bingguo, equivalent to the same dialogue level between China and the United States, a sign from the Chinese side that they took seriously the enhanced role of Ashton in the EU foreign policy system, and its attempt to make use of this reform to move the relationship forward. The first strategic dialogue was held in Guizhou, the hometown of Mr Dai and the capital of one of poorest provinces in China, designed to add personal attachment to the relationship-building and allow Ashton to get a glimpse of the developing part of China. Like the first one, the second strategic dialogue functioned as the platform for the two sides to engage in an in-depth exchange of views on a wide range of issues to enhance mutual strategic trust, and was not intended for for substantive negotiations on concrete issues.[8]

Just few days later, Mr. Van Rompuy the President of the European Council, made his first visit out of Europe to China. The meeting was mainly a get-to-know-each-other one. Besides meetings with Chinese top leaders, Mr Van Rompuy delivered a major speech on EU–China relations at China's Central Party School which trains current and future senior leaders. In the speech, Mr Van Rompuy stressed that, since he took office, he has placed the EU–China relationship 'in the centre of an important internal debate' focusing on the strategic partners of the EU. To his understanding, European leaders have shown a great desire to develop a 'reliable, constructive and forward-looking strategic partnership with China', which should be based 'on the principles of shared responsibility, cooperation and openness'.[9]

On 24 October 2011, Catherine Ashton met Chinese Defence Minister Liang Guanglie in Beijing to explore possible new military cooperation. The two sides exchanged views on promoting China–EU military ties and enhancing maritime escort cooperation and reached several agreements. Maritime escorting in the Gulf of Aden and waters near Somalia has become a new area for cooperation between China and the EU. Both sides have cooperated well during meetings of the UN-led International Contact Group on Piracy off the Coast of Somalia since international escort initiatives began in 2008.[10]

The fourteenth EU–China Summit was held in Beijing on 14 February 2012. The Joint Press Communique released after the summit set a positive tone for the relationship. It said that 'the EU-China Comprehensive Strategic Partnership

---

8   Yuanfang Zhao, 'zhongou zhanlue duihua de "xu" yu "shi"' ['China-EU StrategicDialogue: Its "Conceptual" and "Substantive" Roles'], China Radio International, 13 May 2011.http://gb.cri.cn/27824/2011/05/13/2225s3246082.htm.

9   Herman Van Rompuy, 'Europe and China in an Interdependent World', Speech at the Central Party School, Beijing. 17 May 2011. http://www.consilium.europa.eu/uedocs/cms_data/docs/pressdata/en/ec/122013.pdf.

10   Defence Ministry, China, 'China to Promote Defense Cooperation with EU', 27 October 2011. http://eng.mod.gov.cn/MiltaryExchanges/2011-10/27/content_4309092.htm.

is entering a new important stage of development', with progress 'both in width and in depth'. The two sides expressed 'the determination to set a good example for international cooperation in the 21st century, fully contributing to the cause of making this century one of peace, cooperation and development'. Progresses are mostly in the bilateral relations as they announce a series of new initiatives: establishment of the EU–China High Level People-to-People Dialogue, launching of a new negotiation on an EU–China investment agreement which would promote and facilitate investment in both directions, setting up a new EU–China High-Tech Trade Working Group to facilitate trade in high technology, the establishment of the EU–China Partnership on Urbanisation, the convening of a EU–China High Level Energy Meeting, etc. The two sides also found new common ground on thorny issues (MES and Galileo) in the bilateral relations. On the MES issue, the two sides 'stressed that particular importance should be given to working for the resolution of the Market Economy Status (MES) issue in a swift and comprehensive way'. On the Galileo issue, the two sides 'reaffirmed that they will continue the cooperation on the Civil Global Navigation Satellite System (GNSS)-Galileo following the 2003 Agreement, with an effort to make positive progress in the cooperation, and to seek and foster new cooperation areas in satellite navigation science and its application'.[11]

However, the Communiqué only has six paragraphs to address regional and global issues. Among them, five are about global non-political issues, with only one short and vague paragraph dealing with political and security issues. Leaders from both sides could be satisfied with their cooperation on many non-political issues. China has been vocally supportive of Europe's management of its sovereign debt crisis, either through the IMF or G20. On the climate change issue, after the bitter experience in Copenhagen, both China and the EU adopted more pragmatic approaches, which facilitated better convergence between the EU and China. In the December 2011 climate change conference in Durban, South Africa, the EU committed itself for a prolonged period to the Kyoto Protocol and in return China was flexible to commit itself for a future legally binding global pact. However, on the political front, China and European countries found themselves at odds over the handling of the crises in Libya and Syria. China, along with European countries, supported international sanctions on the Qaddafi regime in February 2011. However, China became increasingly critical of the regime change efforts by the French, British and NATO forces in their Libyan military operation, on the basis that it went beyond the authorization by the UN Security Council resolution 1973 to protect Libyan civilians. China did not support the resolution, but also did not block it. The bad feeling from the Libya case has since prompted China, together with Russia, to veto three draft resolutions sponsored by European countries concerning the Syria crisis.

---

11   Council of the European Union, 'Joint Press Communique of the 14th EU-China Summit', Beijing, 14 February 2012. http://www.consilium.europa.eu/uedocs/cms_data/docs/pressdata/EN/foraff/127967.pdf.

In contrast, the Joint Press Communiqué issued after the EU–India summit just a few days before the EU–China summit had 14 paragraphs on regional and global issues, with eight paragraphs underlining their common grounds and joint approaches in dealing with international political and security challenges,[12] a fact which indicates the serious lack of common grounds in the political and security policies between the EU and China.

The Ongoing European Financial Crisis: Torpedo or Opportunity?

As Lisbon Treaty lifted the EU's institutional capacity to pursue its foreign policy, the EU was almost at the same time hit by a serious sovereign debt crisis in the Eurozone area with profound foreign policy implications for the EU. This section will look at how the crisis has an impact on the building of a strategic partnership with China.

EU countries were heavily hit by the global financial and economic crisis that originated in Wall Street in 2008. As the United States was seemingly pulling itself out of the crisis at the beginning of 2010, Europe was reaching the second wave of the crisis, and this time, it originated from within. Since then, managing the sovereign debt crisis has become the overwhelming priority of the European leaders. On 9 May 2010, EU finance ministers decided to create the European Financial Stability Facility (EFSF), with €440 billion lending capacity to ensure financial stability across Europe. Additional financial support was also secured from the International Monetary Fund (IMF). Substantial bail-out loans were offered to crisis-hit countries, but the contagion still spread to larger economies in Southern Europe. To save the financial stability, European leaders had to engage in numerous summit meetings, which distracted them from their external relations, including relations with key strategic partners of the EU.

In October 2011, the EU scheduled its annual summits with India and China, respectively, on 24 and 26 October. However, a European Council meeting to enlarge the EFSF lending capacity and to decide on the conditions for a second bail-out loan for Greece before these summits had to be postponed to 23 October, due to the deadlocks at the ministerial meetings. Apparently, the EU decided first to postpone the EU–India summit, and hoped that a successful EU Council on 23 October might still allow the EU–China summit to take place. This caused some observers to deplore the fact that the EU was favouring China over India, and 'the EU's Asia policy looks increasingly like a China policy' (Youngs 2011). However, as the prospect for a deal on 23 October became dim, Mr Van Rompuy had to call Premier Wen Jiabao of China to postpone the EU–China summit. A package deal

---

12   Council of the European Union, India-European Union summit – Joint Statement, New Delhi, 10 February 2012. http://www.consilium.europa.eu/uedocs/cms_data/docs/pressdata/EN/foraff/127934.pdf.

among European leaders was reached on 26 October, the cost was first the EU–India summit, and second the EU–China summit.

The financial crisis not only disrupted the EU's handling of its relations with outside players, it also affected the EU's aid policy with regard to emerging powers, including China. In the middle of 2011, the European Commission conducted a review on its development policy. The review argued that the EU needs to focus 'its limited resources in a strategic manner', which implied 'the cessation of EU development assistance, or its diminution' for countries such as Brazil, China, India and South Africa, other G20 members and some middle income countries in Asia and Latin America. Instead, priority aid will be given to 'Neighbourhood' states, sub-Saharan Africa and the world's least developed countries in future (Willis 2011).

In the aftermath of the financial crisis, the EU, which has been a leader in economic liberalization, has witnessed some reversal of the spirit of economic openness. Many new regulations discriminate against non-EU states and companies. Export subsidies have increased significantly. Covert forms of protectionism abound. Scholarly works and official figures all confirm that the EU has resorted to such covert, non-border measures more than any other region since 2008 (Youngs 2011: 6).

Furthermore, to some Europeans, Europe's current crisis has tempered its efforts to build a strategic partnership on EU terms. In the view of the 2012 ECFR report, it is of course easier for member states to cut their own deals with China, especially when they feel other EU member states are not being as supportive as they should be, than to collectively develop a coherent China policy that is able to secure equal access and fair competition. But in putting short-term need above a long-term vision, 'Europe risks reducing its supposedly strategic relationship with Beijing to a profit-making opportunity – for China' (Vaïsse et al. 2012).

The wide reporting of the economic difficulties in Europe also created a tarnished image of Europe in China. Chinese people previously tended to view Europe and the European integration process in a very positive light. As the current crisis exposed the weakness within the EU and also its international standing, Europe is starting to be seen by China as of declining influence. Yang Jiemian, an expert in China on the United States and the head of the influential Chinese think-tank, the Shanghai Institute of International Studies, in his 'Four Groups' theory in early 2010, put Europe in the Losing group, with the EU gradually losing its 'No. 2' status in the world, becoming a reform target in the international institutions, and having to 'transfer' some power and interests in the IMF and World Bank (Yang 2010: 5–6). In January 2011, China's newspaper *Global Times*, an affiliated newspaper to the official *People's Daily*, released its new annual survey on Chinese attitudes towards the outside world. The newspaper has conducted such surveys for five consecutive years. For the first four years, China–Europe relations were seen as the least important bilateral relations that China engaged with major powers, including the United States, Japan and Russia, although it jumped in 2009, almost on par with Japan and Russia, possibly because of the ratification of the

Lisbon Treaty. Nevertheless, in 2010, while Chinese people still overwhelmingly regarded relations with the United States as the most influential one for China, the importance of relations with Europe suffered a dramatic fall, from 19.9 per cent down to 7.3 per cent, which was also significantly lower than in 2006.

Against all these odds, a more positive view would argue that the arrival of the sovereign debt crisis offers a much-needed opportunity for the revitalization of the EU–China strategic partnership.

Over the last three years, the economic relationship between the EU and China has become more balanced in terms of mutual dependence. The EU's yearly growth rate of export to China rose 5.3 per cent, in contrast to an overall decline of 16.2 per cent in 2009. In 2010, while EU exports registered an impressive 23 per cent, its exports to China rose 37.4 per cent.[13] EU exports in both goods and services in 2011 were up to €156.4 billion from €133.3 billion in the previous year. EU imports from China rose only slightly from €299 billion in 2010 to €308 billion in 2011. This clearly shows the EU has reduced its overall trade deficit with China.[14]

At the same time, Europe also becomes a favoured destination of China's overseas direct investment. According to estimates by A Capital, a private-equity firm, in 2011, China's direct investment in European firms surged to $10.4 billion, from $4.1 billion in 2010, which makes Europe the leading destination for Chinese firms' investment abroad in 2011, accounting for 34 per cent of all outbound merger and acquisition activity (Back 2012).

On the finance aspect, as China emerged as the world's largest foreign currency reserve country with $3.3 trillion in hand as of March 2012, China could be of some serious help for the Europeans in dealing with their financial crisis. The current euro crisis, triggered by the debt crisis of Southern EU countries, has erupted at a time when other major developed economies, such as the United States and Japan, are in financial strife. China, in pledging not to divest from euro assets and its gesture to buy further government bonds from EU countries, has contributed to the European efforts to calm the volatile European financial markets, something few other non-EU countries have done. China contributed $50 billion to strengthen the lending capacity of the International Monetary Fund in 2009. During the February 2012 EU–China summit, Premier Wen Jiabao stated publicly that 'China is ready to be more deeply involved in solving the European debt issues and would like to maintain close communication and collaboration with the EU'.[15] In the G20

---

13   DG Trade, European Commission, 'China: Trade Statistics', 12 January 2012. http://trade.ec.europa.eu/doclib/docs/2006/september/tradoc_113366.pdf.

14   'EU-Asian Cooperation in an Era of Transformation', Speech by Commissioner De Gucht at the Foreign Correspondents' Club, Hong Kong, 16 February 2012. http://trade.ec.europa.eu/doclib/docs/2012/february/tradoc_149130.pdf.

15   Chinese Premier Wen Jiabao, European Council President Herman Van Rompuy and European Commission President José Manuel Barroso Jointly Meet Journalists 2012/02/15. http://www.fmprc.gov.cn/eng/zxxx/t905503.htm.

summit meeting of June 2012, China announced its decision to participate in the IMF second round of resource boost with a pledge of $43 billion.[16]

From a Chinese perspective, the difficulties in EU–China relations during the past years are mostly due to assertive European policy towards China, either on normative or economic grounds. As Europe is now in much need of Chinese cooperation, its China policy is bestowed with a growing sense of pragmatism, which might lead to more common ground between China and the EU and hence more substantial cooperation. Accordingly, China should grasp this 'historical opportunity' to strengthen its strategic partnership with Europe (Pang 2012). Surely, Europe would be even less capable to advance its normative political and societal agenda towards China, be they in domestic development in China, or in the handlings of many global and regional affairs. However, a more pragmatic China policy will lead to enhanced cooperation between the EU and China, and strengthen Europe's capacity to deal with its more urgent and important issues, such as economic growth and the debt crisis. It might be difficult for the European side to fully acknowledge this new change, but recent developments in bilateral relations indicate that European leaders are moving in that direction.

Partnerships in Two Levels: To Whose Advantage?

Corresponding to the launching of a China–EU strategic partnership, China announced in 2004 three bilateral strategic partnerships, respectively with France, Italy and the United Kingdom. Strategic partnerships with Spain (2005), Portugal (2005), Denmark (2008), Germany (2010) and Poland (2011) were launched afterwards. While the strategic partnership with Portugal is mainly due to the Macao link between the two countries, clearly, except for the case of Denmark, the rest of the strategic partnerships are all with large member states. China's relations with Poland after the end of Cold War were never warm due to latter's staunch pro-US and anti-communist policy orientation. Therefore, the 2011 launching of a China–Poland strategic partnership signalled a major uplift of China's relations with the biggest new member state, as well as the improvement of China's relations with Central and Eastern European countries at large. A strategic partnership usually means the establishment of intensified high-level dialogues which cover a wide range of important issues. For example, China and the UK established an annual summit mechanism, a vice-premier level economic and financial dialogue, and a vice-ministerial level military strategic consultation mechanism. In the German case, annual inter-governmental consultation meetings were launched in 2011 where government leaders and key cabinet ministers meet to address common problems, a format of dialogue that China has only engaged with Russia before.

---

16 People's Bank of China, 'China Announced Participation in IMF Resource Boost', 20 June 2012. http://www.pbc.gov.cn/publish/english/955/2012/20120628155805079171579/20120628155805079171579_.html.

On 26 April 2012, a China-Central Europe-Poland Economic Forum was held in Warsaw. Speaking to representatives from 16 Central and Eastern European countries, including 14 heads of state or government, Chinese Prime Minister Wen Jiabao announced the creation of a $10 billion credit line to support Chinese investments in Central European infrastructure, new technology and renewable energy, and proposed a goal to reach a volume of $100 billion in trade with Central Europe by 2015 (Milner 2012).

The existence of the EU's two-level foreign policy system explains the persistence of substantive bilateral relationships between individual member states with China. In the common foreign and security policy aspect, as the EU only acts when there is a common position, there are still broad areas that member states need to deal with China directly. For the EU permanent members of the UN Security Council, France and the UK, and a few other member states which occasionally sit in the Security Council as non-permanent members, such as Germany, bilateral contacts with China would be essential for them to pursue an effective role in the Security Council. Also, as China's influence in various regions and other global affairs continues to rise, any member state which has a vested interest in a certain region or a certain policy issue needs to engage in bilateral coordination with China.

Even in the trade policy area where the EU develops a supranational Common Commercial Policy, member states still need to promote their business interests with regard to China. These interests include promoting sales of big items, like Airbus planes and nuclear power plants, to China, lobbying for market access into a particular sector of the Chinese market where a particular member state has a competitive edge, though this is usually done concurrently alongside efforts from the European Commission.

Furthermore, as economies of the member states suffered in the global financial and economic crisis and the ongoing European debt crisis, the re-nationalization of European foreign policy may add new imperatives for member states to engage proactive bilateral relations with third states, including China. As the EU's key member states either run into their own economic difficulties, or take on the heavy burden of bailing out the crisis-hit economies in Southern Europe, a growing number of member states feel the urgency and necessity to seek external help for themselves. Promoting export and seeking inward investment become even more important than before. Coincidentally, Chinese companies are seeking new markets for their direct foreign investments, and the Chinese government is trying to diversify investment of its $3.2 trillion foreign currency reserves. Therefore, attracting Chinese investments in the government bonds or domestic market becomes a new incentive for a member state to develop bilateral ties with China. So far, inward investment is an area where EU common rule and policy is not fully established, therefore is still largely managed by individual states.

The existence of parallel two-level bilateral relations with China produced very complicated consequences. For some Europeans, this means that China can exploit the divisions among EU member states, and hence obtain an upper hand over the EU (Fox and Godement 2009). On the Chinese side, after a period of wishful embracing of the EU as an increasingly important international player, Chinese observers tend to complain of the lack of unity within the EU and deplore the inability of the EU in forming internal consensus on key policy issues with regard to China, like granting China market economy status and lifting the arms embargo. As one retired senior diplomat argued, 'China rather hopes that EU could coordinate internally with regard to its China policy, instead of using internal differences as excuse to shed off responsibilities and run around' (Ding 2009: 32). The immobilism in China–EU relations pushed the Chinese side to rethink its sanguine views about the EU in recent years, and to pay increasing attention to the complicated nature of the EU. As China's former ambassador to Germany later commented, 'we Chinese gradually realize that we have overestimated and been too optimistic about the EU and its attitude towards China. Using the terms of economics, we can say that there are many "bubbles" in there' (Mei 2009: 18). To some extent, such a reassessment leads Chinese observers to reprioritize the member states of the EU. Feng Zhongping, one of leading European experts in China, even goes further to argue the paramount importance of the member states. As he argued, one lesson China possibly learned from China–EU relations over the past years is, no matter whether the issue is a political one or of another sort, the basis for China to deal with and develop relations remains those specific member states. In China's dealings with the EU, China has to remember member states first and EU institutions second. The relationship between the member states and EU institutions can be characterized as the following: it may be very difficult to achieve anything without the EU institutions, but if without the member states, nothing could be achieved (Feng 2009: 66–7).

The resulting mutual frustration suggests that the two sides need to reduce the opportunistic manipulation of the EU's two-level system: China needs to refrain from playing one player in the EU against the other, and the EU institutions and member states need to narrow the credibility gap in the eyes of the Chinese, work together to develop a more coherent and sensible China policy, balancing EU's concerns with Chinese ones, so that future EU–China dialogues and negotiations could lead to mutually beneficial and real results.

Therefore, it is encouraging that EU leaders have made efforts to revitalize the strategic partnership with China, and seemingly attempted to grasp the opportunity that has arisen from the European debt crisis, with some people even floating the idea of some kind of 'great swap' (Phillips 2011).

Conclusion

The new EU foreign policy apparatus added new momentum to the revitalization of the EU–China strategic partnership over the past three years, with the proactive efforts from the new European leaders, such as a special summit on strategic partnership, Lady Ashton's review report on key EU's strategic partnerships, and the dialogues with China via EU–China strategic dialogue, summit meetings and Mr Van Rompuy's visit to China in 2011. Obviously, the European sovereign debt crisis facilitated a more pragmatic approach from the EU side in its dealings with China. The overall tone of the relationship is becoming more positive, and initial steps to deepen the relationships have been fostered, as demonstrated by the encouraging results from the February 2012 annual EU–China summit. Yet, no major breakthroughs have been made so far in the relationship. While overall coordination seems to be improved in the EU, the DG Trade and DG Climate Action are still pursuing assertive sectoral policies towards China. Trade tensions continue while new open confrontation over the EU's carbon tax on airlines using EU airports for destination and departure surfaces, as China seemingly decides to suspend its order for Airbus planes in opposing the EU's carbon tax policy. The EU and member states adopt a more pragmatic approach in their political engagement with China bilaterally, but the EU's more proactive diplomacy in its neighbourhood to foster regime change in Libya and Syria has created new diplomatic rifts with China, a strong supporter of non-interference in domestic affairs. With these in mind, though more possible than before, any major progress in the development of the EU–China strategic partnership remains difficult, requiring the persistent and reciprocal efforts of European leaders and their Chinese counterparts in the coming months or years.

Chapter 11

The Efficiency of European External Action and the Institutional Evolution of EU–Japan Political Relations

Hidetoshi Nakamura

Abstract

For the EU, Japan is not merely one of the strategic partners, but also one of the like-minded partners, sharing 'fundamental values and principles, in particular, democracy, the rule of law and human rights'. This chapter will look back the historical development of institutional interaction between Europe and Japan. We will then examine the efficiency of European external action vis-à-vis Japan. European external action has been focused on economics, and so has Japan. The era of economic friction, during the 1970s and the 1980s, made the Europe–Japan institutional interaction evolve at several significant levels. It was only after the end of the Cold War when they were able to institutionalise the bilateral 'political' dialogue at their highest level: the bilateral summit meetings from July 1991. But, this bilateral institutional evolution has been closely linked with the development of transatlantic relations, and therefore, with the trilateral/multilateral institutional evolution. EU–Japan political relations have been the relationship between the civilian powers, and their interaction has still been responsive to the US policy in many areas. Nevertheless, two civilian powers are now able to cooperate politically, and even militarily. They are also proactive to the United States in such areas as climate change and renewable energy. It would be very hard for the short-term efficiency to be compatible with the long-term effectiveness. We should search for the more efficient European external/diplomatic action, but should not forget about the effectiveness.

Introduction

On 28 April 2010, the Japanese Prime Minister, and the Presidents of both the European Council and the European Commission met in Tokyo for the 19th Summit between Japan and the EU. For about two decades, they have affirmed 'their strong conviction that Japan and the EU are united by a shared commitment to fundamental values and principles, in particular, democracy, the rule of law and human rights'. However, that was supposed to be the special year. Yukio Hatoyama, Herman Van Rompuy and José Manuel Barroso 'recognised that 2010 is a year of renewal' and 'shared the view that this [change] provided an opportunity to renew the Japan-EU relationship, to take it to a higher level and to strengthen cooperation'.[1]

Indeed, the internal practices and institutions dramatically changed for both Japan and the EU in 2009. Each of those changes was made possible in a democratically legitimate way: the change from the Liberal Democratic Party (LDP)-led to the Democratic Party of Japan (DPJ)-led government, indeed the huge swing through the general elections on 30 August 2009; and the change of institutional architecture when the Lisbon Treaty came into force on 1 December 2009, after the long 'period of reflection' and another democratic, but successful, process of ratification. It was natural that we would expect both international actors to have more external effectiveness and efficiency.

In April 2010, the Japanese Prime Minister and Foreign Minister talked with the newly appointed leaders for the newly institutionalised EU external action apparatus: the President of the European Council and the High Representative of the Union for Foreign Affairs and Security Policy. But, in July 2012, are we able to observe that EU–Japan relations have much renewed in an efficient way? When the answer is no, whom should we blame for this external inefficiency?

Undoubtedly, Japan is to be blamed for its malfunction of consistent or innovative foreign policy. Even with the huge majority in the lower house, the DPJ-led government was not able to carry out its renewed and efficient foreign policy under the strong leadership. Even since September 2009, there have been three different Japanese Prime Ministers, and four Foreign Ministers. Van Rompuy and Catherine Ashton need to meet with different individuals as their counterparts. It is not efficient to start any meeting by introducing each other. As shown in Table 11.1, the Japanese leaders have annually changed (again) since the 16th Summit, while the European leaders, particularly the President of the European Council, have not changed since the 19th Summit after the Lisbon Treaty replaced the rotating Presidents with the new type of President.

---

1   'Joint Press Statement', 19th Japan-EU Summit Tokyo, 28 April 2010.

Table 11.1 The annual EU–Japan summit (names of leaders) and the G7/G8 summit

EU–Japan Summit		Place	Japanese Prime Minister	President of the European Commission	President of the European Council	The G7/G8 Summit		Place
1st	19 Jul 1991	The Hague	Toshiki Kaifu	Jacques Delors	Ruud Lubbers (Dutch PM)	17th	15–17 July 1991	London
2nd	04 Jul 1992	London			John Major (British PM)	18th	6–8 July 1992	Munich
3rd	06 Jul 1993	Tokyo	Kiichi Miyazawa	Henning Christophersen (Vice President)	Jean-Luc Dehaene (Belgian PM)	19th	7–9 July 1993	Tokyo
						20th	8–10 July 1994	Naples
4th	19 Jun 1995	Paris	Tomiichi Murayama	Jacques Santer	Jacques Chirac (French Pres.)	21st	15–17 June 1995	Halifax
5th	30 Sep 1996	Tokyo	Ryutaro Hashimoto		John Burton (Irish PM)	22nd	27–29 June 1996	Lyon
6th	25 Jun 1997	The Hague			Wim Kok (Dutch PM)	23rd	20–22 June 1997	Denver
7th	12 Jan 1998	Tokyo			Tony Blair (British PM)	24th	15–17 May 1998	Birmingham
8th	20 Jun 1999	Bonn	Keizo Obuchi	Romano Prodi	Gerhard Schröder (German Ch.)	25th	18–20 June 1999	Köln
9th	19 Jul 2000	Tokyo	Yoshiro Mori		Jacques Chirac (French Pres.)	26th	21–23 July 2000	Okinawa
10th	08 Dec 2001	Brussels	Junichiro Koizumi		Guy Verhofstadt (Belgian PM)	27th	20–22 July 2001	Genoa
11th	08 Jul 2002	Tokyo			Anders Fogh Rasmussen (Danish PM)	28th	26–27 June 2002	Kananaskis
12th	02 May 2003	Athens			Constantinos Simitis (Greek PM)	29th	1–3 June 2003	Evian
13th	22 Jun 2004	Tokyo			Bertie Ahern (Irish PM)	30th	8–10 June 2004	Sea Island
14th	02 May 2005	Luxemburg		José Manuel Barroso	Jean-Claude Juncker (Luxemburg PM)	31st	6–8 July 2005	Gleneagles
15th	24 Apr 2006	Tokyo			Wolfgang Schüssel (Austrian Ch.)	32nd	15–17 July 2006	St Petersburg
16th	05 Jun 2007	Berlin	Shinzo Abe		Angela Merkel (German Ch.)	33rd	6–8 June 2007	Heiligendamm
17th	23 Apr 2008	Tokyo	Yasuo Fukuda		Janez Janša (Slovenian PM)	34th	7–9 July 2008	Hokkaido Toyako
18th	04 May 2009	Prague	Taro Aso		Václav Klaus (Czech Pres.)	35th	8–10 July 2009	L'Aquila
19th	28 Apr 2010	Tokyo	Yukio Hatoyama		Herman Van Rompuy	36th	25–26 June 2010	Muskoka
20th	28 May 2011	Brussels	Naoto Kan			37th	26–27 May 2011	Deauville
21st (*)	2012	Tokyo	Yoshihiko Noda			38th	18–19 May 2012	Camp David

Source: http://www.mofa.go.jp/mofaj/area/eu/shuno.html>; <http://www.euinjapan.jp/relation/chronology/

Note: (*) As of 20 July 2012, the date of the 21st EU–Japan Summit was not decided, and the names of leaders might change.

Through the legitimate way to choose any foreign policy leader, we sometimes end up with an inefficient individual to carry out effective foreign policy. Without a strong leadership, any national institution of external/diplomatic action may well be ineffective. In these regards, the EU, or rather the European External Action Service (EEAS), might also be blamed for its lack of effectiveness and efficiency. However, the Lisbon Treaty institutionalised the EEAS as a more legitimate and efficient foreign policy apparatus than the previous institutions: DG-RELEX and other relevant DGs in the Commission. It should be totally different from the short-lived, rather inefficient, DG IA, which was bureaucratically institutionalised, after the Maastricht Treaty.

From the Japanese perspective, it has always been difficult to carry out any bilateral Japan–Europe negotiation since the 1970s. In his classic description of EC–Japan trade negotiation, Chihiro Hosoya, the Japanese diplomatic historian, regards it as 'asymmetrical bilateral negotiation' (Hosoya 1979: 159–74). Nevertheless, or because of this, Japan has attempted to develop more effective and efficient institutions of bilateral dialogue with the 'European external action' authority: EEAS and its predecessors. In this chapter, we will look back at the historical development of institutional interaction between Europe and Japan. We will then examine the efficiency of European external action vis-à-vis Japan. In the next section, however, we will briefly set up the conceptual framework to explain Europe–Japan political relations.

Conceptual Framework

This section will examine the nature of Europe and Japan as international actors, by introducing two sets of contrasting concepts.

Nature of Actors (1): Civilian Power or Military Power?

By referring to the literature on the concept of civilian power, we will examine the nature of Europe and Japan as the two main actors in this chapter. There has been some literature which, by using the concept of civilian power, explains the behaviour of Europe *or* Japan in the world.[2] Among the existing literature, Hans W. Maull compares Japan and Germany, describing them as 'new civilian powers' (Maull 1990–1, 1994). Indeed, among major European countries, it is Germany which has been reluctant to shoulder security burdens in the West. Britain and

---

2   On Europe as a 'civilian power', see Duchêne (1972, 1973); Shonfield (1972/1973); Bull (1982/1983); Pijpers (1988); Tsakaloyannis (1989); Hill (1990); Lodge (1993); Whitman (1998); Smith (2000); Stavridis (2001); Telò (2007) and Börzel and Risse (2009a). On Japan as a 'civilian power', see Funabashi (1991–2); Aspen Strategy Group (1993); Kamo (1995) and so forth.

France have not had such inhibitions as nation states, but the EC's economically strongest member state has.

However, there is hardly any literature which compares Japan *and* Europe in terms of civilian power,[3] and highlights similarities and differences between the two actors with special reference to the evolution of their political relations. I hope to contribute to rectifying this gap in the literature (see also Reiterer 2006; Ueta and Remacle 2005).

With hindsight, military force did matter in several cases, such as the 1991 Gulf War and the 2003 Iraq War, and there was little cooperation between Japan and Europe. However, even in these hard cases, it may also be true that the US-led multilateral forces would not have liberated Kuwait from Iraq without any moral, financial and logistical support from Europe and Japan. The US-led air forces might well have changed the undemocratic regime of Saddam Hussein, but the difficulty which their land troops faced in Iraq indicate the limits of military force for any post-conflict reconstruction or nation-building (Nakamura 2000). It would therefore be too hasty to conclude this chapter, *à la Realists*, by pointing out the overwhelming logic of military power, without taking serious account of the liberal logic of civilian power.

Nature of Actors (2): Proactive or Responsive Interaction to US Policy

In the 1970s, the United States did not necessarily object to a degree of autonomy in the economic policies of its European and Japanese partners, but it did object to such autonomy in politico-military policy. We can thus argue that 'civilian' activity was a natural emphasis for these 'junior' partners of the United States. The concept of civilian power was related to an attempt to avoid politico-military issues, on which the United States led, and which dealt directly with the USSR. The concept helps to explain why Europe and Japan did not need to consult with each other much on these issues. It also helps us to explore further the inhibitions which held the Europeans and the Japanese back from a more independent politico-military foreign policy. Even in the early 1990s, a similar situation can be observed. For example, the more politico-military the crisis in the Gulf became in 1990, the less assertively Europe and Japan reacted to the crisis.

In order to explain the nature of Europe and Japan as international actors, this section will clarify another conceptual distinction: *proactive* and *responsive* (inter-)action vis-à-vis the US policy (Wallace 1990: 54–5). In the context of this section, we need to explain whether Europe–Japan institutional interaction was proactive or responsive to US policy, as the United States frequently required a tough line of action in politico-military issues.

---

  3   Following Maull's concept of 'civilian power', Hubel (1993) explains the behaviour of Japan and Europe, especially Germany, towards the Gulf conflict.

How to Describe Europe and Japan as International Actors

Our essential assumption is that both Europe and Japan have emerged as international actors since the 1970s, even though they differ from each other in typology. Both of them have been regarded as the 'established powers' in the world, but each of them is different from each other.

It is more difficult to define 'Europe' as a single actor in international affairs as Japan is[4] (Hill and Wallace 1996). Japan's Ministry of Foreign Affairs (MoFA or *Gaimushō*), in its annual *Diplomatic Bluebook*, only referred to its political dialogue with individual West European countries, notably such major countries as Britain, France, West Germany and Italy. It was not until the Joint Declaration was adopted in July 1991 that the *Diplomatic Bluebook* began to refer to Japan's political relations with the EC. Yet, it was the EC together with the collective activities of its member states through European Political Cooperation (EPC) that had political relations with Japan. Even with Common Security and Foreign Policy (CFSP) after the Maastricht Treaty and EEAS after the Lisbon Treaty, the EU is still struggling to become a single actor. In this chapter, we therefore define 'Europe' as the EC/EPC/EU and its major four countries.

Japan is easier than Europe to classify: it is a traditional type of actor, i.e. a nation state. Nevertheless, similar difficulties of definition are encountered when one attempts to define Japan as a single (assertive or autonomous) actor in contemporary international affairs. Europe is a group of states with a range of inhibitions preventing it from pursuing assertive foreign policies independent of the United States, and Japan is a nation state with similar inhibitions. In the mid-1970s, as Hedley Bull argued, next to the United States, the USSR and China, Japan was 'only a potential great power' (Bull 1977/2002: 197). After the Cold War, Daniel Deudney and G. John Ikenberry regard Japan and Germany, rather positively, as 'semi-sovereign and partial great powers' in the Western liberal order (Deudney and Ikenberry 1999). The existing literature on Japanese foreign policy has struggled to describe or prescribe what type of international actor Japan is: a 'new kind of superpower', an 'economic superpower', a 'hesitant superpower', a 'global civilian power' or a 'normal nation'.[5]

In the next section, we observe the institutional evolution of Europe–Japan political dialogue, purely in the bilateral context, and without examining the US involvement in the process. However, in the third section, we argue that the very origins of Europe–Japan political relations can be found in the trilateral context, with special reference to the early years of the Group of Seven (G7) Summit.

---

4   There have been several important 'actors in Europe's foreign policy-making', rather than one single actor solely representing Europe.

5   On each conception, see respectively, Garby and Bullock (1994); Drifte (1996); Bridges (1993); Funabashi (1994) and Ozawa (1994). Hughes (2004) and Serra (2005) describe the more recent development of Japan as an international security actor within the historic context.

Institutional Evolution of Europe–Japan Dialogue: The Bilateral Dimension

An economic relationship between the EC Commission and the Japanese government has emerged and developed since 1970.[6] A bilateral framework has since then been institutionalised. There have been two important facets of this institutionalisation.[7]

Diversified Formal Dialogues: EC–Japan Trade Disputes in the 1970s

The EC and Japan diversified their formal framework of dialogues to deal with trade disputes in the 1970s. In addition to the traditional inter-state dialogues where Europe is defined as the aggregate of West European countries, the diversification can be seen at three levels: administrative officials, cabinet ministers and parliament members.

First, there were talks between the Japanese delegation led by Kiyohiko Tsurumi (Deputy Vice-Minister for Foreign Affairs) and the Commission delegation led by Edmund Wallenstein (Director-General for External Relations) on 12–13 June 1973. These talks were the beginning of the six-monthly high-level consultations, which Masayoshi Ohira (Foreign Minister) had announced at the end of his visit to the Commission on 4 May.[8]

Although, or rather because, Japan began to negotiate with the Commission, Japan engaged in what may be called 'asymmetrical bilateral negotiations' (Hosoya 1979: 167–71). Japan had already negotiated with such major member countries as Britain, France and West Germany. The Japanese government now found it difficult to decide with which 'Europe' it should mainly negotiate: still with the major states and/or solely with the Commission. Some Europeans, on the contrary, saw Japan as being 'directed by a super-efficient interlocking élite of big business (the *zaibatsu* or *keiretsu kigyo*) and government often referred to as "Japan Inc."' (Wilkinson 1980/1991: 139). Neither side was sure with whom to have a dialogue. The Japanese saw a partly-developed EC with several competing major states; and the Europeans saw a closed Japanese system in which prime ministers and foreign ministers changed quite frequently and seemed to wield little political influence. During the 1970s, with this cognitive dissonance between the

---

6   The traditional inter-state dialogue began in the 1960s. Regular consultative meetings at the level of foreign ministers began between Japan and such major West European countries as Britain, France, West Germany and Italy in the early 1960s.

7   Event data, on the EC side, are mostly from the following official publications, unless otherwise stated: the EC Commission, General Report of the European Communities [4th Report – 26th Report], 1970–92; and Bulletin of the European Communities. On the Japanese side, see *Diplomatic Bluebook*, Nos. 15–37, 1971–93.

8   Ohira had talks with François-Xavier Ortoli (President of the Commission) and Christopher Soames (Vice-President of the Commission).

EC and Japan as a background, there emerged a series of trade disputes and the need for more political dialogue.

Second, therefore, meetings at the level of ministers of various kinds, in which the Commission President and/or the Japanese Prime Minister occasionally participated, could be taken as the high point in the process of EC–Japan trade negotiations in 1976–8. Among the Japanese, Nobuhiko Ushiba (Minister of State for International Economic Relations) was instrumental in settling the trade disputes. However, he had been a career diplomat before being allocated to the temporarily established cabinet portfolio.

Third, at the level of members of parliament, the Interparliamentary Conference was also institutionalised in the late 1970s. On 4–5 July 1978, the Japanese Diet sent its first Delegation with 10 of its members to Luxembourg, and on 17–18 October, the European Parliament sent its 10-member Delegation to Tokyo. They exchanged views concerning international political affairs such as the Middle East, Africa and ASEAN, as well as international economic, monetary and trade issues, and EC–Japan trade problems in particular. On 13–14 February 1980, for example, at the third Interparliamentary Conference held at Strasbourg, politicians talked about the Soviet invasion of Afghanistan.[9] This facet of diversified formal dialogue is accompanied by the following facet of the widened scope of issues.

Widened Scope of Issues: Cooperation and Conflict in the 1980s

In the first half of the 1980s, there were still some trade disputes between the EC and Japan. But it is also true that 'cooperation was expanded and strengthened in several sectors',[10] as was conflict/dispute.[11] The scope of issues is widened from investment and industrial cooperation through finance and agriculture to development aid and the environment. On 20–24 January 1986, when Jacques Delors (President of the Commission) visited Japan, he 'ranged over the whole spectrum of bilateral relations, covering their commercial, industrial, financial, monetary and technological aspects'.[12] Throughout the 1980s, EC–Japan relations could still be characterised mostly as economic relations. Indeed, the *Fourteenth General Report*, describing the EC's relations with Japan in 1980, mentioned that the EC and Japan had converged in their 'thinking on political issues, such as the

---

9   Condemning the Soviet invasion, they exchanged the pros and cons of boycotting the Moscow Olympics.

10   Eighteenth General Report of the European Communities, 1984, p. 260.

11   European Policy Unit (1992).

12   Bulletin of the European Communities 1-1986, point 2.2.10.

Middle East'.[13] Yet, it was not until 1989 that the *Twenty-Third General Report* began to re-use the word 'politics'.[14]

Although the Commission was present, Japan discussed political issues with the EPC. On 1 March 1983, the Foreign Ministers of the 10, meeting at Bonn, decided to establish regular political contacts with Japan. Thus, Europe and Japan institutionalised the framework of political consultations between Foreign Ministers of Japan and the EPC Troika (comprising the president of the EC General Affairs Council, his/her predecessor and successor), held biannually on the occasions of OECD ministerial meetings at Paris and of the UN General Assembly at New York. The first Japan–EC Troika Foreign Minister Meeting was held at Paris in May 1983 and such a meeting was held biannually except in 1988 and 1989.

At the fourth meeting held in New York in September 1984, Shintaro Abe (Foreign Minister) proposed the establishment of high-level official meetings of Political Directors (*Seimu-kyokucho*). The first Japan–EC Troika Political Directors Meeting was thus held in March 1985 and followed by 10 more meetings until 1991.[15]

EC/EPC–Japan Joint Declaration in 1991

On 18 July 1991, *the Joint Declaration on Relations between the European Community and Its Member States and Japan* was adopted in The Hague.[16] To some degree, the Declaration summarises the above-mentioned two facets.

The final part of the Joint Declaration is devoted to a 'framework for dialogue and consultations'. Europe and Japan decided to continue such 'existing regular consultation mechanism' as follows: an annual meeting at ministerial level; six-monthly consultations between 'the Foreign Ministers of the Community and the Member of the Commission responsible for external relations (Troika) and the Japanese Foreign Minister'. Significantly, the Declaration decided to institutionalise an annual summit meeting. It is often difficult to carry out any regular consultation mechanism,[17] but they attempt to keep the regularity of holding the newly institutionalised summit meetings. Indeed, the Japan–EC/EU summit meetings have been held annually, with the only exception being 1994.

---

13   *Diplomatic Bluebook* (No. 25, p. 29), reviewing its diplomatic efforts in 1980, mentioned a Europe–Japan dialogue on 'political' issues (e.g. Iran hostage crisis).

14   The *Twenty-Third General Report* (p. 324) says that 'Japan itself has become firmly established over the past few years as a leading financial and economic power and, increasingly, in politics too'.

15   Japanese Ministry of Foreign Affairs, Disclosed document No.04648, 3 October 2001.

16   The text can be found, for example, at www.mofa.go.jp/region/europe/eu/overview/declar.html.

17   For example, the ministerial meetings were held annually, but only in 1984–6.

Concerning the widened scope of issues, the Declaration states that both Europe and Japan will endeavour to strengthen 'their dialogue and cooperation on various aspects of multifaceted relations between both parties in such areas as trade, investment, industrial cooperation, advanced technology, energy, employment, social affairs and competition rules'. It also provides for 'areas of possible cooperation', such as development aid, and 'the issue of environment, the conservation of resources and energy, terrorism, international crime and drugs and related criminal activity', or even 'the field of science and technology' and the area of 'academic, cultural and youth exchange programmes'. Furthermore, Europe and Japan, after setting out the objective of strengthening the UN, declare that they will enhance:

> policy consultation and, wherever possible, policy coordination on …
> international security matters such as the non-proliferation of nuclear, chemical
> and biological weapons, the non-proliferation of missile technology and the
> international transfer of conventional weapons.

They actually drafted the joint proposal for a universal register of conventional arms transfers under the UN auspices, after the end of the Gulf War in 1991.

Chronologically, the EC/EPC–Japan Joint Declaration was adopted about eight months after the EC adopted similar declarations with Canada and the United States, i.e. the Transatlantic Declarations, in November 1990. The initiative was thus taken by the Japanese government, particularly Hisashi Owada (Vice Minister for Foreign Affairs) in December 1990.[18] It took several months for the Declaration to be adopted, mainly because Japan resisted such wordings as 'cooperation in a fair and harmonious way' and 'equitable access to their respective markets'. Just before the end of the Cold War, William Wallace articulated the biggest obstacle of all to a closer understanding between Europe and Japan as follows:

> the reluctance of both potential partners to upset their political patron and
> guarantor of security, the United States, by appearing to be moving publicly
> towards a more independent foreign policy or an explicitly closer direct
> relationship with each other. (Wallace 1988: 9)

It is accordingly assumed that the evolution of the trilateral institution, especially the G7 Summit, has provided one of the most important fora within which Europe–Japan relations have developed and changed their nature. The next section will only briefly examine this assumption.

---

18   This is therefore called the 'Owada Initiative'. See Owada (2001).

The Trilateral Institution of Europe-US-Japan Political Dialogue

The significance of the G7 summits for Europe–Japan relations can be found in the US dimension of the foreign policies of both Europe and Japan. It was the dramatic change in US foreign and economic policies that provided Europe and Japan with the opportunity for creating some multilateral, and some possible bilateral, institutions of political dialogue. While Europe developed its own multilateral institution (namely the EC/EPC), Japan still relied heavily on its bilateral relations with the United States. As a result, the reaction to the change in US policies in the early 1970s was different between the two international actors.

Early Years of Trilateral Relations: Qualitative Account[19]

In the summer of 1971, US President Richard Nixon, together with John Connally (Secretary of the Treasury), made the unilateral announcement on monetary policy that 'shook the world'. The 'Nixon Shock' or the 'Dollar crisis' came on 15 August 1971. Henry Kissinger (Nixon's Assistant for National Security Affairs) was eliminated from this Nixon-Connally initiative, and 'played only a subsidiary part in the negotiations which followed' (Strange 1972: 204; Wallace 1976: 165). In the latter half of 1971, there had originated some ideas of a multilateral summit to seek solutions to the woes of the world economy. Kissinger's idea of a summit among the Atlantic leaders failed to take shape, and was replaced by a series of bilateral talks between Nixon and his European counterparts. Japan also played increasingly important roles in subsequent negotiations specifically on the economic issue.[20]

In 1973, Kissinger prescribed the better idea for forming a multilateral institution, but in a similar vein. In April, he made the 'Year of Europe' speech; and in December, he proposed an 'Energy Action Group'. The American, or the Nixon-Kissinger, initiative did not take shape in 1973–4. It was in 1975 that a trilateral institution began to materialize, not necessarily under US leadership, but rather under European leadership.

In 1975, the initiative to hold economic summits came from Valéry Giscard d'Estaing and Helmut Schmidt, the French and German leaders, to whom the United States responded. As Robert Putnam and Nicholas Bayne explain, the immediate 'genesis' of the G7 Summit is to be found in Helsinki on 31 July: the gathering of four leaders from France, the United States, Britain and West Germany. The French proposal to hold an economic summit meeting among them, together with the Japanese Prime Minister, was on the agenda there (Putnam and Bayne 1984/1987: 25). The Italian Prime Minister joined them, and six leaders

---

19   The description of this particular sub-section heavily relied on Nakamura (2000).

20   In January 1972, Prime Minister Sato proposed a summit of the five major industrialised countries to President Nixon: the United States, Britain, France, West Germany and Japan. However, they did not make any public statement on this proposal.

held their first summit at the Château de Rambouillet on 15–17 November 1975.[21] Indeed, the early G7 summits were to be called 'economic summits'. But, the summits gradually started dealing with 'political issues'.

The starting point can be found in the extra-summit which held among just French, American, British and German leaders on 5–6 January 1979 at Saint François, Guadeloupe. The four leaders discussed China, Iran and mostly the SALT (Strategic Arms Limitation Talks). According to James Callaghan (British Prime Minister), however, the Guadeloupe Summit even began 'with an exchange of views on the problems of the Pacific area, notably the perennial problem of how to secure a more balanced trade with Japan', followed by the issue of China (Callaghan 1987: 544). The Guadeloupe style of informal four-power summit had been held on the occasion of the G7 Summit before January 1979, and it was repeated even at the Tokyo Summit in June 1979. As a host country, however, Japan had still been reluctant to take up political issues on the agenda directly.

In late 1979, however, two events changed the Japanese attitude: the Iranian hostage crisis and the Soviet invasion of Afghanistan. After these events, the G7 Summit finally dealt with 'politics'. At the Venice Summit on 22–23 June 1980, adding to the economic issues, such as inflation, energy, relations with developing countries, monetary problems and trade, and to the issues of hijacking and of refugees, the leaders discussed 'the taking of diplomatic hostages', implicitly the case of the US Embassy in Iran, and 'political topics', especially on 'the Soviet military occupation of Afghanistan'. Japan formally joined the political debate within the West. Zbigniew Brzezinski (National Security Advisor to the Carter Administration) notes that the Guadeloupe Summit was much 'resented by other governments, notably Italy', and that he therefore tried to 'transform the annual Economic Summit into something approximating a Strategic Summit' (Brzezinski 1983: 295–6).

One can certainly argue that the Economic Summit has been politicised since the early 1980s, in that the G7 leaders began to discuss political issues, leading to explicit statements and declarations on most of the issues. Since the Venice Summit of 1980, the G7 countries have held, in the preparatory stage, 'a meeting of Political Directors from Foreign Ministries, to identify the political issues likely to be discussed at the Summit, and offer proposals for any political declarations which the Summit may feel called upon to issue' (Armstrong 1991: 39). At the Williamsburg Summit on 28–30 May 1983, the seven leaders issued the 'Statement on Arms Control and Security', with Yasuhiro Nakasone as one of the new participants. He even argued with/against his French counterpart, François Mitterrand, about the exact wordings of this statement. However, as for the primacy of politics over economics, this summit was rather exceptional even in the 1980s. As for the reason why the Economic Summit was sometimes

---

21 We usually count this summit as the first G7 Summit. Precisely speaking, this was the G6 Summit. But, the Canadian Prime Minister joined the leaders of those six countries as early as 27–28 June 1976 at San Juan.

politicised, one former 'Sherpa' replied: 'a substantial reason ... is the voracious appetite of the press during the course of the proceedings and the perceived need to offer them something to report'.[22]

Quantitative Account of Trilateral Relations

Europe–Japan 'political' relations have thus evolved since the 1970s, or more substantially since the 1980s, within the trilateral context. The United States still played the significant role, either as the leader of Western alliance or as the most significant partner for both Europe and Japan.

In terms of economic relations, particularly trade relations, the United States has still been the most significant partner for both the EU and Japan. As shown in Table 11.2, from the perspectives of the EC/EU, the United States has been the No. 1 trade partner. Japan has never occupied that position, and only became No. 2 as the exporter from 1983 to 2000. In 1988, the share of European imports from Japan was the highest over the half century, 12.2 per cent, but those from the United States still accounted for 20.1 per cent. On the other hand, the share of European exports to Japan has always been lower than, for example, Switzerland. The highest share Japan has ever occupied was 6.4 per cent in 1990, and the US share was 21.5 per cent in the same year. It was rather the trade imbalance between Europe and Japan that often led to the politically sensitive trade negotiations particularly in the 1980s.

Recently, China replaced the position of Japan in the EU's trade relations. The share of European exports to China has been higher than Japan since 2004, and the share of imports since 2002. China partially replaced the US position. The share of European imports from China has been higher than the United States since 2006. This structural change is partly reflected by the increasing role of the Group of 20 (G20), rather than the G7 trilateral institution, as a provider of global governance in many economic areas.

Politically, nevertheless, the trilateral institution of Europe–US–Japan political dialogue is still substantial in setting the global standards and in diffusing some normative values to the world.

---

22 The former 'Sherpa', answering my question after his speech, Oxford, 4 February 1994.

The EU's Foreign Policy

Table 11.2 EC/EU trade with the United States, Japan and China, 1958–2010

	Exports			Imports			
	US	Japan	China	US	Japan	China	
1958	10.5	0.9	1.9	17.4	0.7	0.7	(*EC6)
1960	11.5	1.1	1.2	19.7	0.8	0.8	
1970	14.7	2.2	0.8	19.8	2.7	0.6	
1975	10.9	1.8	n.a.	16.4	3.8	n.a.	(*EC9)
1976	11.5	1.9	n.a.	15.9	4.0	n.a.	
1977	12.5	1.9	n.a.	15.0	4.5	n.a.	
1978	13.3	2.1	0.9	15.9	4.9	0.5	
1979	12.9	2.4	1.1	15.5	4.4	0.6	
1980	12.0	2.1	0.8	16.1	4.6	0.7	
1981	13.9	2.1	0.7	16.3	5.3	0.8	(*EC10)
1982	15.0	2.2	0.7	16.7	5.6	0.7	
1983	16.6	2.4	0.9	16.2	6.2	0.8	
1984	20.0	2.6	1.0	16.2	6.4	0.8	
1985	21.5	2.7	1.7	16.0	6.8	1.0	
1986	22.0	3.3	1.9	16.9	9.9	1.3	(*EC12)
1987	21.2	4.0	1.6	16.5	10.2	1.5	
1988	23.1	5.5	1.9	20.1	12.2	2.1	
1989	22.0	6.0	1.8	21.6	11.8	2.3	
1990	21.5	6.4	1.5	21.0	11.4	2.6	
1991	19.5	6.1	1.5	20.9	11.9	3.4	
1992	19.5	5.4	1.8	20.3	12.0	3.9	
1993	19.6	5.2	2.6	19.3	10.9	4.5	
1994	20.1	5.6	2.6	19.4	10.1	4.7	
1995	18.0	5.7	2.6	19.9	10.8	4.5	(*EC15)
1996	18.2	5.7	2.3	20.4	9.7	4.8	
1997	19.4	5.0	2.3	21.7	9.7	5.2	
1998	21.4	4.3	2.4	22.1	10.1	5.5	
1999	24.1	4.7	2.6	20.6	9.1	6.4	
2000	24.6	4.7	2.7	19.2	8.4	6.8	
2001	24.3	4.6	3.1	19.0	7.4	7.4	
2002	24.3	4.3	3.4	17.7	6.9	8.3	
2003	22.6	4.1	4.1	15.3	6.7	9.7	
2004	24.2	4.5	5.0	15.3	7.2	12.3	(*EC25)
2005	23.5	4.1	4.8	13.7	6.2	13.4	
2006	22.7	3.8	5.4	12.8	5.7	14.2	
2007	20.9	3.5	5.8	12.1	5.5	16.2	(*EC27)
2008	19.1	3.2	6.0	11.9	4.8	15.8	
2009	18.7	3.3	7.5	13.2	4.7	17.7	
2010	18.0	3.2	8.4	11.3	4.4	18.7	

Source: EUROSTAT, External Trade: Statistical Yearbook, 1958–79; EUROSTAT, External and Intra-EU Trade: Statistical Yearbook, 1958–99, 1958–2003 and 1958–2010.

Note: Unit: Share of EC/EU Import and Export (%)

EU–Japan Political Relations in the 1990s and the 2000s

As we saw the EC/EPC–Japan Joint Declaration was adopted after the EC adopted the transatlantic declarations with Canada and the United States. These three declarations of the EC with what we now call the strategic partners, or rather the like-minded partners, were efficiently adopted, while the Europeans were negotiating a new treaty of their own.

After the Maastricht Treaty

The Maastricht Treaty, the second pillar of which revolved around CFSP, was adopted in December 1991, and came into force in November 1993. What type of new elements did this introduce into EU–Japan relations?

The Japanese government was not solely represented by the MoFA, nor the European Commission by DG I, the Directorate General responsible for external relations. The interpenetration of 'external' and 'internal' policy concerns made the role of DG I in internal coordination more important (Smith 1994: 254–5). A Deputy Head of Unit at DG I (F1, relations with Japan) pointed out that DG I should negotiate with Japan, mostly the MoFA, in better coordination with DG II on the issue of macro-economic matters and with DG III on the issue of industrial cooperation.[23] The so-called 1992 programme for completing the internal market had many external implications, but DG III was responsible for the issue. The status of DG I was 'rather like that of US Trade Representative (USTR) in Washington, trying to coordinate and moderate the needs and interests of powerful internal baronies' (Smith 1994: 255).

The Maastricht Treaty made the Commission adjust to a newly conceptualised area of activity. The reformation was twofold (Nuttall 1992: 300). First, in December 1992, the Delors Commission informally decided that the responsibility for political and economic external relations would be split. The three commissioners held the following new portfolios: Hans van den Broek, for external political relations and CFSP; Leon Brittan, for external economic relations mostly with developed countries; and Manuel Marin, for cooperation and development, or external economic relations with developing countries. The ministerial meeting held in November 1994, in which only Brittan participated, showed that EU–Japan relations were still characterised mostly as economic relations.

Second, in March 1993, the Commission established DG IA, the new Directorate General for external 'political' relations, which made the old DG I confine its responsibility only to external 'economic' relations. DG I had one independent unit for relations with Japan (F1). However, DG IA also had a unit (C2) which would be responsible for political relations with Japan, China and Far Eastern countries, and Australia and New Zealand. The newly appointed Head of the Unit came from the Danish foreign office, and talked with his counterpart in

---

23 Interview, Brussels, 6 May 1994.

Japan about such political issues as developments both in Asia and Europe, those in Russia, UN peace-keeping operations, relations with the United States, or even developments in the Korean Peninsula.[24]

The Action Plan and the Decade of EU–Japan Cooperation

With a slightly innovative institutional reform inside the Commission, from DG IA to DG-RELEX (Carta 2012: 66–7), the EU has gradually broadened the scope of political cooperation with Japan. The MoFA has also experienced the internal institutional reform and the division which deals with the EU has moved from the International Economy Division of the Economic Affairs Bureau to the European Policy Division of the European Affairs Bureau. During those institutional reforms inside the Commission and MoFA, the EU and Japan were entering the second decade of their partnership.

On 8 December 2001, Junichiro Koizumi, Romano Prodi and Guy Verhofstadt met in Brussels, and adopted the Action Plan for EU–Japan Cooperation, which was entitled as 'Shaping Our Common Future'. They decided 'to launch a Decade of Japan-Europe Cooperation' in the various fields. They set up the four major objectives: (1) promoting peace and stability; (2) strengthening the economic and trade partnership utilising the dynamism of globalisation for the benefit of all; (3) coping with global and societal challenges; and (4) bringing together people and cultures. Under those objectives, they listed a series of action plans. The Japanese and European leaders agreed that they 'will coordinate regularly, and update the Action Plan as necessary at the annual EU-Japan Summit'. At the following summits, they have issued the statement, in which they reviewed the progress of fulfilling the above-mentioned objectives.

Takahiro Shinyo, who was instrumental in the Europe–Japan joint drafting of the UN register of conventional arms in 1991, claimed that 'Japan entered into a strategic partnership with the EU in December 2001' (Shinyo 2003: 7). At the 17th EU–Japan Summit in April 2008, it was stated that European and Japanese 'leaders are determined to further promote the Japan-EU strategic partnership'.

The New Decade of the 2010s

A decade after the Joint Action, there was the high expectation from both the EU and Japan towards the next decade of closer cooperation.[25] However, a new agreement/document has yet to be adopted. For a while, MoFA would have been

---

24 Interview, Brussels, 3 May 1994. In early days of DG IA, they were ambitious enough to commit themselves to be the part of KEDO (The Korean Peninsula Energy Development Organization) together with South Korea, Japan and the United States.

25 For example, Yohei Kohno, who made the monumental speech on EU–Japan relations as the Foreign Minister in 2000, expressed his expectations at the symposium held by European Union Institute in Japan at Waseda University (EUIJ Waseda) in cooperation

satisfied with a new Action Plan for the new decade, but DG-RELEX/EEAS would have needed a more sustainable agreement.

Separately, Japan needed an Economic Partnership Agreement (EPA) with the EU. The EU was reluctant to start any Free Trade Agreement (FTA) negotiations with Japan, however. Ambassador Hans Dietmar Schweisgut was appointed the new Head of the Delegation of the European Union to Tokyo in January 2011, as one of the first appointments under the new EEAS procedures. At first, he was also sceptical about an EU–Japan FTA/EPA.

However, the triple disaster on 11 March 2011, the earthquakes, the tsunami, and the accidents at Fukushima nuclear power plants, changed the atmosphere in some of the major European capitals, including London. The EU was still willing to negotiate for a Framework Agreement, and sceptical about a lifting of non-tariff barriers in the Japanese market. But, on 28 May 2011, Van Rompuy and Barroso met with Naoto Kan at the 20th EU–Japan Summit, and they 'agreed to start the process for parallel negotiations' for the following two agreements:

1. A deep and comprehensive FTA/EPA, addressing all issues of shared interest to both sides including tariffs, non-tariff measures, services, investment, Intellectual Property Rights, competition and public procurement.
2. A binding agreement, covering political, global and other sectoral cooperation in a comprehensive manner, and underpinned by their (Japan and EU) shared commitment to fundamental values and principles.

EEAS and MoFA concluded the 'scoping exercise' for a Framework/Political Agreement in April 2012. The Commission and MoFA also concluded the 'scoping exercise' for FTA/EPA. However, the Council and EU member states have yet to provide EEAS and the Commission with the mandate of official negotiations with Japan. On 13 June, the European Parliament voted by 517 votes to 74, with 89 abstentions, to '[ask] the Council not to authorise the opening of trade negotiations until Parliament has stated its position on the proposed negotiating mandate'.[26] Meanwhile, on 18 July, Karel De Gucht (European Commissioner for Trade) made a speech, expressing that the Commission 'decided to ask Member States for the green light to open free trade negotiations with a major political and economic partner for us: Japan'. He mentioned as follows:

> Japan is our second biggest trading partner in Asia and a key partner with which we share common values like democracy and the rule of law. If growth in the

---

with the Delegation of the European Union to Japan on 12 January 2010. See http://www.euij-waseda.jp/eng/.

26 European Parliament, 'Resolution of 13 June 2012 on EU Trade Negotiations with Japan', P7_TA-PROV(2012)0246. See also http://www.europarl.europa.eu/news/lv/pressroom/content/20120613IPR46762/html/EU-Japan-trade-talks-MEPs-fear-for-EU-car-market.

next twenty years is likely to come from Asia, then overlooking Japan would be a serious mistake in our trade strategy.[27]

An official start of negotiations for a FTA/EPA and/or a Framework/Political Agreement has been announced for the 2012 EU–Japan Summit.

Conclusion

In 1973, Kissinger posed the famous question about the evolving EPC: 'Who do I call if I want to call Europe?' However, he also feared a common front between Europe and Japan against the United States.

On 6 October 1973, the 'Kippur War' broke out. This Arab-Israeli conflict made 'the accumulated tensions' between the United States and Europe erupt (Kissinger 1982: 707). On 6 November, the EC Foreign Ministers met in Copenhagen, and issued a declaration on the Middle East. On French initiative, a Euro-Arab dialogue was proposed. By November, as Kissinger recalls, 'Japanese leaders, just like their European counterparts, began to feel – with some reluctance – that their national interest might require them to dissociate themselves from American policy in the Middle East' (Kissinger 1982: 740). Although the Japanese Foreign Minister was put under pressure to detach Japan from American, pro-Israeli policy, he made an effort not to change Japan's policy in the Middle East immediately without prior consultation with the United States (Ohira 1979: 119–20).[28] On 22 November, Japan officially announced an intention to change its policy in the Middle East, towards a more pro-Arab policy. This change in Japanese foreign policy caused Kissinger to contemplate the possibility of a Europe–Japan front against US diplomacy. Kissinger reminisces as follows: [29]

> If Japan followed the line of the European Community, we would be able to do no better than be silent; if forced to comment, we would have to be critical.
> (Kissinger 1982: 742)

Could Europe and Japan have started the autonomous, effective and efficient coordination of foreign policy even in 1973? Unfortunately, the answer is no, and both actors should be blamed for the failure.

---

27   Karel De Gucht, 'Why We Should Open Free Trade Negotiations with Japan', speech in Brussels, 18 July 2012. http://trade.ec.europa.eu/doclib/docs/2012/july/tradoc_149791.pdf.

28   On 14 November, Kissinger visited Japan on his way back to the United States after a visit to the Middle East. Ohira 'took advantage of the occasion to explain to him the Japanese government's new Arab policy and asked for his views'.

29   With Ohira's efforts of prior consultation in mind, Kissinger (1982: 741) said that '[though] formally similar to Europe's, Japanese policy differed radically in spirit'.

As we observe, European external action has been focused on economics vis-à-vis Japan. The era of economic friction, during the 1970s and the 1980s, made the Europe–Japan institutional interaction evolve at several significant levels. It was only after the end of the Cold War when they were able to institutionalise the bilateral 'political' dialogue at their highest level: the summit meetings from July 1991. But, even this has been closely linked with the development of transatlantic relations, and of the trilateral G7 institutions. As shown in Table 11.1, half of the EU–Japan summits were held within a few days before/after the G7/G8 summits.

As advanced economies, the EC/EU and Japan have formed and developed the G7 institutions since the 1970s. They became the like-minded partners within a Western alliance during the Cold War. However, EU–Japan political relations have still been the relationship between the civilian powers, and their interaction has still been responsive to the US policy in many areas. But, using some military capabilities, the EU and Japan have jointly committed to more political cooperation, for example, the anti-piracy operations off the coast of Somalia.[30] In such areas as climate change and renewable energy, the EU and Japan would be more proactive to the US policy: the United States is not able to inhibit both civilian powers from a bilateral policy coordination.

Of course, the EU and Japan do not share every single value or norm. For example, one of the conflicting issues between the two civilian powers is over the conservation of bluefin tuna, which was debated at the Convention of International Trade in Endangered Species (CITES) in March 2010.

Another is the issue of the death penalty (Bacon 2011).[31] The EU/EEAS has asked Japan to adopt the moratorium on the death penalty, if not abolish it. This may well be the test case for the efficiency and effectiveness of EEAS. Indeed, the efficiency of EEAS towards three East Asian 'strategic partners', i.e. Japan, China and South Korea, can be observed over the issue of human rights. Japan attempts to follow the EU–Korea FTA. But, it may have been easier for South Korea to conclude the Framework Agreement with the EU, partly because South Korea has not carried out the execution of prisoners since 1998. The DPJ-led government in Japan has stopped the executions for 20 months, but on 29 March 2012, the new Justice Minister decided to execute three prisoners. The High Representative Ashton efficiently stated on the day: 'The EU deeply regrets the execution … and the fact that this marks the resumption of executions in Japan'. The efficiency of the EU's human rights diplomacy has yet to resemble to its effectiveness.

Carrots and sticks are always necessary for any efficient and effective foreign policy or diplomacy. Kissinger liked using them. As any great power in the past faced, however, the short-term efficiency would not automatically lead to the long-term effectiveness: sending a diplomatic message is easier than achieving

---

30 See, for example, http://www.eunavfor.eu/2011/01/coordination-between-eu-navfor-and-the-japanese-navy/.

31 The EU is also different from many US states. See 'The EU Memorandum on the Death Penalty', from http://www.eurunion.org/legislat/deathpenalty/eumemorandum.htm.

diplomatic objectives, the latter of which requires more sophisticated instruments. We should search for the more efficient European external/diplomatic action, but should not forget about the effectiveness.

Chapter 12

The Efficiency of the EU's External Actions and the EU–India Relationship

Ummu Salma Bava

Abstract

The end of the Cold War had a profound impact on the political development of the EU and its further evolution as an actor in international politics and its engagement with emerging powers. In 2003, the European Security Strategy identified not only the security challenges but also drew attention to addressing these problems within the framework of effective multilateralism and with global partnerships – identifying countries like Russia, China, Japan and India. It is in this context that this chapter will examine the EU's relation with emerging power India especially from the perspective of the efficiency of the EU's external actions which have evolved over the years. Although the relationship goes back to 1963, this chapter analyses the transformation of EU–India relations since the end of the Cold War which has resulted in a strategic partnership and that seeks to create a win-win relationship for both actors.

Introduction

The end of the Cold War had a profound impact on the political development of the EU and its further evolution as an actor in international politics and its engagement with emerging powers. In 2003 the European Security Strategy identified not only the security challenges but also drew attention to addressing these problems within the framework of effective multilateralism and with global partnerships – identifying countries like Russia, China, Japan and India. In addition, the Lisbon Treaty could be considered path-breaking in giving the EU a new character as it finally acquired a legal personality and could be treated as a full actor in international politics. However, the Treaty rests on the structures created before – Maastricht, Amsterdam and Nice – and points to the incremental nature of the growth of the EU, its institutions and processes and, to that extent, it remains a work in progress.

It is in this context that this chapter will examine the EU's relation with emerging power India especially from the perspective of the efficiency of the EU's external actions which have evolved over the years. Although the relationship goes back to 1963, this chapter analyses the transformation of EU–India relations since the end of the Cold War which has resulted in a strategic partnership and that seeks to create a win-win partnership for both actors.

EU's Asia Strategy and Relation with India in the Post-Cold War Period

The relations between India and the European Union (EU) have evolved over a long period. India was the first among the developing countries to establish diplomatic relations with the European Economic Community (EEC) in 1963. This engagement has expanded and subsequently been transformed because both India and the EU (since 1992) have assumed a growing significance in post-Cold War international politics (Bava 2010b). Incremental steps have over the years elevated the relationship from commercial and trade relations to political and security cooperation between both. The EC for a long time was India's largest economic partner. The 1980s witnessed enhanced trade and commercial relations, with the EEC constituting 22.8 per cent of Indian trade between 1980 and 1988, which grew to a robust 29.36 per cent in 1990–1 (Gupta 1995: 168). However, it was the end of the Cold War that provided the economic and political impetus to move the relations forward beyond trade.

The end of the Cold War took away the terrain with which India was familiar and it 'undermined the foundations of India's foreign policy' (Ganguly 2002: 41). 1990 offered India new opportunities for engagement as it was freed from the Cold War rubric. A strong domestic economic growth that came in the wake of an economic liberalisation programme that the country adopted in 1992 subsequently brought India political visibility as well. 'The shift in the economic policy can be seen as a watershed moment in India's development trajectory that also set a new course to its political growth as an emerging power' (Bava 2010a: 119). 'Responding to a changing international order and an increasing diffusion of threats, India was slowly moving towards what can be called a "strategically engaged foreign policy"' (ibid.). But more significantly, it was the nuclear tests by India in 1998 and a steadily performing economy that changed not only India's perception of itself but the world's perception of India (Bava 2007).

The political and economic developments at the global level provided both India and the EU with new opportunities for engagement. As India moved towards liberalization of its economy in the early 1990s and reorienting its foreign policy to an emerging world order, the EEC also underwent a transformation into the European Union together with the launching of a Common Foreign and Security Policy. It was in this context that the New Asia Strategy of the European Union was adopted in 1994 which sought to give 'priority to relations with Asia in light of the growing economic and political power of this region'. As the document states, it was a first attempt to take an integrated and balanced view of the relations between the EU and its Asian partners. The 1994 Asia Strategy was, however, aimed primarily at East Asia and Southeast Asia and it resulted in the launch of the Asia-Europe Meeting (ASEM) in 1996. The economic rise of East Asia brought it far greater political visibility and engagement as well. 'The increasing strategic value of East Asia provided a timely and welcome additional impetus to intensified EU approach towards East Asia' (Park 2008). South Asia and India did not get the kind of strategic attention that East Asia got despite the launch of the new Asia strategy.

This can be explained by the fact that India had just embarked on its economic liberalisation and not yet emerged as a major economic actor at this time and thus there was a time lag before the EU extended its recognition to India as a critical partner. What is significant is that the EU's focus on Southeast Asia coincided with India's launch of its own Look East policy in 1991. An economically vibrant and emerging Southeast Asia attracted both the EU's and India's attention. In addition, there were many factors driving both to engage the region, but what distinctly stood out was the rapid economic growth of Southeast Asia, the rise of the Asian tigers and growing influence of China, which was transforming the region. However, in 1994, EU–India relations were given a small boost through the Co-operation Agreement, which provided the legislative framework for cooperation and led to a broad political dialogue.

It is, nonetheless, revealing that even after the launch of the EU's Asia Strategy, the real transformation in the EU–India relationship did not come until the next decade. The EU's external relations still viewed India through the development frame. The 1998 nuclear test by India marked a turning point in the global engagement with India. Having broken into the privileged nuclear club through its own indigenously developed technology, the world took note of a rising India. Within the EU, Germany and Denmark stopped aid programmes, but most EU members did not apply any sanctions. The EU was not far behind in recognising an emerging India but it was individual countries like France that helped India to renegotiate its place within the international nuclear regime. The step-by-step upgrading of the India–EU political and economic relationship to the summit level in Lisbon in June 2000 can be viewed as a signal by the EU of its intentions to enhance its political relations with India. But the enhancing of this summit-level relationship to a strategic partnership in 2004 was driven largely by other factors that influenced the EU to define its own strategic concept.

One can read the EU's intentions about the region in its revised Asia Strategy of 2001 called 'Europe and Asia: A Strategic Framework for Enhanced Partnership'. The EU had set for itself the task to 'follow a forward-looking policy of engagement with Asia, both in the region and globally' (European Commission 2001). The strategy identified six objectives: contributing to peace and security, promoting mutual trade and investment flows, protection of human rights, to build global partnerships and enhance the awareness of Europe in Asia and vice versa. The first review of the Commission's strategic framework for action in Asia took place in May 2007. Subsequently, the Commission set up a Regional Programming for Asia Strategy Document 2007–13 and identified three priority areas: support to regional integration; policy and know-how based cooperation in environment, energy and climate change; and support to uprooted people.

Although the 2001 document laid the blueprint for a more enhanced engagement with Asia, other factors contributed to this policy shift within the EU. A major trigger for the shift in the EU's engagement with different countries were the 11 September 2001 attacks on the United States and the dissonance created by the events that followed in Iraq. The EU's response to the US attack on Iraq could at best be described as incoherent – while France and Germany sought legitimacy within a UN mandate, Italy and Spain favoured a US strike, and Britain stood resolute in supporting the United States. The much-proclaimed CFSP launched a decade earlier in 1992 stood shattered. The EU found its CFSP in total disarray and it was this that forced stocktaking by the Union. The EU's external image was severely blunted and the internal incoherence further strengthened the external perception of the EU as a weak and disjointed actor.

It was against this backdrop of incoherence that the EU adopted the European Security Strategy (ESS) in the European Council in December 2003, titled 'A Secure Europe in a Better World'. After a long time, there was a presentation of a coherent policy document that indicated the EU's strategic perception of threats, objectives and the policy implications for Europe. For the first time the Union also identified the 'need to develop a strategic culture that fosters early, rapid and when necessary, robust intervention' (Council of the European Union 2003). The ESS also signalled new lines of partnership and cooperation and to enhance those that exist within a framework of 'effective multilateralism'. The ESS could be read as the Union's intentionality in its external actions of value preferences and the kind of global engagement it would like to construct and strengthen. This document also forms the backdrop for the EU–India strategic partnership.

EU–India Relation: Building a Strategic Partnership

In retrospect, one can say that the launch of the EU–India strategic partnership in 2004 was the recognition by the EU of India as a regional power that was gradually exerting a growing influence on many international issues. Internationally, recognising India's importance has led to a new rationale for engagement and building up the partnership with it. Emerging or rising India's potential has endorsed it as a likely partner in providing stability and order not merely in South Asia but to Asia as a whole. Four years after the launch of the annual summits in 2000 at Lisbon between India and the EU, at The Hague Summit in 2004, it was decided to upgrade the EU–India relationship to a strategic partnership.

In contrast to India, the EU's relations with the other big Asian power, China, only began in 1975 and this late engagement was quickly upgraded as in 1985 the EU and the PRC concluded the Trade and Cooperation Agreement that governs the relationship. China's growing significance in the region and globally also propelled the EU to launch a comprehensive strategic partnership with it in 2003.

In retrospect, 2004 signalled the new EU visibility at the regional and global level. The EU had enlarged and become 25 member states – extending democracy, rule of law, human rights and market economy to Central and Eastern Europe. This was an affirmation of its normative values and the consequence it brought to the new member states. Beyond Europe, the EU was successfully engaging three major economic powers of Asia in tandem – since 2001 with Japan through the Action Plan, with China since 2003 and finally India since 2004. The EU's expansion of cooperation with Japan, China and India can be also seen as a way to strengthen existing relationships. Although each of these strategic relations emphasised different aspects, it indicates the EU's efforts to harness the changing power equations in the post-Cold War period, especially in Asia through enhancing the engagement with the new emerging powers – China and India.

In 2005, the EU and India adopted a detailed Joint Action Plan (JAP) at New Delhi. The JAP is an ambitious agenda and emphasises a strong political, economic and civil society engagement. It 'offers a roadmap for future bilateral relations' (Wagner 2008: 103). The Joint Action Plan committed itself to the following issues (Council of the European Union 2005):

1. strengthening dialogue and consultation mechanisms;
2. deepening political dialogue and cooperation;
3. bringing together people and cultures;
4. enhancing economic policy dialogue and cooperation;
5. developing trade and investment

The Joint Action Plan was reviewed at the 2008 summit held in Marseille, which has since focused on promoting four priorities areas: peace and comprehensive security, sustainable development, research and technology, and people-to-people and cultural exchanges.

In terms of the objectives laid out in the JAP, political dialogue and cooperation with respect to security and defence between India and the EU and bilaterally with London, Paris and Berlin have grown extensively in the aftermath of the Mumbai attacks in 2008. There has been an increase in the dialogue on terrorism at all levels. The 2005 India–EU Joint Action Plan had identified counter-terrorism as an area of cooperation. This was reiterated in the 2009 EU–India Summit Declaration. However, there is a need to revitalise and restructure the cooperation which has so far been bilateral rather than multilateral. This point was also reiterated by the EU–India Forum on Effective Multilateralism in October 2009 in New Delhi. It said in its recommendations that 'there is a need to establish an India-EU Joint Working Group on counter terrorism to develop a common understanding of issues related to terrorism and response mechanisms' (Devare et al. 2009).

In 2006, at the Helsinki Summit, both sides endorsed a proposal to negotiate a free trade agreement, negotiations for which are still under way in 2012. India's growing economic performance has also translated into it taking a harder stand on trade related matters. Negotiations for the free trade agreement called the Bilateral

Trade and Investment Agreement (BTIA), which began in 2007 covering trade in goods and services, investments, intellectual property rights and government procurement, have not yet been concluded. The latest figures show that the 'EU-India trade has grown impressively and more than doubled from €28.6 billion in 2003 to over €67.9 billion in 2010. EU investment to India has more than tripled since 2003 from €759million to €3 billion in 2010 and trade in commercial services has tripled from €5.2billion in 2002 to €17.9 billion in 2010' (EU Delegation). It is not surprising that supporters on both sides speak of the overwhelming positive impact it will have on trade between India and the EU.

However, the delay in concluding the FTA points to major problems in some key areas. One such area is the liberalisation of trade and investment in banking services in India. The EU is seeking a larger market access for its banks; in particular, this is being pursued aggressively by the UK and Germany. Undoubtedly, the profitability of the Indian economy attracts foreign banks to India. Most foreign banks in India are reporting high profits. As of March 2010, there were nine EU-based banks operating in India and they are keen to concentrate on niche marketing in the metropolitan areas rather than on social and developmental banking in rural areas. India will need to tread with caution in the light of the last financial crisis that also enveloped European banks. In the absence of adequate regulations, the EU's desire for an unrestricted investment environment in India could cause major repercussions for the economy (Singh 2011).

Another key area of discord between India and the EU pertains to intellectual property rights in the field of medicine. The EU would like to include data exclusivity, which would impact the production of generic drugs in India. In fact, the EU is supported by leading pharmaceutical companies in Europe, which would like this provision to be incorporated in the FTA. Such generic drugs are exported to Africa and other poor regions to combat endemic diseases such as HIV/AIDS, tuberculosis and malaria. Given that generic drugs are cheaper than patented drugs, these have played an important role in the fight against these diseases. Interestingly, there is protest within the EU civil society itself against this issue. The CEO, a watchdog group specialising in revealing the influence that European industries exert over the EU's investment and trade relations with the developing world, accuses the EU 'of discriminating in favour of corporate lobby groups and of violating the EU's transparency rules' (Godoy 2011).

The slowness in negotiating the FTA also underscores the point that beyond ideational proximity, states negotiate trade issues from a strong position of national interest. While India and the EU have shared values based on democracy and human rights, there had been a tendency in the past for the EU to lecture India on its human rights practice. In stark contrast, the EU has actively engaged China although it is not a democracy. This reiterates the fact that despite the emphasis on normative values, the EU is driven by realistic considerations of trade (Bava 2008: 109). Although the EU is an undisputed global economic actor, it does not yet have the commensurate political or military strength. Its inability to articulate a common foreign policy position even after the adoption of the Lisbon Treaty was once again evidenced by the deep divisions over the engagement in the wake of the unrest in Libya and the strong bilateral positions articulated by individual member states have also diminished its credibility as a critical security player for India. India sees very few security deliverables that the EU can bring to the table and the perception here is grounded in reality.

The distinct feature of the strategic partnership has been the growing significance of India not only as an economic but political partner as well for the EU. The EU has represented itself at the global level with references to a foreign policy guided by values and principles. Ascribing higher normative values to EU action abroad and purely national interest to India assumes that the EU has no national/collective interest, which is clearly not the case if one were to read the 2003 European Security Strategy that highlights the challenges confronted by the EU and the proposed action. The ambiguity with which the EU appears to treat the two Asian emerging powers, China and India, only emphasises the need for a serious strategic dialogue with India that goes beyond the enumeration of normative principles to concrete action that acknowledges India's real and nascent potential as a major global actor. 'Europe, as the "norm entrepreneur" is a satiated power, whereas India is trying to become a norm setter, seeking to change the status quo in matters of global governance. The fact that the US and the EU engage a rising Asia in different ways, underscores who shapes what aspect of global politics' (Bava 2008: 112–13). To reflect the growing depth of their relations, the EU and China upgraded their strategic partnership in 2010 to include foreign affairs, security matters and global challenges such as climate change and global economy governance. The Chinese however feel that while India got a Joint Action Plan, they did not benefit from such political engagement. This also points to how the EU's engagement of its partners is quite varied and does not follow a uniform template.

The undercutting of India–EU relations is partially due to the remarkable development in India's bilateral relationships with many European countries. Strong bilateral relationships between India and the UK, France and Germany, have led to a weak relationship with the EU as a whole. In fact, it is often felt in New Delhi that the lack of coherence in the EU can be offset by a stronger engagement of bilateral relations rather than multilateral. Managing the relations when numerous actors are involved both within the EU and with member states has meant that the coherence in policy articulation from member states has won over Brussels.

The EU's External Actions and Visibility as a Cohesive Actor

Coherence in policy objectives and action is critical and is one of the benchmarks for evaluating the performance of an actor in international politics (Bretherton and Vogler 2006). It must be stressed here that the lack of a coherent response by the EU to numerous crises including the handling of the current euro crisis has led to comments such as 'how irrelevant it is becoming to the rest of the world' (Mahbubani 2010). In a speech titled – *The Challenges for Europe in a Changing World* – President of the Council Mr Herman Van Rompuy drew attention to review and strengthen the EU's relationship with key partners, namely the United States, Canada, Russia, China, Japan, India and Brazil. He concluded by saying 'To get in the deal-making game, the Union needs to assert itself politically. The first step is to carefully choose our allies, to reflect about what we can do together with them' (Van Rompuy 2010).

'The idea of foreign policy implies both politics and coherence' (Hill 2002: 4). If the EU is unable to present itself as a cohesive actor, it risks not being taken seriously by other actors. However, building coherence for the EU has not been an easy task (Gauttier 2004; Nuttall 2005; Tietje 1997). Barroso has also clearly illustrated a keen awareness of the challenges faced by the EU in the strategic dimension. In his State of the Union address in 2010 he argued forcibly that:

> As the strategic partnerships of the 21st century emerge, Europe should seize the chance to define its future. I am impatient to see the Union play the role in global affairs that matches its economic weight. Our partners are watching and are expecting us to engage as Europe, not just as 27 individual countries. If we don't act together, Europe will not be a force in the world, and they will move on without us: without the European Union but also without its Member States.

The Lisbon Treaty has undoubtedly reshaped some of the architecture of the Union by reforming existing institutions and creating new ones (Buzek 2011). The permanent President gives continuity and visibility, the merged positions leading to a new enhanced High Representative for Foreign Affairs and Security Policy and the newly created office of Foreign Affairs and Security Policy (FASP) to be assisted by a European External Action Service. According to article 21(3) of the Lisbon Treaty the Union was tasked to 'ensure consistency between the different areas of its external action and between these and its other policies'. This is not an easy task. For example, although the External Action Service has been created, there are many critical areas such as trade and development assistance that continue to remain with the Commission and so coordinating these entirely diverse tasks pose major challenges. Since the Lisbon Treaty entered into force in December 2009, the EU and not the member states has become a contracting party to international agreements. However, Declaration 13 and 14 of the CFSP provisions clearly reveals that the member states' sovereignty in foreign policy has in no way been infringed by the Lisbon Treaty (Koehler 2010).

As a consequence, the EU suffers at two levels to be considered a critical actor. First, 'it suffers from a deficit of recognition as a political actor enjoying the full array of traditional attributes of power' (de Vasconcelos 2008: 17). Second, the lack of political consensus within the EU on foreign policy issues prevents New Delhi from considering Brussels a critical political actor. Observers speak of 'divided sovereignty' (Cannizzaro 2002): that there is a distribution of foreign policy powers between the EU and the member states. Thus despite the Lisbon Treaty, the fragmentation of power continues to exist and there is a situation of divided sovereignty.

Consequently, despite a considerable ideational convergence between India and the EU, it does not automatically translate into cooperation. Things in the past happened more by chance and less by intent. Undoubtedly, there has been a shift in the focus of relations, by changing the political equation and taking it beyond rhetoric. India's foreign policy today sees a pragmatic blend of its security and economic imperatives. 'As the relative capabilities of India have grown, the assessment of other countries about India has also slowly shifted' (Bava 2010a: 125).

Conclusion

The EU's ability 'to influence global change is limited unless Europeans demonstrate a willingness to identify clear strategic priorities and to combine their efforts under the same flag' (Duke 2011: 83). Duke further quotes what the then High Representative, Javier Solana, noted in 2006, 'on our own we are political midgets. Policy takers' (ibid.). There is scepticism on how much the EU can influence the emerging powers such as China and India. Rather it would appear that the EU would like to co-opt these states in its value preference to create an enabling multilateral framework that would be beneficial to its interests.

In the early 1990s as the Yugoslavia conflict corroborated, the EU was a long way off from being a cohesive political actor. It had a potential to be a power, but was at best a 'Would-Be World Power' (Majone 2009) and politically was not capable of exercising influence in conflict situations. Although Lisbon was successful in creating certain institutional mechanisms that would 'help' project coherence in EU CFSP, the current responses to the Arab Spring, the fiasco in Libya, all point to the reluctance of member states to foster a collective decision-making on matters pertaining to foreign and security policy in Brussels. This is despite the fact that the ESS in 2003 pointed out 'Greater coherence is needed not only among EU instruments but also embracing the external activities of the individual member states'. The net result is: a disconnect between the stated intentions and the actual practice of the Union's external relations when seeking to present itself as an effective and coherent actor.

'Europe the "norm entrepreneur" is a satiated power, whereas India is also trying to be a norm creator currently seeks to change the status quo in matters of global governance' (Bava 2008: 112). For example, on the issue of the UNSC reform, the EU member states have remained divided and are also unable to formulate a common EU position. It is no coincidence that it is the member states who are members of the UN and not the EU.

The United States has discovered the power potential of India, critical to the Asian strategic calculus and has sought to overcome the Cold War legacy of mutual estrangement. In contrast the EU seeks to create a multipolar world in which it identifies India and China as the emerging Asian power centres and seeks to engage India because of its economic growth. However, there is a deficit in the India–EU relationship because the EU is not perceived as a strategic security actor and its ability to bring security deliverables to the partnership is extremely limited (Bava 2008: 113).

The EU and India have different political priorities and preferences shaped by their past history and politics and current experiences. While the EU negotiates internally to a more post-modern and cohesive decision-making of the 27; India's preference is for sovereignty and non-interference in the domestic affairs of other states. The challenge is to bring a post-Westphalian EU and a Westphalian India to find a win-win partnership. The integration of the EU has raised performance and visibility expectations globally and more so in its strategic partnerships. According to Grevi, 'Entering strategic partnerships constitutes a key test for the Union as an international actor' (Grevi 2008: 154). However, Europe's lack of political cohesion and military visibility of the EU have also contributed to additional problems in that its political effectiveness is diluted. At a global level, while the EU is the most successful example of regional integration and extended durable peace between countries, however, 'the idea of Europe does not trigger any sense either of excitement or attraction'. The biggest challenge in assessing the EU as a global economic and political and security actor lies in the fact that it is constantly evolving. In effect, the challenge for EU–India relations is, on the one hand, to manage expectation and capability and, on the other hand, find a balance between norms and realism (Bava 2008).

Bibliography

Abélès, M., Bellier, I. and McDonald, M. (1993) *Approche anthropologique de la Commission européenne*, Brussels: European Commission.

Acharya, A. (2011) 'Norm Subsidiarity and Regional Orders: Sovereignty, Regionalism, and Rule-Making in the Third World', *International Studies Quarterly*, 55(1), 95–123.

Adebahr, Cornelius (2011) *The Comprehensive Approach to Crisis Management in a Concerted Weimar Effort*, Stiftung Genshagen, Genshagener Papiere 6.

Aggarwal, V.K. (1998) 'Analyzing Institutional Transformation in the Asia-Pacific', in V.K. Aggarwal and C. Morrison (eds), *Asia-Pacific Crossroads: Regime Creation and the Future of APEC*, New York: St. Martin's Press, pp. 23–64.

Alcaro, R. and Haubrich-Seco, M. (eds) (2012) *Rethinking Western Policies in Light of the Arab Uprisings*, Rome: Istituto Affari Internazionali/Edizioni Nuova Cultura.

Allen, D. (1998) 'Who Speaks for Europe? The Search for an Effective and Coherent External Policy', in J. Peterson and H. Sjursen (eds), *A Common Foreign Policy for Europe?*, London: Routledge, pp. 42–58.

Allison, G.T. and Zelikow, P. (1971) *Essence of Decision: Explaining the Cuban Missile Crisis*, New York: Longman.

Allison, G.T. and Zelikow, P. (1999) *Essence of Decision*, 2nd edition, New York: Longman.

Anderson, Perry (2009) *The New Old World*, London: Verso.

Applebaum, Anne (2011) 'Will the Libya Intervention Bring the End of NATO?', *The Washington Post*, 11 April.

Armstrong of Ilminster, Lord (Robert T.) (1991) 'Summits: A Sherpa's Eye View', 44th Montague Burton Lecture on International Relations, given at Leeds, 4 February 1991, in *The University of Leeds Review 1991–92*, pp. 31–44.

Arrighi, Giovanni (1994) *The Long Twentieth Century: Money, Power and the Origins of Our Times*, London: Verso.

Aspen Strategy Group, The (1993) *Harness The Rising Sun: An American Strategy for Managing Japan's Rise as a Global Power*, Maryland and London: University Press of America.

Ashton, C. (2010) *CFSP Annual Report*.

Ashton, C. (2011a) Speech at Corvinus University, Budapest, 25 February. Accessed at http://europa.eu/rapid/pressReleasesAction.do?reference=SPEECH/11/126.

Ashton, C. (2011b) *CFSP Annual Report*.

Attinà, F. (2003) 'The Euro-Mediterranean Partnership Assessed: The Realist and Liberal Views', *European Foreign Affairs Review*, 8(2), 181–99.

Bacevich, Andrew J. (2011) 'Last Act in the Middle East', *Newsweek*, 3 April.

Back, A. (2012) 'China Turns Investment Eye to Europe', *The Wall Street Journal*, 14 February.

Bacon, P. (2011) 'Human Rights, Transformative Power and EU-Japan Relations', in Koji Fukuda (ed.), *Multi-layered Governance of the EU* [title in Japanese: *Tagenka-suru EU gabanansu*], Tokyo: Waseda University Press, ch. 9.

Badr, Mayssa (2011) 'The European Commission One Year On: So Far, Not So Good', 9 February. Accessed 11 July 2012 at http://burson-marsteller. be/2011/02/barroso2-survey-results/.

Barnett, M. and Duvall, R. (eds) (2005) *Power in Global Governance*, Cambridge: Cambridge University Press.

Barnett, Thomas P. (2009) *Great Powers: America and the World After Bush*, New York: Putnam's.

Barysch, Katinka, Grant, Charles and Valasek, Tomas (2011), 'A New Opportunity for EU Foreign Policy', *CER Bulletin*, No. 76, February/March.

Bates, Gill (2008) 'The United States and the China-Europe Relations', in David Shambaugh, Eberhard Sandschneider and Zhou Hong (eds), *China-Europe Relations: Perceptions, Policies and Prospects*, Routledge: London, pp. 270–87.

Bava, Ummu Salma (2001) 'Emerging Power Alliances in Perspective: IBSA, BRIC, BASIC', in Francis A. Kornegay and Lesley Masters (eds), *From BRIC to BRICS, Berlin: Friedrich Erbert Stiftung*, pp. 55–63.

Bava, Ummu Salma (2006) 'India – An Emerging Power in International Security?', in A.C. Vaz (ed.), *Intermediate States, Regional Leadership and Security: India, Brazil and South Africa*, Brasilia: University of Brasilia, pp. 71–86.

Bava, Ummu Salma (2007) 'India's Role in the Emerging World Order', *Dialogue on Globalization*, FES Briefing Paper, pp. 1–7.

Bava, Ummu Salma (2008) 'The EU and India: Challenges to a Strategic Partnership', in Giovanni Grevi and Alvaro de Vasconcelos (eds), *Partnerships for Effective Multilateralism*, Paris: Institute for Security Studies, No. 109, pp. 105–13.

Bava, Ummu Salma (2010a) 'India: Foreign Policy Strategy between Interests and Ideas', in Daniel Flemes (ed.), *Regional Leadership in the Global System: Ideas, Interests and Strategies of Regional Powers*, Surrey: Ashgate, pp. 11–126.

Bava, Ummu Salma (2010b) 'India and the European Union: From Engagement to Strategic Partnership', *International Studies*, 47(2–4), 373–86.

Bava, Ummu Salma (2011) 'Emerging Power Alliances in Perspective: IBSA, BRIC, BASIC', in F. Kornegay and L. Masters (eds), *From BRIC to BRICS: Report on the Proceedings of the International Workshop on South Africa and Emerging Power Alliance: IBSA, BRIC, BASIC*. Cape Town and Berlin: Institute for Global Dialogue and Friedrich Ebert Stiftung, pp. 55–61.

Beck, U. (2011) 'Créons une Europe des citoyens!', *Le Monde*, Paris, 27 December.

Berridge, G.R. (2010) *Diplomacy: Theory and Practice*, 2nd edition, Basingstoke: Palgrave Macmillan.

Bicchi, F. and Carta, C. (2011) 'The Lisbon Treaty and the Common Foreign and Security Policy: A Leap Forward or More of the Same?', *European Foreign Policy Unit Working Paper No. 2011/2.*

Bicchi, F. and Gillespie, R. (eds) (2012) *The Union for the Mediterranean*, London: Routledge.

Bickerton, C. (2011) *European Foreign Policy from Effectiveness to Functionality*, London: Palgrave.

Bretherton, Charlotte and Vogler, John (2006) *The European Union as a Global Actor*, London: Routledge.

Biscop, Sven (2008) 'Permanent Structured Cooperation and the Future of the ESDP: Transformation and Integration', *European Foreign Affairs Review*, 13(4), 431–48.

Biscop, Sven (2012) *EU Grand Strategy: Optimism is Mandatory*, Brussels, Egmont Policy Brief No. 36.

Blom-Hansen, J. (2011) 'The EU Comitology System: Taking Stock before the New Lisbon Regime', *Journal of European Public Policy*, 18(4), 607–17.

Börzel, Tanja and Risse, Thomas (2003) 'Conceptualizing the Domestic Impact of Europe', in Keith Featherstone and Claudio Radaelli (eds), *The Politics of Europeanisation*, Oxford: Oxford University Press, pp. 57–80.

Börzel, T.A. and Risse, T. (2009a) 'Venus Approaching Mars? The European Union as an Emerging Civilian World Power', *Berlin Working Paper on European Integration*, No. 11, April.

Börzel, T.A. and Risse, T. (2009b) *The Transformative Power of Europe: The European Union and the Diffusion of Ideas*, Berlin: Kolleg-Forschergruppe (KFG) Working Paper No. 7.

Breslin, Shaun (2007) *China and the Global Political Economy*, London: Palgrave Macmillan.

Bretherton, Charlotte and Vogler, John (2006) *The European Union as a Global Actor*, 2nd edition, London: Routledge.

Bridges, B. (1993) *Japan: Hesitant Superpower*, London: Research Institute for the Study of Conflict and Terrorism.

Brimmer, Esther (ed.) (2002) *The EU's Search for a Strategic Role: ESDP and its Implications for Transatlantic Relations*, Washington, DC: Centre for Transatlantic Relations.

Brzezinski, Z. (1983) *Power and Principle: Memoirs of the National Security Adviser 1977–1981*, London: Weidenfeld & Nicolson.

Bull, H. (1977/2002) *The Anarchical Society: A Study of Order in World Politics*, London: Macmillan, 1977; 3rd edition, 2002.

Bull, H. (1982/1983) 'Civilian Power Europe: A Contradiction in Terms?', in Loukas Tsoukalis (ed.), *The European Community: Past, Present and Future*, Oxford: Basil Blackwell, 1983, pp. 149–74.

Bulmer, S. Jeffery, C. and Padgett S. (eds) (2010) *Rethinking Germany and Europe: Democracy and Diplomacy in a Semi-Sovereign State*, Basingstoke: Palgrave Macmillan.

Bulmer, S. and Paterson, W. (2010) 'Germany and the European Union: From "Tamed Power" to Normalized Power?', *International Affairs*, 86(5), 1051–70.

Buzek, Jerzy (2011) 'State of the Union: Three Cheers for the Lisbon Treaty and Two Warnings for Political Parties', *Journal of Common Market Studies*, 49, 7–18.

Byman, D. and Waxman, M. (2002) *The Dynamics of Coercion, American Foreign Policy and the Limits of Military Might*, Cambridge: Cambridge University Press.

Cafruny, Alan and Ryner, Magnus (2007) *Europe at Bay: In the Shadows of US Hegemony*, Boulder: Lynne Rienner.

Calder, K. and Fukuyama, F. (eds) (2008) *East Asian Multilateralism*, Baltimore: Johns Hopkins University Press.

Callaghan, J. (1987) *Time and Chance*, London: Collins.

Cameron, F. (2012) *An Introduction to European Foreign Policy*, London: Routledge.

Cannizzaro, Enzo (2002) *The European Union as an Actor in International Relations*, The Hague: Kluwer Law International.

Carothers, Thomas (2008) 'Is a League of Democracies a Good Idea?', New York, Carnegie Endowment for International Peace, May. Accessed at http://carnegieendowment.org/2008/05/19/is-league-of-democracies-good-idea/aiy.

Carta, C. (2012) *The European Union Diplomatic System: Preferences, Ideas and Identities*, London: Routledge.

Carta, C. (forthcoming, 2013) 'The Geneva Convention: The External Representation of a System of Governance', *European Journal of Contemporary Research*.

Casarini, Nicola (2009) *Remaking Global Order: The Evolution of Europe–China Relations*, New York: Oxford University Press.

Chaban, Natalia, Elgström, Ole and Holland, Martin (2006) 'The European Union as Others see it', *European Foreign Affairs Review*, 11(2), 245–62.

Chen Zhimin (2012) 'The Chinese Foreign Policy', in M. Telò (ed.), *Globalization, State and Multilateralism*, Dordrecht: Springer, pp. 79–97.

Christiansen, T. (1997) 'Tensions of European Governance: Politicized Bureaucracy and Multiple Accountability in the European Commission', *Journal of European Public Policy*, 4(1), 73–90.

Colombo, S. and Tocci, N. (2012) 'The EU Response to the Arab Uprisings: Old Wine in New Bottles?', in R. Alcaro and M. Haubrich-Seco (eds), *Rethinking Western Policies in Light of the Arab Uprisings*, Rome: Istituto Affari Internazionali/Edizioni Nuova Cultura, pp. 71–96.

Commission of the European Communities (2010) Commission Decision: Organigramme pour le nouveau FPIS (Foreign Policy Instrument Service), SEC(2010) 1307 final, Bruxelles, 27 October.

Commission of the European Communities (2011) Communication from the Commission to the Council and the European Parliament, *Financing of Civilian and Crisis Management Operations*, Brussels, 28.11.2001 COM(2001) 647 final.

Cooper, A.F., Hughes, C.W. and De Lombaerde, P. (2007) *Regionalization and Global Governance: The Taming of Globalization?* London: Routledge.

Cooper, R. (2004) *The Breaking of Nations*, New York: Atlantic Monthly Press.

Council [of the European Union] (2003) *European Security Strategy: A Secure Europe In A Better World*, Brussels. Accessed at http://www.consilium.europa.eu/uedocs/cmsUpload/78367.pdf.

Council [of the European Union] (2005) *The India-EU Strategic Partnership*. Joint Action Plan. 11984/05. Brussels.

Council [of the European Union] (2008) *Declaration on Strengthening Capabilities*, 11 December. Accessed 11 July 2012 at http://register.consilium.europa.eu/pdf/en/08/st16/st16840.en08.pdf.

Council [of the European Union] (2009b) *Council Decision on 1 December 2009 adopting the Council's Rules of Procedure* (2009/937/EU). OJ L 325/35-61.

Council [of the European Union] (2009a) *Council Decision Laying Down Measures for the Implementation of the European Council Decision on the Exercise of the Presidency of the Council, and on the Chairmanship of Preparatory Bodies of the Council*. 16517/09. Brussels.

Council [of the European Union] (2009c) *European Council Decision of 1 December 2009 on the Exercise of the Presidency of the Council* (2009/881/EU). OJ L 315/50.

Council [of the European Union] (2010) *The Stockholm Programme – An Open and Secure Europe Serving and Protecting Citizens*, 5731/10, Brussels, 3 March.

Cox, R. (1986) 'Production, Power and World Orders', in R.O. Keohane (ed.), *Realism and Its Critics*, New York: Columbia University Press, pp. 204–53.

Cramme, Olaf (2009) *Rescuing the European Project: EU Legitimacy, Governance and Security*, London: Policy Network.

Crawley, A. (2006) 'Europe-Latin America (EU-LAC) Relations: Toward Interregional Coalition Building?', in H. Hänggi, R. Roloff and J. Rüland (eds), *Interregionalism and International Relations*, London: Routledge, pp. 167–81.

Czempiel, E.O. (1999) *Kluge Macht: Außenpolitik für das 21. Jahrhundert*, München: C.H. Beck.

Daalder, Ivo and Lindsay, James (2007) 'Democracies of the World, Unite', *The National Interest*, January/February. Accessed at http://www.the-american-interest.com/article.cfm?piece=220.

Daalder, Ivo and Stavridis, James (2012) 'NATO's Victory in Libya: The Right Way to Run an Intervention', *Foreign Affairs*, 91(2).

Damro, C. (2011) 'Market Power Europe', paper delivered at EUSA 2011.

Daviter, F. (2007) 'Policy Framing in the European Union', *Journal of European Public Policy*, 14(4), 654–66.

Department of Defense [DoD] (2012) *Sustaining US Global Leadership. Priorities for 21st Century Defense*. Accessed at http://www.defense.gov/news/Defense_Strategic_Guidance.pdf.

De Schoutheete, Philippe and Andoura, Sami (2007) 'The Legal Personality of the European Union', *Studia Diplomatica*, LX/1, 1–9.

Deudney, D. and Ikenberry, J.G. (1999) 'The Nature and Sources of Liberal International Order', *Review of International Studies*, 25(2), 179–96.

Devare, S.T., de Vasconcelos, A. and Peral, L. (2009) *Report on the India-EU Forum on Effective Multilateralism*, Paris: EUISS.

De Vasconcelos, A. (2008) 'Multilateralising Multipolarity', in G. Grevi and A. de Vasconcelos (eds), *Partnerships for Effective Multilateralism*, Paris: Institute for Security Studies, No. 109, pp. 11–32.

Dewatripont, M. and Legros, P. (2009) 'EU Competition Policy in a Global World', in M. Telò (ed.), *EU and Global Governance*, London: Routledge, pp. 87–102.

Dimier, V. (2003) 'L'institutionnalisation de la Commission Européenne (DG Développement): du rôle des leaders dans la construction d'une administration multinational 1958–1975', *Revue Études internationales*, 34(3), 401–27.

Ding Yuanhong (2009) 'Jingshouzhu shijian kaoyan de zhongou guanxi' [China–Europe Relations after the Test of Time], *Ouzhou Yanjiu* [*Chinese Journal of European Studies*], 5, pp. 29–33.

Doidge, M. (2011) *The European Union and Interregionalism*, London: Ashgate.

Dony, M. (ed.) (2008) *Démocratie, cohérence et transparence*, Bruxelles: Université de Bruxelles.

Drent, M. and Zandee, D. (2010) *Breaking Pillars: Towards a Civil-Military Security Approach for the EU*, Clingendael security paper, The Hague.

Drifte, R. (1996) *Japan's Foreign Policy in the 1990s: From Economic Power to What Power?*, London: Macmillan, in association with St Antony's College, Oxford.

Driss, A. (2012) 'The EU Response to the Arab Uprising: A Show of Ambivalence', in R. Alcaro and M. Haubrich-Seco (eds), *Rethinking Western Policies in Light of the Arab Uprisings*, Rome: Istituto Affari Internazionali/Edizioni Nuova Cultura, 97–110.

Duchêne, F. (1972) 'Europe's Role in World Peace', in Richard Mayne (ed.), *Europe Tomorrow: Sixteen Europeans Look Ahead*, London: Fontana/Collins for Chatham House/PEP, pp. 32–47.

Duchêne, F. (1973) 'The European Community and the Uncertainties of Interdependence', in Max Kohnstamm and Wolfgang Hager (eds), *A Nation Writ Large? Foreign-Policy Problems before the European Community*, London: Macmillan [*Zivilmacht Europa -Supermacht oder Partner?* (Frankfurt am Main: Suhrkamp, 1973)], pp. 1–21.

Duke, S. (2006) 'Consistency as an Issue in EU External Activities', *EIPA Working Paper*, 99/W/06.

Duke, S. (2009) 'Providing for European-Level Diplomacy after Lisbon: The Case of the European External Action Service', *The Hague Journal of Diplomacy*, 4, 211–33.

Duke, S. (2011) 'Pax or Pox Europeana after the Lisbon Treaty?', *The International Spectator*, 46(1), 83–99.

EDA (2011) 'EDA's Pooling and Sharing', 2 December. Accessed at http://www.eda.europa.eu/Libraries/Documents/factsheet_-_pooling_sharing_-_301111.sflb.ashx.

EDA (2012) 'Taking Pooling and Sharing to the Next Level', *European Defence Matters*, 1, May–July. Accessed 11 July 2012 at http://www.eda.europa.eu/publications/12-05-21/European_Defence_Matters_-_Issue_1.

Eeckhout, P. (2005) *External Relations of the EU: Legal and Constitutional Foundation*, Oxford: Oxford University Press.

Eichengreen, Barry (1996) *Globalising Capital: A History of the International Monetary System*, Princeton: Princeton University Press.

Emerson, M., Balfour, R., Corthaut, T., Wouters, J., Kaczynski, P.M. and Renard, T. (2011) *Upgrading the EU's Role as Global Actor: Institutions, Law and the Restructuring of European Diplomacy*, Brussels: Centre for European Policy Studies.

Engberg, Katarina (2011) *The EU's Collective Use of Force: Exploring the Factors Behind its First Military Operations*, Uppsala: Universitet.

Erlanger, Steven (2011) 'Libya's Dark Lesson for NATO', *New York Times*, 3 September.

European Commission (1994) 'Towards a New Asia Strategy', *Communication from the Commission to the Council* COM(94)314 final, Brussels.

European Commission (2001) 'Europe and Asia: A Strategic Framework for Enhanced Partnerships', *Communication from the Commission to the Council* COM(2001) 469 final, Brussels.

European Commission and High Representative of the Union for Foreign Affairs and Security Policy (2011a) Joint Communication to the European Council, the European Parliament, the Council, the European Economic and Social Committee and the Committee of the Regions, *A Partnership for Democracy and Shared Prosperity with the Southern Mediterranean*, Brussels, 8 March, COM(2011) 200 final.

European Commission and High Representative of the Union for Foreign Affairs and Security Policy (2011b) Joint Communication to the European Parliament, the Council, the European Economic and Social Committee and the Committee of the Regions, *A New Response to a Changing Neighbourhood*, Brussels, 25 May, COM(2011) 303.

European Policy Unit (1992) *Europe and Japan: Cooperation and Conflict*, Summary of Conference Proceedings, Conference held at Florence: European University Institute, 4–6 June.

Everett, S. (2003) 'The Policy Cycle: Democratic Process or Rational Paradigm Revisited?', *The Australian Journal of Public Administration,* 62(2), 65–70.

Feng Zhongping (2009) 'Zhongou xuyao jianshexing jiechu' [China and Europe: Constructive Engagement Needed], *Ouzhou Yanjiu* [*Chinese Journal of European Studies*], 5, pp. 59–67.

Fox, J. and Godemont, F. (2009) 'A Power Audit of EU-China Relations', London: European Council on Foreign Relations (ECFR), 17 April. Accessed at http: // ecfr. eu/page/-/documents.

Friedberg, Aaron (2011) *A Contest for Supremacy: China, America, and the Struggle for Master in Asia*, New York: Norton.

Fukuyama, Francis (1992) *The End of History and the Last Man*, London: Hamish Hamilton.

Fukuyama, Francis (2006) *Nation-Building: Beyond Afghanistan and Iraq*, Baltimore: Johns Hopkins University Press.

Funabashi, Y. (1991–2) 'Japan and the New World Order', *Foreign Affairs*, 70(5), 58–74.

Funabashi, Y. (ed.) (1994) *Japan's International Agenda*, New York: New York University Press.

Gamble, Andrew (2009) *The Spectre at the Feast: Capitalist Crisis and the Politics of Recession*, London: Palgrave Macmillan.

Gamble, A. (2012) 'The Changing World Order: From the Opening of the Berlin Wall to the Financial Crisis', in M. Telò (ed.), *State, Globalization, Multilateralism*, Dordrecht: Springer, pp. 45–60.

Gamble, A. and Lane, D. (eds) (2009) *The European Union and World Politics*, Basingstoke: Palgrave.

Ganguly, Sumit (2002) 'India's Multiple Revolutions', *Journal of Democracy*, 13(1), 38–51.

Garby, C. and Bullock, M.B. (eds) (1994) *Japan: A New Kind of Superpower?*, Washington, DC: The Woodrow Wilson Center Press; Baltimore and London: Johns Hopkins University Press.

Garton Ash, Timothy (2005) *Free World: America, Europe and the Surprising Future of the West*, New York: Vintage.

Gates, R. (2011) 'The Security and Defense Agenda: The Future of NATO', Speech by Secretary of Defense Robert M. Gates, 10 June. Accessed at http://www.defense.gov/Speeches/Speech.aspx?SpeechID=1581.

Gauttier, P. (2004) 'Horizontal Coherence and the External Competencies of the European Union', *European Law Journal*, 10, 23–41.

Gebhard, C. (2011) 'Coherence', in C. Hill and M. Smith (eds), *International Relations and the European Union*, 2nd edition, Oxford: Oxford University Press, pp. 101–27.

Giandomenico, M. (2009) *Europe as the Would-be World Power: The EU at Fifty*, Florence: European University Institute.

Gillespie, R. (2011a) 'The Union for the Mediterranean: An Intergovernmentalist Challenge for the European Union?', *Journal of Common Market Studies*, 49(6), 1205–25.

Gillespie, R. (2011b) 'Adapting to French "Leadership": Spain's Role in the Union for the Mediterranean', *Mediterranean Politics*, 16/1, 59–78.

Gillespie, R. (2012) 'The UfM Found Wanting: European Responses to the Challenge of Regime Change in the Mediterranean', in F. Bicchi and R. Gillespie (eds), *The Union for the Mediterranean*, London: Routledge, pp. 211–23.

Gilpin, R. (1981) *War and Change in World Politics*, Cambridge: Cambridge University Press.

Gilson, J. (2002a) *Asia Meets Europe: Interregionalism and the Asia–Europe Meeting*, London and Cheltenham: Edward Elgar.

Gilson, J. (2002b) *Defining Inter-Regionalism: The Asia-Europe Meeting (ASEM)*, Presentation for the University of Sheffield – School of East Asian Studies (24 April), 1st published on the SEAS Website (http://213.207.94.236/files/gilson_DefiningInterRegionalism.pdf).

Gilson, Julie (2005) 'New Interregionalism? The EU and East Asia', *Journal of European Integration*, 27(3): 307–26.

Glaesner, H.J. (1994) 'The European Council', in D. Curtin and T. Heukels (eds), *Institutional Dynamics of the European Union: Essays in Honour of Henry G. Schermers*, Dordrecht: Martinus Nijhoff, p. 103.

Glyn, Andrew (2006) *Capitalism Unleashed: Finance, Globalisation and Welfare*, Oxford: Oxford University Press.

Gnesotto, N. (2011) *L'Europe a-t-elle un avenir stratégique?*, Paris: A. Colin.

Godoy, Julio (2011) 'EU Trade Deal with India Stalemated by Threat to Affordable Drugs', Inter Press Service News Agency, Berlin. Accessed at http://www.ipsnews.net/2011/05/eu-trade-deal-withindia-stalemated-by-threat-to-affordable-drugs/.

Goldstein, Judith and Keohane, Robert (eds) (1993) *Ideas and Foreign Policy: Beliefs, Institutions and Political Change*, Cornell: Cornell University Press.

Gowan, R. (2011) 'Multilateralism without Money', Article on E!Sharp webpage: http://esharp.eu/oped/richard-gowan/6-multilateralism-without-money/.

Gowan, R. and Brantner, F. (2011) *The EU and Human Rights at the UN: 2011 Review*, Policy Memo, The European Council on Foreign Relations.

Graesli, Ingeborg (MEP) (2011) 'The Creation of the European External Action Service: A Critical Analysis', Fondation Robert Schuman, 14 February.

Gratius, S. (2011) *The EU and the 'Special Ten': Deepening or Widening Strategic Partnerships?* Policy Brief 76, FRIDE.

Green, M. and Gill, B. (eds) (2009) *Asia's New Multilateralism*, New York: Columbia University Press.

Grevi, G. (2008) 'The Rise of Strategic Partnerships: Between Interdependence and Power Politics', in G. Grevi and A. de Vasconcelos (eds), *Partnerships for Effective Multilateralism: EU Relations with Brazil, China, India and Russia*, Paris: Institute for Security Studies, No. 109, pp. 145–72.

Grevi, G. (2010) 'Making EU Strategic Partnerships Effective', Working Paper 105, FRIDE.

Grevi, G. (2011a) 'Strategic Partnerships: Smart Grid or Talking Shops?', in G. Grevi with G. Khandekar (eds), *Mapping EU Strategic Partnerships*, Madrid: FRIDE book.

Grevi, G. (2011b) 'The Performance of the EU in International Institutions', *Journal of European Integration*, 33(6).

Gros-Verheyde, N. (2011) 'Le Priorités 'défense' de la présidence polonaise: Ashton Absente', Brussels, 2–3 July.

Guess, G. and Farnham P. (2011) *Cases in Public Policy Analysis*, Washington, DC: Georgetown University Press.

Gupta, K.R. (1995) *World Trade*, Delhi: Atlantic Publishers.

Haas, E. (1964) *Beyond the Nation-State: Functionalism and International Organizations*, Stanford: Stanford University Press.

Habermas, J. (2006) *The Divided West*, Cambridge: Polity Press.

Habermas, J. (2012) *The Crisis of the European Union: A Response*, Cambridge: Polity Press.

Hänggi, Heiner (1999) 'ASEM and the Construction of the New Triad', *Journal of the Asia Pacific Economy*, 4(1), 56–80.

Hänggi, Heiner (2000) 'Interregionalism: Empirical and Theoretical Perspectives', Paper Prepared for the Workshop 'Dollars, Democracy and Trade. External Influence on Economic Integration in the Americas', Los Angeles, CA, 18 May.

Hänggi, H. (2006) 'Interregionalism as a Multi-Faceted Phenomenon: In Search of a Typology', in H. Hänggi, R. Rolof and Rüland J. Heydemann (eds), *Interregionalism and International Relations*, London: Routledge, pp. 31–63.

Halliday, Fred (2000) *The World at 2000*, Basingstoke: Palgrave.

Halper, Stefan (2010) *The Beijing Consensus: How China's Authoritarian Model will Dominate the Twenty-First Century*, New York: Basic Books.

Hannay, David (2011) 'Benchmarking the EU's New Diplomatic Service', *Europe's World*, 21 January.

Hay, Colin and Marsh, David (1999) *Demystifying Globalisation*, New York: St Martin's Press.

He Jingjun (2009) 'Jialilue yu beidou yuanhe fenfei' [Why Galileoand Beidou Can Not Cooperate?], *Wenhui Daily*, 31 March.

Held, David and McGrew, Anthony (2007) *Globalisation/Anti-Globalisation: Beyond the Great Divide*, Cambridge: Polity.

Hettne, B. (2007) 'Interregionalism and World Order: The Diverging EU and US Models', in M. Telò (ed.), *European Union and New Regionalism*, London: Ashgate, pp. 107–127.

Hettne, B. and Söderbaum, F. (2005) 'Civilian Power or Soft Imperialism? EU as a Global Actor and the Role of Interregionalism', *European Foreign Affairs Review*, 10(4), 535–52.

Heydemann, S. (2012) 'Embracing the Change, Accepting the Challenge? Western Response to the Arab Spring', in R. Alcaro and M. Haubrich-Seco (eds), *Rethinking Western Policies in Light of the Arab Uprisings*, Rome: Istituto Affari Internazionali/Edizioni Nuova Cultura, pp. 21–30.

High Representative for Foreign Affairs and Security Policy Council (2010) *Proposal for a Draft Decision Establishing the Organization and Functioning of the EEAS*, 8029/10 25 March 2010.

High Representative of the Union for Foreign Affairs and Security Policy (2010) *Annex to the Proposal for a Council Decision Establishing the Organisation and Functioning of the European External Action Service*, 8870/10, Brussels, 22 April 2010.

Hill, C. (1990) 'European Foreign Policy: Power Bloc, Civilian Model – or Flop?', in R. Rummel (ed.), *The Evolution of an International Actor: Western Europe's New Assertiveness*, Boulder: Westview Press, pp. 31–55.

Hill, C. (1993) 'The Capabilities-Expectations Gap, or Conceptualising Europe's International Role', *Journal of Common Market Studies*, 31(3), 305–28.

Hill, C. (ed.) (1996) *The Actors in Europe's Foreign Policy*, London: Routledge.

Hill, C. (1998) 'Closing the Capability–Expectations Gap', in J. Peterson and H. Sjursen (eds), *A Common Foreign Policy for Europe*, London: Routledge, pp. 18–38.

Hill, C. (2002) *The Changing Politics of Foreign Policy*, London: Palgrave.

Hill, C. and Smith, M. (eds) (2005) *International Relations and the European Union*, Oxford: Oxford University Press.

Hill, C. and Smith, M. (eds) (2011) *International Relations and the European Union*, 2nd edition, Oxford: Oxford University Press.

Hill, C. and Wallace, W. (1996) 'The Actors in Europe's Foreign Policy-Making', in C. Hill (ed.), *The Actors in Europe's Foreign Policy*, London: Routledge, pp. 1–16.

Hillion, C. (2009) 'Mixity and Coherence in EU External Relations: The Significance of the Duty of Cooperation', CLEER Working Papers, 2.

Hollis, R. (2012) 'No Friend of Democratization: Europe's Role in the Genesis of the "Arab Spring"', *International Affairs*, 88(1), 81–94.

Hooghe, L. (2001) *The European Commission and the Integration of Europe: Images of Governance*, Cambridge: Cambridge University Press.

Hosoya, C. (1979) 'Relations between the European Communities and Japan', *Journal of Common Market Studies*, 18(2), 159–74.

Howard, C. (2005) 'The Policy Cycle: A Model of Post-Machiavellian Policy Making?', *Australian Journal of Public Administration*, 64(3), 3–13.

Howorth, Jolyon (2007) *Security and Defence Policy in the European Union*, London: Palgrave.

Howorth, J. (2011) 'The New Faces of Lisbon: Assessing the Performance of Catherine Ashton and Herman Van Rompuy on the Global Stage', *European Foreign Affairs Review*, 16, 303–23.

Hubel, H. (1993) 'Europa, Japan und der Krieg um Kuwait', in Hanns W. Maull (ed.), *Japan und Europa: Getrennte Welten?*, Frankfurt and New York: Campus Verlag, pp. 482–502.

Hughes, C.W. (2004) *Japan's Re-emergence as a 'Normal' Military Power*, Adelphi Paper 368-9, London: The International Institute for Strategic Studies.

Hurrell, A. (2007) *On Global Order. Power, Values, and the Constitution of International Society*, Oxford: Oxford University Press.

Hutton, Will (2006) *The Writing on the Wall: Why We Must Embrace China as a Partner or Face it as an Enemy*, New York: Free Press.

Ikenberry, John (2004) 'Liberalism and Empire: Logics of Order in the American Unipolar Age', *Review of International Studies*, 30, 609–30.

Isis [Europe] (2012) *Missions Map*. Accessed 11 July 2012 at http://www.csdpmap. eu/mission-chart.

Johnson, A. and Mueen, S. (eds) (2012) *Short War, Long Shadow: The Political and Military Legacies of the 2011 Libya Campaign*, London: RUSI.

Jones, B. (2011) *Beyond Blocs: The West, Rising Powers and Interest-Based International Cooperation*, Policy Analysis Brief, The Stanley Foundation.

Jørgensen, K.E. and Wessel, R.A. (2011) 'The Position of the European Union in (other) International Organizations: Confronting Legal and Political Approaches European Foreign Policy', in P. Koutrakos (ed.), *European Foreign Policy: Legal and Political Perspectives*, Cheltenham: Edward Elgar Publishing, pp. 261–86.

Jung, K. (2012) 'Willing or Waning? NATO's Role in An Age of Coalitions', *World Affairs*, 16(2) (see http://www.worldaffairsjournal.org/article/willing-or-waning-nato%E2%80%99s-role-age-coalitions).

Kagan, R. (2002) *Paradise and Power: America and Europe in the New World Order*, London: Atlantic.

Kagan, R. (2012) *The World America Made*, New York: Knopf.

Kaletsky, Anatole (2010) *Capitalism 4.0: The Birth of a New Economy*, London: Bloomsbury.

Kamo, T. (1995) 'Views about Security in Japan', paper prepared for delivery at the 36th Annual Convention of the International Studies Association (ISA), Chicago, 21–25 February, 22pp.

Kaplan, Fred (2011) 'NATO's Last Mission? The Military Crisis in Libya Highlights an Existential Crisis for NATO', *Slate*, 14 April.

Katzenstein, P. (2005) *A World of Regions: Asia and Europe in the American Imperium*, Ithaca and London: Cornell University Press.

Kennedy, Paul (1988) *The Rise and Fall of the Great Powers: Economic Change and Military Conflict from 1500–2000*, London: Unwin Hyman.

Keohane, R.O. (ed.) (1986) *Neorealism and its Critics*, New York: Columbia University Press.

Keohane, R.O. (2004) *After Hegemony: Cooperation and Discord in the World Political Economy*, Princeton: Princeton University Press.

Keukeleire, S. (2004) 'EU Structural Foreign Policy and Structural Conflict Prevention', in Vincent Kronenberger and Jan Wouters (eds), *The European Union and Conflict Prevention: Policy and Legal Aspects*, Den Haag: TMC Asser Institute, pp. 151–73.

Keukeleire, S. and Justaert, A. (2010) 'Structural Diplomacy, Contextual Difference, and the Process of Learning', UACES, Bruges, 6–8 September.

Keukeleire, S. and Justaert, A. (2012) 'EU Foreign Policy and the Challenges of Structural Diplomacy: Comprehensiveness, Coordination, Alignment and Learning', Brussels: DSEU Policy Paper no. 12.

Keukeleire, S. and MacNaughtan, J. (2008) *The Foreign Policy of the European Union*, Houndmills: Palgrave Macmillan.

Keukeleire, S., Mattlin, M., Hooijmaaijers, B., Behr, T., Jokela, J., Wigell, M. and Kononenko, V. (2011) *The EU Foreign Policy towards the BRICS and Other Emerging Powers: Objectives and Strategies*, Directorate General for External Policies, European Parliament.

Keukeliere, S., Delreux, T. and Drieskens, E. (2012) *The Foreign Policy of the European Union*, Houndmills: Palgrave Macmillan.

Kingdon, J.W. (1984) *Agenda, Alternatives, and Public Policies*, New York: HarperCollins College Publishers.

Kingdon, J.W. (2003) *Agenda, Alternatives, and Public Policies*, 2nd edition, New York: Longman Classics in Political Science.

Kishore, M. (2010) 'Europe's Errors', *Time*, 8 March. Accessed at http://www. time.com/time/magazine/article/0,9171,1967700,00.html.

Kissinger, H.A. (1982) *Years of Upheaval*, London: Weidenfeld & Nicolson, and Michael Joseph.

Koehler K. (2010) 'European Foreign Policy after Lisbon: Strengthening the EU as an International Actor', *Caucasian Review of International Affairs*, 4(1), 57–72.

Koo, Richard (2009) *The Holy Grail of Macroeconomics – Lessons from Japan's Great Recession*, New York: Wiley.

Korski, Daniel (2011) 'Lay Off the Lady', *E'Sharp*, 15 May.

Kostanyan, H. and Nasieniak, M. (2012) 'Moving the EU from a Laggard to a Leader in Democracy Assistance: The Potential Role of the European Endowment for Democracy', *CEPS Policy Brief No. 273*, 15 June.

Krasner, S. (1999) *Sovereignty: Organized Hypocrisy*, Princeton: Princeton University Press.

Krauthammer, C. (2011) 'The Obama Doctrine: Leading from Behind', *Washington Post*, 28 April. Accessed at http://www.washingtonpost.com/opinions/the-obama-doctrine-leading-from-behind/2011/04/28/AFBCy18E_story.html.

Krugman, Paul (2009) *The Return of Depression Economics and the Crisis of 2008*, New York: Norton.

Kupchan, C.A. (2012) *No One's World: The West, the Rising Rest and the Coming Global Turn*, Oxford: Oxford University Press.

Laaitikainen, K.V. (2010) 'Multilateral Leadership at the UN after the Lisbon Treaty', *European Foreign Affairs Review*, 15(4), 475–93.

Lasswell, H.D. (1956) *The Decision Process: Seven Categories of Functional Analysis*, College Park: University of Maryland Press.

Lavallée, C. (2011) 'The European Commission's Position in the Field of Security and Defence: An Unconventional Actor at a Meeting Point', *Perspectives on European Politics and Society*, 12(4), 371–89.

Lehne, Stefan (2011) 'More Action, Better Service: How to Strengthen the EEAS', *Carnegie Policy Outlook*, 16 December.

Lehne, S. (2012) *More Action, Better Service: How to Strengthen the EEAS*, Carnegie Europe.

Leonard, M. (2005) *Why Europe Will Run the 21st Century*, London: Fourth Estate.

Leonard, M. (2012) *Europe will Leave G20 with a Unilateral Future*, European Council of Foreign Relations Communication. Accessed at http://ecfr.eu/content/entry/commentary_europe_will_leave_g20_with_a_unilateral_future.

Lequesne, C., Jamet, F. and Chopin, T. (2012) *L'Europe d'après. En finir avec le pessimisme*, Paris: Lignes de repères.

Lindblom, C.E. (1959) 'The Science of Muddling Through', *Public Administration Review*, 19(2), 79–88.

Lizza, Ryan (2011) 'The Consequentialist: How the Arab Spring Re-made Obama's Foreign Policy', *New Yorker*, 2 May.

Lodge, J. (1993) 'From Civilian Power to Speaking with a Common Voice: The Transition to a CFSP', in J. Lodge (ed.), *The European Community and the Challenge of the Future*, 2nd edition, London: Pinter, pp. 227–51.

Lucarelli, S. and Fioramonti, L. (eds) (2010) *External Perceptions of the European Union as a Global Actor*, London and New York: Routledge.

Lucarelli, Sonia, Cerutti, Furio and Schmidt, Vivien (2011) *Debating Political Identity and Legitimacy in the European Union*, London: Routledge.

Mahbubani, Kishore. (2010) 'Europe's Errors', *Time*, 8 March. Accessed at http://www.time.com/time/magazine/article/0,9171,1967700,00.html.

Majone, Giandomenico (2009) *Europe as the Would-be World Power: The EU at Fifty*, Florence: European University Institute.

May, J.P. and Wildavsky, A. (ed.) (1978) *The Policy Cycle*, Beverly Hills: Sage.

Mandelbaum, Michael (2010) *The Frugal Superpower: America's Global Leadership in a Cash-Strapped Era*, New York: Public Affairs.

Manners, J. (2002) 'Normative Power Europe: A Contradiction in Terms?', *Journal of Common Market Studies*, 40/2, 234–58.

Marchesi, D. (2008) 'The EU Foreign and Security Policy in the EU Security Council: Between Representation and Coherence', 2008 Garnet Conference, Brussels, 24–26 April.

Marquand, David (2011) *The End of the West: The Once and Future Europe*, Princeton: Princeton University Press.

Martiningui, A. and Youngs, R. (eds) (2011) *Challenges for European Foreign Policy in 2012: What Kind of Geo-economic Europe?* Madrid: FRIDE. Accessed 15 December 2011 at http://www.fride.org/publicacion/971/desafios-para-la-politica-exterior-europea-en-2012.-una-europa-geoeconomica.

Maull, H.W. (1990–1) 'Germany and Japan: The New Civilian Powers', *Foreign Affairs*, 69(5), 91–106.

Maull, H.W. (1994) 'Germany and Japan: The Powers to Watch?', paper prepared for the IPSA Congress, Berlin, 20–25 August, 27pp.

Maull, H.W. (2006) 'Zivilmacht Deutschland', in G. Hellmann and S. Wolf Schmidt (eds), *Handbuch zur deutschen Außenpolitik*, Opladen: VS Verlag, pp. 73–84.

Maull, H.W. and Tanaka, A. (1997) 'The Geopolitical Dimension', in Council for Asia-Europe Cooperation (ed.), *The Rationale and Common Agenda for Asia-Europe Cooperation*, CAEC Task Force Reports, pp. 31–41.

Mayer, H. (2008a) 'Is it Still Called "Chinese Whispers"? The EU's Rhetoric and Action as a Responsible Global Institution', *International Affairs*, 84(1), 61–79.

Mayer, H. (2008b) 'The Long Legacy of Dorian Gray: Why the European Union Needs to Redefine its Role in Global Affairs', *Journal of European Integration*, 30(1), 7–25.

Mayer, H. and Vogt, H. (eds) (2006), *A Responsible Europe? Ethical Foundations of EU External Relations*, Basingstoke: Palgrave.

Mei Zhaorong (2009) 'Dui zhongou guanxi de zai renshi' [A Further Understanding of China–Europe Relations], *Ouzhou Yanjiu* [*Chinese Journal of European Studies*], 5, pp. 15–19.

Menon, Anand (2011) 'European Defence Policy from Lisbon to Libya', *Survival*, 53(3), 75–90.

Menotti, R. and Vencato, F. (2008) 'The European Security Strategy and the Partners', in S. Biscop and J.J. Andersson (eds), *The EU and the European Security Strategy*, Abingdon: Routledge, pp. 103–22.

Metz, Stephen (2011) 'Swan Song: Is Libya the End of NATO?', *The New Republic*, 15 April.

Mikail, B. (2011) 'France and the Arab Spring: An Opportunistic Quest for Influence', FRIDE (Madrid) Working Paper, 110, October.

Milner, C. (2012) 'Beijing Sets its Sights on Central Europe', *Spiegel Online International*, 18 May. Accessed at http://www.spiegel.de/international/ europe/with-10-billion-dollar-credit-line-china-deepens-presence-in-central-europe-a-833811.html.

Missiroli, A. (2001) 'European Security Policy: The Challenge of Coherence', *European Foreign Affairs Review*, 6(2), 177–96.

Missiroli, Antonio (2010a) 'The EU Foreign Service Under Construction', European University Institute, Florence, Robert Schuman Centre for Advanced Studies, Policy Paper 2010/04.

Missiroli, A. (2010b) 'The New EU "Foreign Policy" System after Lisbon: A Work in Progress', *European Foreign Affairs Review*, 15, 427–52.

Mölling, Christian (2011) 'Europe Without Defence', *SWP Comments* No. 38, November 2011.

Mols, Manfred (1990) 'Cooperation with ASEAN: A Success Story', in E. Regelsberger and G. Edwards (eds), *Europe's Global Links: The European Community and Inter-Regional Cooperation*, London: Pinter Publishers, pp. 66–83.

Monar, J. (2010) 'The European Union Institutional Balance of Power after Lisbon', online paper. Accessed at ec.europa.eu/education/jean.../monarb_ en.pdf.

Moravscic, A. (1998) *The Choice for Europe: Social Purpose and State Power from Messina to Maastricht*, Ithaca: Cornell University Press.

Müller, P. (2012) *EU Foreign Policymaking and the Middle East Conflict: The Europeanization of National Foreign Policy*, Abingdon: Routledge.

Murphy, E. (2012) 'Problematizing Arab Youth: Generational Narratives of Systemic Failure', *Mediterranean Politics*, 17(1), 5–22.

Nakamura, H. (2000) 'The G7 Summit for Japan: A Western Security Community or another US-led Hegemonic Alliance?', *Journal of the Faculty of Global Communication, Siebold University of Nagasaki*, 1, 165–94.

Nossal, K.R.; Roussel, S. and Paquin, S. *Politique internationale et défense au Canada et au Québec* Montréal: Les Presses de l'Université de Montréal, 2007), p. 646.

Nugent, N. (2003) *The Government and Politics of the European Union*, Basingstoke: Palgrave Macmillan.

Nugent, N. and Rhinard, M. (2011) 'The European Commission and the European Union's External Relations after the Lisbon Treaty', Paper prepared for the Twelfth Biennial Conference of the European Union Studies Association, Boston, 3–5 March.

Nuttall, S.J. (1992) *European Political Co-operation*, Oxford: Clarendon Press.

Nuttall, S.J. (2000) *European Foreign Policy*, Oxford: Oxford University Press.

Nuttall, Simon (2005) 'Coherence and Consistency', in Christopher Hill and Michael Smith (eds), *International Relations and the European Union*, Oxford: Oxford University Press, pp. 91-113.

Nye, J. (1971) *Peace in Parts: Integration and Conflict in Regional Organization*, New York: Little Brown and Company.

Nye, Joseph (2003) *The Paradox of American Power: Why the World's Only Superpower Can't Go it Alone*, New York: Oxford University Press.

Nye, Joseph (2011) *The Future of Power*, New York: Public Affairs.

Obama, Barack, Cameron, David and Sarkozy, Nicolas (2011) 'Libya's Pathway to Peace', *New York Times*, 14 April.

Ochmann, Cornelius (2012) 'The New EU: The Consequences of the Polish Presidency', Bertelsmann Stiftung, *Spotlight Europe* No. 2012/01, January.

O'Donnell, Clara Marina (2012) 'Poland's U-Turn on European Defence: A Missed Opportunity?', London, Centre for European Reform Policy Brief, March.

Ohira, M. (1979) *Brush Strokes: Moments from My Life*, Tokyo: Foreign Press Center, Japan.

Ongaro, E. (2010) 'Building the European External Action Service after the Lisbon Treaty: Reflections on some Key Organisational Issues', Working Paper.

[Open Letter] (2011) 'EU Foreign Policy Must Not Become a Casualty of the Euro Crisis', *European Voice*, 16 December. Accessed at http://euobserver.com/7/114664.

Owada, H. (2001) 'The Japan-EU Joint Declaration and its Significance toward the Future', *Studia Diplomatica*, 54(1–2), 11–26.

Ozawa, I. (1994) *Blueprint for a New Japan: The Rethinking of a Nation*, Tokyo: Kodansha International.

Pang Zhongying (2012) 'Gei Ouzhou kai Zhang zhonhyaofang' [Offer Europe a Chinese Medicine Prescription], *Huanqiu Shibao* [*Global Times*], 15 February.

Park, Sung-Hoon (2008) 'The Asia Strategy of the European Union and Asia–EU Economic Relations: History and New Developments', in Richard Balme and Brian Bridges (eds), *Europe Asia Relations: Building Multilateralism*, Hampshire: Palgrave Macmillan, pp. 66–83.

Patten, Chris (2009) 'A Vision-free Leadership', *European Voice*, 26 November.

Perruche, Jean-Paul (2011) *L'Europe de la Défense post-Lisbonne: illusion ou défi?*, Paris: IRSEM. (*Etudes de l'Irsem*, No. 11, 249pp.).

Peters, D., Wagner, W. and Deitelhoff, N. (2010) 'Parliaments and European Security Policy: Mapping the Parliamentary Field', *European Integration Online Papers*, 14. – see http://eiop.or.at/eiop/index.php/eiop/article/view/2010_012a

Pfaff, William (2010) *The Irony of Manifest Destiny: The Tragedy of America's Foreign Policy*, New York: Walker.

Pflimlin, Edouard (2011) 'l'UE relance la coopération militaire treize ans après Saint-Malo', *Le Monde*, 20 December.

Phillips, L. (2011) 'EU Recovery from Debt Crisis "Vital" to Chinese Investments', *EU Observer*, 17 June.

Pigman, G. (2011) *Contemporary Diplomacy*, London: Polity.

Pijpers, A. (1988) 'The Twelve Out-of-Area: A Civilian Power in an Uncivil World?', in A. Pijpers, E. Regelsberger and W. Wessels (eds), *European Political Cooperation in the 1980s: A Common Foreign Policy for Western Europe?*, Dordrecht: Martinus Nijhoff, pp. 143–65.

Piris, J.-C. (2012) *The Future of Europe: Towards a Two-Speed EU?*, Cambridge: Cambridge University Press.

Plantey, A. (2007) *International Negotiation in the 21st Century*, London: Routledge.

Ponjaert, F. (2008) 'Cross-Regional Dynamics: Their Specific Role and Contribution to Global Governance Efforts within the International System', in J.-L. de Sales Marques, R. Seidelmann and A. Vasilache (eds), *Asia and Europe: Dynamics of Inter- and Intra-Regional Dialogues*, Baden Baden: Nomos, pp. 177–97.

Ponjaert, F. and Bardaro, M.-E. (2013, forthcoming) 'China within the Emerging Asian Multilateralism and Regionalism as Perceived through a Comparison with the European Neighbourhood Policy', in J.-M. Beneyto, X. Song and D. Chun (eds), *China and the European Union: Future Directions*, London: Edward Elgar.

Portela, C. (2010) *EU Sanctions and Foreign Policy*, London: Routledge.

Portela, C. and Raub, K. *Revisiting Coherence in EU Foreign Policy*, Hamburg Revue of Social Sciences (HRSS) – Special Issue on Coherence in EU Foreign Policy, 3(1), 1–10. – see http://www.hamburg-review.com/fileadmin/pdf/03_01/Completely_finished.pdf

Putnam, R.D. and Bayne, N. (1984/1987) *Hanging Together: Cooperation and Conflict in the Seven-Power Summits*, London: RIIA (1984; revised and enlarged edition, London: SAGE Publications, 1987).

Rachman, Gideon (2011) 'Libya, a Last Hurrah for the West', *Financial Times*, 28 March.

Raube, K. (2012) 'The European External Action Service and the European Parliament', *The Hague Journal of Diplomacy*, 7, 65–80.

Regelsberger, E. and Edwards, G. (1990) *Europe's Global Links: The European Community and Inter-Regional Cooperation*, London: Printer Publisher.

Reiterer, M. (2006) 'Japan and the European Union: Shared Foreign Policy Interests', *Asia Europe Journal*, 4(3), 333–49.

Renard, T. (2011) 'The Treachery of Strategies: A Call for True EU Strategic Partnerships', Egmont Paper 45, Egmont Institute, Brussels.

Rettman, A. (2010) 'Ashton Pragmatic on China in EU Foreign Policy Blueprint', *EU Observer*, 17 December.

Rettman, A. (2011) 'EU to Keep China Arms Embargo Despite Massive Investment', *EU Observer*, 5 January.

Reynaert, V. (2011) 'Preoccupied with the Market: The EU as a Promoter of "Shallow" Democracy in the Mediterranean', *European Foreign Affairs Review*, 16(5), 623–37.

Rodrigues, M.J. (2011) 'Global Economic Governance and the EU's External Action', *Studia diplomatiica*, LXIV, 85–101.

Rogers, James (2011) 'The Sly Return of Civilian Power', European Geostrategy blog, 2 March. Accessed at http://europeangeostrategy.ideasoneurope. eu/2011/03/02/the-sly-return-of-civilian-power/.

Rosencrance, R. (1987) *Rise of the Trading State: Commerce and Conquest in the Modern World*, London: Basic Books.

Rubio Plo, A.R. (2008) 'La política mediterránea de Francia: del imperio latino de Alexandre Kojève al neogaullismo de Henri Guaino', Madrid: Real Instituto Elcano, ARI Paper 86.

Ruger, Carolin (2011) 'A Position under Construction: Future Prospects of the High Representative after the Treaty of Lisbon', in Gisela Müller-Brandeck-Boquet and Carolin Ruger (eds), *The High Representative for the EU Foreign and Security Policy – Review and Prospects*, Baden Baden: Nomos, pp. 201–35.

Rüland, Jürgen (1996) *The Asia-Europe Meeting (ASEM): Towards a New Euro-Asian Relationship?*, Universität Rostock: Rostocker Informationen zu Politik und Verwaltung, Heft 5.

Rüland, Jürgen (1999a) 'The Future of the ASEM Process: Who, How, Why and What', in Wim Stokhof and Paul van der Velde (eds), *ASEM. The Asia-Europe Meeting. A Window of Opportunity*, London and New York: Kegan Paul International, pp. 126–51.

Rüland, Jürgen (1999b) 'The EU as an Inter-regional Actor: The Asia-Europe Meeting', Paper presented at the Conference on 'Asia and Europe on the Eve of the 21st Century', 19–20 August 1999 in Bangkok at Chulalongkorn University, published in: Suthiphand Chirathivat, Franz Knipping, Poul Henrik Lassen and Chia Siow Yue (eds), *Asia-Europe on the Eve of the 21st Century*, Bangkok: Saksopha Press, 2001, S. 43–56.

Rüland, J. (2002) 'ASEM and the Emerging System of Global Governance', Paper prepared for the Meeting in Conjunction, Round Table: Asia-Europe Meeting (ASEM), at the Annual Meeting of the Association for Asian Studies, 4–7 April 2002, Washington, DC, USA.

Rüland, J. (2006) 'Interregionalism: An Unfinished Agenda', in H. Häggi, R. Rolof and J. Rüland Heydemann (eds), *Interregionalism and International Relations*, London: Routledge, pp. 295–314.

Rupp, Richard E. (2006) *NATO after 9/11: An Alliance in Continuing Decline*, New York: Palgrave.

Rynning, Sten (2005) *NATO Renewed: The Power and Purpose of Transatlantic Cooperation*, New York: Palgrave.

Sabatier, P.A. (1991) 'Toward Better Theories of the Policy Process', *Political Science and Politics*, 24, 147–56.

Sabel, C. and Zeitlin, J. (eds) (2010) *Experimentalist Governance in the EU*, Oxford: Oxford University Press.

Sanger, David E. (2011) 'Letting Others Lead in Libya', *New York Times*, 23 April.

Santander, S. (2012). 'Invariances et ruptures dans le Mercosur', in S. Santander (ed.), *Relations internationales et régionalisme. Entre dynamiques internes et projections mondiales*, Liège: Presses Universitaires de Liège.

Santander, S. and Ponjaert, F. (2009) 'The EU and its Far Abroad: Interregional Relations with Other Continents', in M. Telò (ed.), *The EU and Global Governance*, London: Routledge, pp. 283–306.

Sapir, André (ed.) (2007) *Fragmented Power and the Global Economy*, Brussels: Bruegel Book.

Schalk, J., Torenvlied, R., Jeroen, W. and Stokman, F. (2007) 'The Power of the Presidency in EU Council Decision-Making', *European Union Politics*, 8(2), 229–50.

Scharpf, F. et al. (1996) *Governance in the European Union* (with Gary Marks, Philippe C. Schmitter, Wolfgang Streeck), London: Sage.

Schmidt, V. (2008) 'Discursive Institutionalism: The Explanatory Power of Ideas and Discourse', *Annual Review of Political Science*, 11, 303–26.

Schmidt, V. (2012a) 'The State and Political Economic Change: Beyond Rational Choice and Historical Institutionalism to Discursive Institutionalism', in M. Telò (ed.), *Globalization State and Multilateralism*, Berlin: Springer, pp. 99–117.

Schmidt, V. (2012b) 'European Member State Elites' Diverging Visions of the European Union: Diverging Differently since the Economic Crisis and the Libyan Intervention?', *Journal of European Integration Studies*, 34(2), pp. 169–90.

Schmitt, Eric (2012) 'NATO Sees Flaws in Air Campaign Against Libya', *New York Times*, 14 April.

Schwartz, Herman (2000) *States versus Markets: The Emergence of a Global Economy*, London: Macmillan.

Seidelmann, R. (2009) 'The EU's Neighbourhood Policies', in M. Telò (ed.), *The EU and Global Governance*, London: Routledge, pp. 261–83.

Serra, R. (2005) *L'Evolution Stratégique du Japon: Un enjeu pour l'Union*, Occasional Paper No. 59, Paris: Institut d'Etudes de Sécurité.

Shambaugh, David (2004) 'China and Europe: The Emerging Axis', *Current History*, September, pp. 243–8.

Shinyo, T. (2003) 'EU-Japan Political-Security Co-operation', *EurAsia Bulletin*, 7(4), 7–10.

Shonfield, A. (1972/1973) *Europe: Journey to an Unknown Destination*, The BBC Reith Lectures, 1972; expanded version, London: Allen Lane and Penguin, 1973.

Singh, Kavaljit (2011) 'India-EU Free Trade Agreement: Rethinking Banking Services Liberalization', Briefing Paper No. 1, New Delhi: Madhyam.

Slaughter, A.-M. (2004) *A New World Order: Government Networks and the Disaggregated State*, Princeton: Princeton University Press.

Smith, K.E. (2000) 'The End of Civilian Power EU: A Welcome Demise or Cause for Concern?', *The International Spectator*, 35(2), 11–28.

Smith, K.E. (2003) *European Union Foreign Policy in a Changing World*, Cambridge: Polity Press.

Smith, K.E. (2006) 'Speaking with One Voice? European Union Co-ordination on Human Rights Issues at the United Nations', *Journal of Common Market Studies*, 44(1), 113–37.

Smith, M. (1994) 'The Commission and External Relations', in Geoffrey Edwards and David Spence (eds), *The European Commission*, London: Longman, pp. 249–86.

Smith, M. (2011) 'Strategic Diplomacy in Action? The Diplomacy of the EU's "Strategic Partnership" with China', Conference on 'Conceptualising and Analysing Strategic and Structural Diplomacy', Katholieke Universiteit Leuven, 7–8 April 2011.

Smouts, M.C. (1999) 'Que reste-t-il de la politique étrangère?', *Pouvoirs*, 88, 5–15.

Söderbaum, F. and Van Langenhove, L. (2005) 'Introduction: The EU as a Global Actor and the Role of Interregionalism', *Journal of European Integration*, 27(3), 249–62.

Soetendorp, B. (1999) *Foreign Policy In The European Union*, London and New York: Longman.

Soler i Lecha, E. and Viilup, E. (2011) 'Reviewing the European Neighbourhood Policy: A Weak Response to Fast Changing Realities', CIDOB (Barcelona), *Notes Internacionals*, 36, June.

Solingen, E. and Şenses Ozyrt, S. (2006) 'Mare nostrum? The Sources, Logic and Dilemmas of the Euro-Mediterranean Partnership', in E. Adler, F. Bicchi, B. Crawford and R. Del Sarto (eds), *The Convergence of Civilizations: Constructing a Mediterranean Region*, Toronto: University of Toronto Press, pp. 51–82.

Sommer, T. (2012) *Diese NATO hat ausgedient: Das Bündnis muss europäischer werden*, Hamburg: Körber Stiftung.

Spence, D. (2012) 'The Early Days of the European External Action Service: A Practitioner's View', *The Hague Journal of Diplomacy*, 7, 115–34.

Stavridis, S. (2001) *Why the 'Militarising' of the European Union is Strengthening the Concept of a Civilian Power Europe*, EUI Working Papers, Florence: European University Institute.

Stelzenmüller, Constanze (2011) 'Gates was Far Too Nice about NATO's Failings', *Financial Times*, 15 June.

Strange, S. (1972) 'The Dollar Crisis 1971', *International Affairs*, 48(2), 191–216.

Sudhir, D.T., de Vasconcelos, A. and Peral, L. (2009) *Report on the India-EU Forum on Effective Multilateralism*, Paris: EUISS.

Swaine, Michael (2011) *America's Challenge: Engaging a Rising China in the Twenty-First Century*, Washington, DC: Carnegie.

Tallberg, J. (2006) *Leadership and Negotiation in the European Union*, Cambridge: Cambridge University Press.

Telò, M. (2005) *Europe: A Civilian Power? European Union, Global Governance, World Order*, Houndmills: Palgrave Macmillan.

Telò, M. (ed.) (2007) *European Union and New Regionalism: Regional Actors and Global Governance in a Post-Hegemonic Era*, Aldershot: Ashgate.

Telò, M. (ed.) (2009) *The European Union and Global Governance*, London: Routledge.

Telò, M. (ed.) (2012) *Globalization, State and Multilateralism*, London: Springer.

Terrain, F. (2010) *La politique étrangère,de sécurité et de defence de l'Union Europèenne*, Paris: La Documentation française.

Thompson, Helen (2010) *China and the Mortgaging of America: Economic Interdependence and Domestic Politics*, London: Palgrave Macmillan.

Tietje, Christian (1997) 'The Concept of Coherence in the Treaty on European Union and the Common Foreign and Security Policy', *European Foreign Affairs Review*, 2, 211–33.

Timmermann, M. and Tsuchiyama, J. (eds) (2008) *Institutionalizing North-East Asia*, Tokyo: UN University.

Tsakaloyannis, P. (1989) 'The EC: From Civilian Power to Military Integration', in Juliet Lodge (ed.), *The European Community and the Challenge of the Future*, London: Pinter, pp. 241–55.

Tsoukalis, Loukas (2009) *An EU 'Fit for Purpose' in the Global Age*, London: Policy Network.

Ueta, T. and Remacle, E. (eds) (2005) *Japan and Enlarged Europe: Partners in Global Governance*, Brussels: P.I.E.-Peter Lang.

Vaïsse, J. and Kundnani, H. (2011) *European Foreign Policy: Scorecard 2010*, London: European Council of on Foreign Relations.

Vaïsse, J. and Kundnani, H. (2012) *European Foreign Policy: Scorecard 2012*, London: European Council of on Foreign.

Valasek, Tomas (2011) 'Race to the Bottom', London: Centre for European Reform, Insight, 24 August. Accessed at http://centreforeuropeanreform. blogspot.com/2011/08/race-to-bottom.html.

Vasalek, T., Barysch, K. and Grant, Charles (2011) *A New Opportunity for EU Foreign Policy*, London: Centre for European Reform.

van der Pijl, Kees (2006) *Global Rivalries from the Cold War to Iraq*, London: Pluto.

Vanhoonacker, S., Pomorska, K. and Maurer, H. (2011) 'The Council Presidency and European Foreign Policy – Challenges for Poland in 2011', report prepared in cooperation with Konrad Adenauer Foundation in Poland, Center for International Relation.

Van Rompuy, Herman (2010) *The Challenges for Europe in a Changing World*, PCE 34/10, Bruges, 25 February.

Vanoverbeke, D. and Ponjaert, F. (2007) 'Japan in East Asia: The Dynamics of Regional Cooperation from a European Perspective', *Japan – European Union: A Strategic Partnership in the Making, Studia Diplomatica*, LXI(1) (Special Issue), 5–19.

Van Langenhove, L. (2011) *Building Regions*, Burlington: Ashgate.

Vogel, Toby (2012) 'Ashton on Defensive over EU's Diplomatic Service', *European Observer*, 5 January.

Wagner, C. (2008) 'The EU and India: A Deepening Partnership', in Giovanni Grevi and Alvaro de Vasconcelos (eds), *Partnerships for Effective Multilateralism: EU Relations with Brazil, China, India and Russia*, Paris: Institute for Security Studies, No. 109, pp. 87–103.

Walker, N. (ed.) (2003) *Sovereignty in Transition*, Oxford: Hart.

Wallace, W. (1976) 'Issue Linkage among Atlantic Governments', *International Affairs*, 52(2), 163–79.

Wallace, W. (1988) 'Western Europe and Japan: Political Dimensions of the Relationship', Paper for the UK–Japan 2000 Group, the fourth conference, Elvetham Hall, 15–18 January, 13pp.

Wallace, W. (1990) *The Transformation of Western Europe*, London: Pinter/Royal Institute of International Affairs.

Werner, J. and Wegrich, K. (2007) 'Theories of the Policy Cycle', in F. Fisher, G.J. Miller and M.S. Sydney (eds), *Handbook of Public Policy Analysis: Theory, Politics and Methods*, London: CPR Press, pp. 43–62.

Wessels, W. (1997) 'An Ever Closer Fusion? A Dynamic Macropolitical View on Integration Processes', *Journal of Common Market Studies*, 35(2), 267–99.

Wessels, W. (2005) 'The Constitutional Treaty: Three Readings from a Fusion Perspective', *Journal of Common Market Studies, Annual Review, 2004/2005, The European Union*, 11–36.

Whitman, R. (1998) *From Civilian Power to Superpower? The International Identity of the European Union*, London: Macmillan.

Wilkinson, E. (1980/1991) *Japan versus The West: Image and Reality*, first published, Tokyo: Chuokoron-sha Inc., 1980; newly revised edition published under the present title, with revisions, London: Penguin Books, 1991.

Willis, A. (2011) 'EU Aid Policy to Target Fewer States and Good Governance', *EU Observer*, 31 May.

Witney, Nick (2011) 'How to Stop the De-militarisation of Europe', London, European Council on Foreign Affairs, November.

Wolcock, S. (2012) *European Union Economic Diplomacy: The Role of the EU in External Economic Relations*, Farnham: Ashgate.

Wong, R. (2005) 'The Europeanization of Foreign Policy', in C. Hill and M. Smith (eds), *International Relations and the EU*, Oxford: Oxford University Press, pp. 134–53.

Wong, R. (2006) *The Europeanization of French Foreign Policy: France and the EU in East Asia*, Basingstoke: Palgrave.

Wouters, J., Coppens, D. and De Meester, D. (2008) 'The European Union's External Relations after the Lisbon Treaty', in S. Griller and J. Ziller (eds), *The Lisbon Treaty: EU Constitutionalism without a Constitutional Treaty?*, Vienna: Springer, pp. 143–203.

Yang Jiemian (2010) 'Lun "sishi qunti" he Guoji liliang chongzu de shidai tedian' [On the Features of Contemporary Regrouping of International Forces], *Shijie Jingji yu Zhengzhi* [*World Economy and Politics*], 3, 5–6.

Youngs, R. (2011) 'The EU and the Arab Spring: From Munificence to Geo-Strategy', FRIDE (Madrid), Policy Brief 100, October.

Zeitlin, J. (ed.) (2009) *Experimental Governance*, Oxford: Oxford University Press.

Zimmerling, Ruth (1991) *Externe Einflüsse auf regionale Integrationsprozesse: Zentralamerika und Adenpakt*, Fort Lauderdale and Saarbrücken: Breitenbach.

Index